"The Grief Recovery with Individualized Evidence-Based Formulation (GRIEF) approach provides insightful guidelines for survivors of those who have died from traumatic circumstances. The authors focus on how violent, unnatural deaths create their own set of challenges not only for survivors but for the clinicians who strive arduously to offer help. They make clear that clinician self-care is another essential component of ensuring the delivery of effective bereavement care for survivors of traumatic deaths."

> —**Holly G. Prigerson, PhD**, endowed professor of diagnosi
> at Weill Cornell Medicine, lead scientist on grief for DSI
> and director of the Cornell Center for Research on End-c

"This book is an incredible resource for providers working with adult survivors of traumatic death loss. The GRIEF model combines evidence-based strategies from psychotherapies for post-traumatic stress disorder (PTSD), depression, and persistent grief into a comprehensive, eight-module package that can be tailored to the unique needs of each survivor. The authors provide guidance on treatment planning, as well as selection, sequencing, and implementation of practice elements. I highly recommend it."

> —**Joan M. Cook, PhD**, professor at the Yale School of Medicine

"Right out of the gate, this clinician's resource focuses on APPROACH—that is, overcoming avoidance—as a key component in the GRIEF treatment strategy. Dealing with traumatic loss is difficult, and this guide provides an evidence-based pathway for the informed clinician to effectively help those seeking solace and recovery. The authors outline a science-based approach to treating traumatic grief in such a direct and clear way that effective implementation, even by those new to the area, is likely."

> —**Ron Acierno, PhD**, Faillace Professor of Psychiatry and vice chair for
> Veterans Affairs at the University of Texas Health Sciences Center
> at Houston; and senior clinical research scientist at the Ralph H. Johnson
> Veterans Affairs Medical Center in Charleston, SC

"The authors synthesize a highly relevant, evidence-based intervention (GRIEF) for those distressed and disabled with trauma, grief, and depression after sudden or violent death. The modules for patterns of distress are clinically illustrated in a protocol that guides the timing and application of these modules in a relevant therapeutic structure for the clinician or counselor."

> —**Ted Rynearson, MD**, emeritus clinical professor of psychiatry at
> the University of Washington

"*Treating Traumatic Loss* provides a comprehensive integration of relevant theory, assessment, and evidence-informed clinical practices to support adults exposed to traumatic loss. With its assessment-driven, modularized, and flexible approach, this book serves as an invaluable resource to clinicians dedicated to addressing the wide-ranging mental health needs of those grappling with traumatic deaths."

> —**Julie Kaplow, PhD**, executive director of the Trauma and Grief Center at the Meadows Institute, professor of psychiatry at Tulane, and author of *Multidimensional Grief Therapy*

"This manual fills a critical gap in the field by offering clinicians a unique, compassionate, and non-stigmatizing approach to grief. Unlike other resources, this manual avoids pathologizing grief, instead focusing on understanding and supporting clients through their healing process. Its step-by-step, reader-friendly format is suitable for clinicians at all levels, providing practical tools for assessing and treating grief while promoting resilience."

> —**Angela Moreland, PhD**, clinical psychologist, and expert in child and adult trauma and grief

"As leaders in the bereavement field, Rheingold and her colleagues have developed a highly useful, long-overdue, and much-needed traumatic loss treatment manual that will be invaluable for grief therapists looking to cultivate or strengthen their skills in treating traumatic death loss. Using an easy-to-follow format and numerous true-to-life narratives and clinical vignettes, this high-caliber resource should be a mandatory component of every graduate-level grief training program."

> —**Laurie Burke, PhD**, clinical psychologist specializing in traumatic loss, and coeditor of *The Restorative Nature of Ongoing Connections with the Deceased*

"*Treating Traumatic Loss* provides clinicians with an integrative, empirically informed approach to address the complexities and unique experiences of traumatically bereaved adults. The guide is written in a way that makes it easy for clinicians to use. This modular and flexible model, along with the clinician tips and handouts, is an excellent resource for all clinicians working with traumatically bereaved adults."

> —**Alison Salloum, PhD, LCSW**, professor in the School of Social Work at the University of South Florida, and author of *Grief and Trauma in Children*

TREATING TRAUMATIC LOSS

A Clinician's Guide to Helping Clients Cope with a Sudden, Violent, or Difficult Death Using the GRIEF Approach

ALYSSA A. RHEINGOLD, PHD
JOAH L. WILLIAMS, PHD
MEGAN M. WALLACE, LISW-CP
JAMISON S. BOTTOMLEY, PHD

New Harbinger Publications, Inc.

Publisher's Note

This publication is designed to provide accurate and authoritative information in regard to the subject matter covered. It is sold with the understanding that the publisher is not engaged in rendering psychological, financial, legal, or other professional services. If expert assistance or counseling is needed, the services of a competent professional should be sought.

NEW HARBINGER PUBLICATIONS is a registered trademark of New Harbinger Publications, Inc.

New Harbinger Publications is an employee-owned company.

Copyright © 2025 by Alyssa A. Rheingold, Joah L. Williams, Megan M. Wallace, and Jamison S. Bottomley
New Harbinger Publications, Inc.
5720 Shattuck Avenue
Oakland, CA 94609
www.newharbinger.com

All Rights Reserved

Cover design by Amy Shoup

Acquired by Elizabeth Holllis Hansen

Edited by Iris van de Pavert

Library of Congress Cataloging-in-Publication Data on file

Printed in the United States of America

27	26	25									
10	9	8	7	6	5	4	3	2	1		First Printing

This manual is dedicated to all those whose lives were tragically cut short by violence and preventable injuries and the loved ones who grieve for them. You are not alone.

Contents

	Foreword	vii
Chapter 1	Understanding Traumatic Loss	1
Chapter 2	Introduction to GRIEF Approach	16
Chapter 3	Using This Manual: Assessment and Treatment Planning	26
Chapter 4	Module 1: Psychoeducation About Grief, Types of Loss, and Traumatic Loss Reactions	40
Chapter 5	Module 2: Identifying Emotions and Processing Thoughts	54
Chapter 6	Module 3: Identifying and Building Strengths	71
Chapter 7	Module 4: Managing Strong Emotions	78
Chapter 8	Module 5: Building Healthy Support Networks	94
Chapter 9	Module 6: Meaningful Behavioral Activation	103
Chapter 10	Module 7: Revising Bonds	113
Chapter 11	Module 8: Therapeutic Exposure	126
Chapter 12	Putting It All Together	147
Chapter 13	Self-Care for Providers	158
	References	167
	Index	181

Foreword

As both the daily news and official statistics relentlessly document, the world is awash in traumatic loss. Wars take the lives of countless combatants and civilians, their remains often buried in the rubble of what once were cities. Refugees flee countries to escape the chaos and violence, leaving their dead to save their children's lives and their own. Homicide is a weekly occurrence in American urban centers, particularly in those communities with the fewest resources for mitigating their impact on surviving family members and intimate others. Suicide rates have climbed in many nations over the last two decades, with these statistics further shadowed by the burgeoning toll of drug-related deaths, whether intentional, unintentional, or subintentioned. Add to these the surging deaths from vehicular accidents, deadly weather events, floods, fires, and other natural disasters, and it is clear why it is the rare family that has been untouched by tragic loss at some point in its history. And of course, for the most vulnerable of minoritized populations, such loss is a tragically frequent visitor.

Considering these statistical and public-health realities, it is ironic that psychotherapists, who arguably are best positioned to meet survivors of such loss in their complex grief and desolation, are often unprepared to do so. Indeed, the average social worker, psychologist, or counselor can graduate from a masters or even a doctoral program without having read a single article or heard a single lecture on grief—or worse, having been given only a regurgitated rendition of a generic and outdated stage model of grieving that dramatically simplifies the human encounter with even normative death through progressive illness, much less prepares them to address the complex conjunction of trauma and loss that follows sudden or violent death bereavement. In the virtual absence of relevant training, clinicians can therefore be forgiven for offering little more than an empathic listening ear, combined with vague normalization of the person's experience, and the implicit or explicit message that time will heal the wounds inflicted by a cruel, often unanticipated and senseless loss.

In *Treating Traumatic Loss*, Rheingold, Williams, Wallace, and Bottomley have delved into the toolbox of contemporary cognitive behavioral therapy to offer practical resources and guidance to clinicians who confront such losses in the hospital, community, and private practice settings in which they work. Organizing their model into an evidence-informed protocol of twelve to sixteen sessions, they draw on familiar CBT techniques of psychoeducation, emotion identification, cognitive restructuring, mindfulness and relaxation, behavioral activation, and building social support, bringing these to bear on the pain and trauma of tragic loss and the common tendency of clients to attempt to mitigate them through avoidance. In addition, they selectively include interventions arising in narrative and meaning-oriented approaches to assist the bereaved with reaffirming and revising their attachment bonds with the deceased and undertaking the sort of prolonged exposure to retelling the story of complicated loss that promotes its integration. The result is a protocol with four core modules applied to all clients, as well as four optional modules applied to cases with prominent features of major depression, PTSD, or prolonged grief disorder.

In each module, the authors offer guidance about considering distinctive features of the client's cultural context and offer detailed scripts for delivering the treatment or countering client reluctance to approach difficult material, something that is likely to be appreciated by novice therapists looking for models that link theory and practice. Recommendations of appropriate clinical assessments that aid in the modification of the protocol to address client symptomatology and to track clinical progress supplement the "how-to" coverage of the modules themselves.

In short, readers looking to apply well-researched CBT techniques to traumatic bereavement will find in these pages a logical and straightforward structure for doing so. Its accessibility recommends it to both graduate students in the helping professions and to therapists looking for practical tools for addressing the amalgam of complex trauma and loss that clients present, often in settings that are themselves underresourced and overstretched in the care they provide. *Treating Traumatic Loss* goes some distance toward filling this gap.

—Robert A. Neimeyer, PhD
Director, Portland Institute for Loss and Transition
Editor, *Death Studies*
Author, *Living Beyond Loss: Questions and Answers about Grief and Bereavement*

CHAPTER 1

Understanding Traumatic Loss

Donna, a sixty-four-year-old grandmother and mother of two, was suddenly awakened one cool spring morning to the sound of the doorbell ringing. The sun hadn't come up yet, and she still felt sleepy as she walked downstairs. When she opened the door and saw two police officers who asked her to confirm her name and her daughter's name, she remembered initially feeling confused. Her daughter had just left five hours before; her car packed and ready to begin the three-hour trip to her new home, where she was about to start a new job and planned to get married in just a few short months. Donna's confusion quickly gave way to an overwhelming sense of horror when she heard one of the officers utter the word "killed." Donna's daughter had been struck in a head-on collision by a drunk driver on the interstate about thirty minutes after leaving her mother's house.

Joe, a twenty-year-old college athlete, still remembers getting the phone call from his mother early one Saturday morning. He knew something was wrong by the sound of her voice. She was talking with a sense of urgency—crying and almost screaming, "Joe, you've got to come home. Someone killed him." "Mom, slow down. Who? Someone killed who?" When he heard his brother's name, Joe remembered saying, "I'll be right there, Mom. Hold on," and hung up the phone. In the midst of frantically trying to pack for the one-hour drive home, Joe paused long enough to open his laptop. He quickly learned from several online news sources that his older brother was the identified victim in a random shooting that had taken place the night before in front of a popular bar near campus.

Alexis, a forty-seven-year-old married mother of two, received a call at work from her husband, who sounded off and not like himself. He had been struggling with depression on and off for several years, but it worsened since he lost his job nine months ago, and he began drinking more frequently. While on the phone, Alexis assumed he had been drinking and encouraged him to lie down to take a nap. She tried calling him a few times after several hours, but he did not answer his phone. She decided to swing by their house to check on him before heading to pick up their children from their after-school program. At home, she found her husband dead in his car, which was running in the garage. There was a letter on the kitchen table apologizing for failing their family.

Dave, a fifty-six-year-old grandfather and father of three, had just finished making breakfast for his granddaughter when he walked upstairs to his son's room to invite him down for breakfast. His son, the second of his three children, had just moved back into the family home two months prior after separating from his long-time partner. Dave knocked on his son's bedroom door and called his name but heard no response. He continued knocking and called his son's name one more time as he slowly opened the door and walked into his son's room. Initially, Dave didn't notice anything out of the ordinary—his son, who was still lying in bed, was a notoriously heavy sleeper. As he approached his son's bed, however, Dave was quickly overwhelmed with terror as he noticed his son's color was off, his body cold to the touch, and a syringe still dangling from his arm.

The circumstances are different, but Donna, Joe, Alexis, and Dave's stories illustrate several common elements of traumatic loss. These often involve a sense of suddenness, and at least on some level, they are preventable, as in a result of direct human action or negligence. Often, traumatic losses involve serious injuries to the deceased, leaving survivors with a sense of violation against their loved one. In the case of homicide and interpersonal violence, there is a person(s) responsible for inflicting these violating injuries. In the case of suicide or drug overdose, their loved one may have intentionally or unintentionally inflicted injuries upon themselves. When a death is accidental or disaster-related, there may not be a single person who was responsible for a loved one's violating injuries, though surviving family members or friends may find ways that personal or social action (or inaction) ultimately made their loved one vulnerable to those injuries.

As clinicians and professionals who bring our own lived experiences to this work, we recognize that the death of a loved one under any circumstance can be inherently difficult. Our professional and lived experiences have also shown us that when a death is perceived as sudden, preventable, and a violation of our most basic assumptions in life, it can lead to unique complications that require special considerations for treatment, from psychological trauma surrounding the death itself to prolonged grief. In our work with traumatic loss survivors over the past several decades, time and time again we felt the need to pull various aspects from different linear-based, disorder-specific manuals to address the complexities of traumatic loss. There was not a manual that seemed to capture the complexities of traumatic loss guided by evidence-based practices of common trauma and grief-related mental health disorders. This led us to create our own manual; the one you are reading right now. This manual provides an introduction to GRIEF Approach—a transdiagnostic intervention for survivors of traumatic death losses.

Throughout the manual, we will use the term *survivors* to refer to family and friends grieving the traumatic loss of a loved one. We will also use the term *clinicians* to refer to behavioral health and other mental health care professionals who work with survivors after the traumatic loss of a loved one. This chapter provides an introduction to traumatic loss and bereavement-related mental health problems commonly associated with these deaths.

Prevalence of Traumatic Loss

Traumatic loss in all of its forms poses a significant public health burden on families and communities around the world. Highlighting the global impact of traumatic loss, the World Health Organization (WHO) recently reported that nearly 4.4 million deaths occur each year from intentional injuries (such as homicide or suicide) and unintentional injuries (including those resulting from road traffic crashes, falls, drowning, and so forth), accounting for nearly 8 percent of global deaths annually (WHO, 2024). Despite international efforts to curb this trend, many regions are seeing increases in rates of traumatic loss. In the United States (US), deaths due to traumatic loss from intentional and unintentional injury increased from over 240,000 deaths in 2018 to over 306,000 deaths in 2021 (Centers for Disease Control and Prevention [CDC], 2023b). This is a nearly 27 percent increase driven in large part by parallel epidemics in opioid misuse and gun violence.

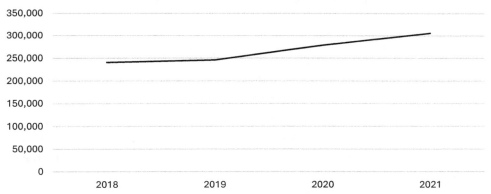

Data available from the CDC's WISQARS Fatal and Nonfatal Injury Reports

During the same period, for example, the US saw a nearly 23 percent increase in deaths due to firearm injuries and a nearly 67 percent increase in unintentional deaths due to drug-related poisoning and overdoses (CDC, 2023b). Among the youngest Americans, and reflective of national trends in gun violence, intentional firearm injuries due to homicide and suicide became the leading cause of death for children and adolescents in the US in 2020, with pediatric firearm deaths increasing over 41 percent from 2018 to 2021 (Roberts et al., 2023).

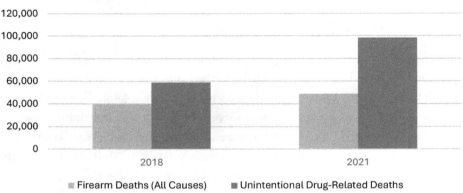

All Cause Firearm and Unintentional Drug-Related Deaths in the United States, 2018–2021

Data available from the CDC's WISQARS Fatal and Nonfatal Injury Reports

Of course, mortality rates alone only partially capture the scope of traumatic loss, which often has lasting impacts on family, friends, and entire communities. In the case of traumatic loss, it has been estimated that as many as 7–10 individuals close to the deceased are substantially impacted for each death that occurs and as many as 135 people in the deceased person's community may be exposed to the death (Cerel et al., 2019; Redmond, 1989).

Traumatic loss of a loved one is one of the most common and typically worst traumatic experiences many people will experience during their lifetime. National studies have shown that as many as 50 percent of adults in the US have experienced the unexpected death of a loved one at some point during their lifetime and tend to identify these losses as worse than other types of traumatic events they may have experienced (Keyes et al., 2014; Kilpatrick et al., 2013). Together, these findings underscore just how commonplace traumatic loss is in contemporary society. A closer look, however, also reveals that traumatic loss is both a result of and contributor to major health disparities, which has implications for treatment with this population.

Health Disparities in Traumatic Loss

Traumatic loss affects individuals across all segments of our society but disproportionately affects some individuals and communities. Demographically, traumatic loss survivors tend to be younger than individuals grieving other kinds of losses (Rheingold et al., 2024), a finding that parallels national trends showing that the majority of deaths due to traumatic loss involve children and young adults (CDC, 2023a). Because both survivors and their deceased loved ones tend to be younger than individuals grieving other kinds of losses, traumatic loss survivors are more likely to be grieving the death of a sibling, partner or spouse, or close friend than a parent or nonnuclear family member (Rheingold et al., 2024). This can have immediate impacts on available sources of social support for survivors. Bereaved parents are also disproportionately represented among traumatic loss survivors. The fact that the majority of these deaths involve young people can have profound implications for how survivors grieve, often violating social norms and personal expectations about the natural life course and how much time survivors expected to have with their loved ones.

Males and individuals from racially and ethnically minoritized groups are also disproportionately affected by traumatic loss. Of the nearly 306,000 deaths from intentional and unintentional injuries in the US in 2021, nearly 70 percent involved males, and despite making up a little over 13 percent of the population, nearly 18 percent of these deaths involved Black and African Americans (CDC, 2023b). Disparities in prevalence of traumatic loss among Black and African Americans are most pronounced when looking at firearm injury deaths. They are nearly seven times more likely to die from firearm-related homicides in the US than Whites (Young & Xiang, 2022). Given the criminal nature of homicide death, they often have to deal with added stresses of having a loved one's death deemed worthy of media attention and legal investigation and prosecution—challenges faced by many homicide survivors from marginalized and racialized communities (Bordere et al., 2021). Over the last two decades, Black and African Americans also saw the biggest increase in deaths due to motor vehicle crashes compared to White and Latinx/Hispanic Americans (Cherpitel et al., 2021), highlighting yet another growing disparity in the prevalence of traumatic loss among these communities.

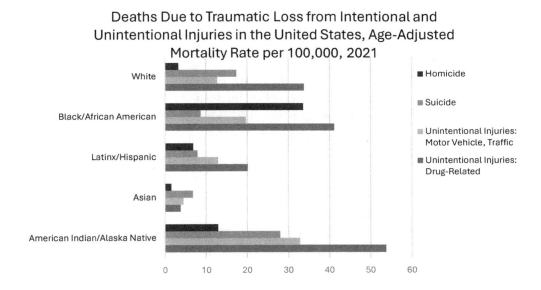

Data available from the CDC's WISQARS Fatal and Nonfatal Injury Reports

Traumatic loss also disproportionately affects individuals and families in socioeconomically under-resourced communities. Several community-level socioeconomic characteristics are associated with death due to intentional injury from homicide and suicide, including residential instability, poverty, and income inequality (Gobaud et al., 2022; Wilkins et al., 2019). County poverty level has also been associated with higher mortality rates for all causes of unintentional injury, including motor vehicle crashes and poisonings (Karb et al., 2016). For survivors living in socially and economically under-resourced communities, the loss of social, financial, and other resources that often accompanies the death of a loved one can further compound social and economic disadvantage—stressors that often interfere with survivors' psychological adaptation to traumatic loss.

Contemporary Theories of Psychological Adaptation to Traumatic Loss

Many contemporary theories frame psychological adaptation to the traumatic loss of a loved one by the ways that survivors cope with and make meaning of both the trauma and grief associated with the death. Some of these contemporary theories are drawn from broader theories of how people grieve more generally, while others were developed based on clinical and research experiences with traumatic loss survivors themselves. More recent theories have also started to take into account the broader impact of environmental deprivation and death-related resource losses on psychological adaptation to traumatic loss, recognizing the impact of persistent inequities in the prevalence of traumatic loss. In this section, we review some of these major theories that informed the development of the GRIEF Approach model and discuss their implications for survivors' adjustment to traumatic loss.

Dual Process Model of Bereavement

Stroebe and Schut's (1999) dual process model of bereavement (DPM) considers psychological adaptation to death as a process of coping with different daily stressors that are likely to occur for survivors. According to the DPM, survivors often oscillate between two types of coping strategies to help them adapt to loss: loss-oriented coping and restoration-oriented coping. The former involves intentional efforts to cope with some aspect of the death or lost relationship with the deceased. It can include rumination about the death or deceased, yearning for the deceased and engaging in behaviors that give survivors a sense of connection to the deceased (for example, looking at pictures), and avoidance of activities and relationships that do not involve the deceased. Conversely, restoration-oriented coping involves intentional efforts to cope with secondary stressors associated with the death, particularly stressors that increase survivors' awareness of the reality and finality of the death. This can include coping with the stress of managing new tasks (such as ones the deceased may have previously done for the survivor), taking on new roles, and building new relationships.

Both loss- and restoration-oriented coping can be important for survivors at different times as they grieve, although complications can arise when efforts to cope with one set of stressors undermine a survivors' ability to cope with other stressors. For example, primarily relying on avoidance in the context of loss-oriented coping can have a significant impact on survivors' ability to function in multiple domains and maintain other important relationships. Similarly, feeling overwhelmed with the demands of multiple restoration-oriented tasks can limit survivors' ability to process important aspects of the loss and its implications for their life moving forward. It can even limit doing things that were once important in the survivors' life, increasing risk for bereavement-related mental health problems, which we will discuss in the next section.

Meaning Reconstruction and Narrative Models of Bereavement

Neimeyer's meaning reconstruction model of bereavement (see Neimeyer, 2019; Neimeyer, 2023) similarly frames psychological adaptation to loss as an active attempt to cope with stress but focuses in particular on the ways survivors make meaning of their loved one's death. Each person is assumed to have a core set of personal meaning structures related to their understanding of the world in terms of how to approach and prioritize daily activities and responsibilities, personal identities, interpersonal relationships, outlook on the future, spiritual and philosophic beliefs, and participation in social communities. In some cases, these meaning structures can be used to help survivors explain or make sense of a loved one's death.

However, in circumstances where the death of a loved one is seen as inconsistent with the meanings we attach to the world, such as might occur in the context of a traumatic loss, survivors may experience distress as they realize that the ways they understand the world are inconsistent with the nature of what occurred. These threats to personal understandings of oneself and the world are notably prominent in bereavement-related mental health problems, such as post-traumatic stress and prolonged grief. This model assumes that this distress will prompt survivors to begin a process of meaning reconstruction by trying to make sense of the death, finding benefit in their experiences, and changing personal identities. The result of this process of meaning making is that survivors ultimately reconstruct some of their personal meanings and begin to understand the world in new ways or continue searching for meaning in the loss.

Drawing on several decades of clinical experience with homicide survivors in particular, Rynearson (2012) developed a narrative model of traumatic dying that complements and has continuity with the meaning reconstruction model of bereavement by focusing on the unique challenges of traumatic loss, including an often intense effort to make sense of the death of a loved one. According to Rynearson (2012), a central feature of the death event in the context of traumatic loss is that the death occurred as a result of preventable intentional or unintentional injuries. Survivors seeking to make meaning of the loss will often find this incompatible with preexisting personal meaning structures (such as our personal sense of being able to control outcomes in our lives and protect loved ones). Survivors trying to come to terms with a world in which their loved one was traumatically injured may then become focused on the nature of the death event itself, which they experience as recurrent reenactment imagery of their loved one's dying moments.

Reenactment imagery typically involves highly vivid, visual replays of a loved one's dying moments, whether real or imagined, that are simultaneously countered by imagined reunion with a loved one, either as they were in life or in an afterlife (Williams et al., 2022). This imagining of a loved one's death alongside imagined reunion reflects another core assumption of the narrative model of traumatic loss that survivors will often construct secondary stories around the death event to mentally "undo" the death, alleviate distress, and restore some sense of coherence to one's personal meaning structures (Rynearson et al., 2006).

These secondary stories can include imagined themes of revenge or retaliation against a person(s) deemed responsible for causing a loved one's death to restore a sense of justice or even themes of remorse and guilt for not having been able to prevent a loved one's death. The latter may be commonplace as survivors try to make sense of the loss through preexisting meaning structures. Through replaying and making sense of these stories, survivors ultimately reconstruct new meanings that allow for greater understanding of the world, although the imagery connected to these narrative themes of traumatic dying, reunion, and remorse feature prominently in several bereavement-related mental health problems.

Multidimensional Grief Theory

Originally developed as a model for understanding grief reactions in bereaved youth, multidimensional grief theory (Kaplow et al., 2013; Layne et al., 2017) suggests that psychological adaptation to loss is a process that involves and is shaped by individual-level factors, such as personal coping styles, and socio-environmental factors, such as family communication style. Both factors can impact grief responses in three different domains: circumstance-related distress, existential/identity-related distress, and separation distress.

The first of these domains, circumstance-related distress, involves distress associated with the circumstances of the death, especially when a death occurs under traumatic circumstances. This type of distress encompasses a wide range of adaptive and maladaptive responses similar to the narrative themes proposed in Rynearson's (2012) narrative model of traumatic death, such as preoccupation with how a loved one died, persistent feelings of guilt and remorse, and desire for revenge when someone is perceived to be responsible for the death.

The second domain, existential/identity-related distress, involves distress associated with managing new roles, routines, and identities brought on by the death, similar to the tasks involved in restoration-oriented coping as described in the DPM (Stroebe & Schut, 1999). The third domain, separation distress, involves distress associated with missing the lost loved one. This can include actions similar to those described as loss-oriented coping in the DPM, such as an intense yearning for or seeking reunion with a lost loved one and other common grief reactions.

Multidimensional grief theory further suggests that distress in each of these various domains can be elicited by reminders of the death event and loss, noting that maladaptive coping strategies, such as excessive avoidance and emotional suppression, can contribute to the persistence of distress in some or all of these domains (Kaplow et al., 2014; Kaplow et al., 2012). Besides the role of maladaptive coping strategies in multidimensional grief theory, contemporary social justice theories of loss also highlight the importance of intersectional identities and persistent disparities in the prevalence of traumatic death in shaping adaptation to traumatic loss.

Social Justice Conceptualizations of Loss and Traumatic Loss

Social justice conceptualizations of loss (Harris & Bordere, 2016) focus on ways that personal identities and social positionality contribute to psychological adaptation to loss. These have been applied to the experience of traumatic loss survivors as well (Bordere et al., 2021). That is, social positionality and identities based on socioeconomic status, race, ethnicity, gender, sexuality, and ability status, among other identities, all determine the extent to which an individual's grief may be recognized by others in their community. This can potentially contribute to a sense of disenfranchisement and invisibility that can interfere with adaptation to the death of a loved one. For example, homicides involving firearms, multiple victims, children and young people, and strangers are likely to receive more media attention than homicides involving socially marginalized populations (Waters et al., 2017), which can lead helping professionals across multiple sectors to underestimate the prevalence and impact of traumatic loss in marginalized communities.

As a consequence, communities and professionals risk pathologizing or suffocating natural grief responses in socially marginalized communities (for instance, a Black man is written up by his supervisor at work for expressing anger at a coworker following the homicide of a family member). Resources, such as funding for grief support at a community level, may then be channeled elsewhere, adding to secondary resource loss that commonly accompanies traumatic loss.

Stage Models of Grief

We would not go amiss without acknowledging early theories of grief that have widespread reach, as many survivors' understanding of their grief experiences and that of those around them may rely on such theories. Numerous early theories focused on a stage-based model of grief (Bowlby, 1980; Kübler-Ross, 1969; Parkes, 2009). For instance, Elisabeth Kübler-Ross's stages of grief (1969), initially intended to describe the reactions to the imminent death of terminally ill individuals, have been applied to bereavement. The model suggests we grieve in five stages: denial, anger, bargaining, depression, and acceptance. Although not her intention, many interpret it as that individuals need to pass through each stage sequentially. We have learned from subsequent grief research that we do not grieve according to Kübler-Ross's stages and that grief responses are more complex and dynamic in nature, requiring a more sophisticated framework (see Stroebe et al., 2017 for summary of concerns).

Mental Health Complications of Traumatic Loss

Survivors can experience several mental health complications while grieving traumatic losses because psychological adaptation to traumatic loss involves adaptation to the traumatic nature of the death event in addition to losing a loved one and other personal and environmental resources. Research over the last two decades has shown that the most common psychological problems that result from these primary sources of distress during adaptation to traumatic loss include persistent post-traumatic stress, depression, and prolonged grief reactions.

Post-Traumatic Stress

In the months after her daughter's death, Donna found herself unable to drive her car, overwhelmed with horrific images of what she imagined her daughter's dying moments were like every time she tried to sit behind the wheel. A previously independent woman who took pride in taking her grandchildren to the park or a movie, she now relied on her husband to drive her places when needed and carefully mapped out routes that avoided the interstate where her daughter had been killed. Donna also experienced occasional nightmares about her daughter's death and even got extremely upset with family and friends who rang the doorbell at her home when they came to visit her—the same doorbell the police rang the morning her daughter was killed.

Post-traumatic stress reactions in the context of traumatic loss are generally related to the circumstances of the death event and can include intrusive mental images of a loved one's death, distress associated with and avoidance of reminders of the death, changes in beliefs about oneself and the world, and increased physical and mental arousal. Among traumatic loss survivors, increased arousal can often take the form of heightened concern about the safety and well-being of surviving family and loved ones (such as worries about allowing children to leave the home or attend social events). Post-traumatic stress reactions in and of themselves are extremely common among traumatic loss survivors, especially in the early aftermath of a traumatic loss. However, some of these reactions, like intrusive images of a loved one's death, can persist for months or even years after the death. One study, for example, found that as many as 80 percent of treatment-seeking survivors who were, on average, more than three years postloss reported experiencing intrusive imagery of a loved one's death in the month prior to seeking treatment, even though the majority of survivors reported they did not directly witness the death (Baddeley et al., 2015). Accordingly, clinicians should be mindful that even survivors who were not present at the time of their loved one's death may still experience recurrent, persistent post-traumatic stress reactions in the wake of a traumatic loss, especially when repeatedly confronted with graphic details about the death from police, media reports, and other sources.

For the majority of survivors, post-traumatic stress reactions will naturally decline over time in the absence of formal mental health treatment, though for some survivors, these reactions will persist and lead to post-traumatic stress disorder (PTSD), significantly impairing multiple life domains (American Psychiatric Association [APA], 2022). Traumatic loss is responsible for more new cases of PTSD globally than any other single type of traumatic experience (Kessler et al., 2017). Several studies in the US have found high prevalence rates of PTSD among traumatic loss survivors, with prevalence ranging from 18 to 40 percent among homicide survivors (McDevitt-Murphy et al., 2012; Rheingold & Williams, 2015; Rheingold et al., 2024) with similar rates found internationally (e.g., van Denderen et al., 2016). Among suicide survivors, the prevalence rate was 55 percent (Tal et al., 2017), 43 percent among adults bereaved by fatal overdose (Bottomley et al., 2022), and 30 percent among survivors of motor vehicle crash fatalities (Hardt et al., 2020).

PTSD symptoms after traumatic loss often co-occur with other bereavement-related mental health problems, like depression (e.g., McDevitt-Murphy et al., 2012; Rheingold & Williams, 2015; Rheingold et al., 2024), and have been associated with an increased risk of experiencing prolonged grief reactions (Glad et al., 2022; Rheingold et al., 2024).

Depression

Hoping to better support his mother after his brother's death, Joe moved back home and transferred to a community college in the town where his mother lived. Although he kept in touch with many of his old college friends on social media and sometimes phone, he mostly spent time alone. Other than his friends at college, Joe's brother and mother had been his primary sources of support. Joe found himself reluctant to seek support from his mother, not wanting to put added stress on her and feeling it was his responsibility to support her. Joe's loneliness added to the sadness and anger he felt over his brother's death, and he began to feel increasingly guilty for not having been able to do something to prevent the death or soothe his mother's anguish.

While PTSD symptoms are generally tied to the nature of the death event, traumatic loss often has an immediate and wide-ranging impact on multiple aspects of a survivor's life, from available social support to financial resources and access to other basic needs. Perhaps a lost loved one who lived in the home with the survivor was their primary source of social support and connection to the broader community, leaving survivors with a sense of despair about the future. In other cases, maybe the lost loved one left behind children, and extended family members may find themselves suddenly responsible for raising them, limiting their ability to draw on personal social support or do things they previously enjoyed doing.

This loss of personal resources and sources of support can often be a precursor to depression among survivors, leaving those already coping with grief with a pervasive sense of sadness or hopelessness about the future. Symptoms commonly associated with depression can include persistent feelings of sadness, loss of interest in things survivors used to enjoy, changes in diet or sleep, loss of energy, difficulty concentrating, and excessive feelings of guilt or worthlessness (APA, 2022). Excessive feelings of guilt associated with depression in traumatic loss survivors often involve intense remorse about having not been able to prevent a loved one's death or even inappropriately blaming oneself for the death (Rynearson et al., 2006; Shear & Mulhare, 2008), although survivors may also experience intense guilt about things they perceive having done or not done with their loved one in life. Suicidal ideation and thoughts of death can also be an important indicator of depression (APA, 2022), though it is important to note that this is also associated with several bereavement-related mental health problems among survivors and is not specific to depression (Williams, Eddinger et al., 2018).

Several studies suggest that depression is the most common mental health problem experienced by traumatic loss survivors; the prevalence estimates for depression range from 36 to 69 percent in different samples of survivors (Bottomley et al., 2022; Hardt et al., 2020; McDevitt-Murphy et al., 2012; Rheingold & Williams, 2015; Rheingold et al., 2024; Tal et al., 2017). Although depression can appear similar to many common grief reactions, especially in the first few months after a traumatic death, it is distinct from grief and prolonged grief in several important ways that can call for different approaches to treatment.

Prolonged Grief

Over a year after her husband's death, Alexis still found there was only one place where she found any real sense of comfort—her shared bedroom with her husband. Their bedroom and bathroom looked exactly the way it had the afternoon her husband died by suicide, with his clothes still lying in a pile in front of the closet, his glass of water by his bedstand, and his toothbrush still next to the sink. It was here that Alexis could talk to her husband and feel some sense of connection with him—something that, it seemed to her, no one else in her life could understand. This perceived lack of understanding also meant that Alexis regularly turned down invitations from family and friends to spend time together. For now, it seemed, the only prospect for joy she could find was inside the walls of her bedroom.

Grief is a nearly universal reflection of separation distress but can vary from person to person and may appear in different ways, depending on several personal and cultural factors unique to each survivor. Grief reactions include a wide range of cognitive, emotional, and behavioral reactions to being separated from a loved one, including shock and disbelief about the death, yearning for reunion and preoccupation with a lost loved one, changes in one's personal sense of identity after a loved one's death, and intense emotional reactions like bitterness and sorrow related to the death (APA, 2022; Bonanno & Kaltman, 2001).

Similar to depression, grief reactions can also include feelings of loneliness, difficulty reengaging in things the survivor used to enjoy, and feeling that life is meaningless. However, in the context of grief, these reactions are directly related to being separated from a loved one and are not as generalized as they might be in depression (APA, 2022). In depression, these reactions are also generally accompanied by a sweeping sense of sadness and inability to experience pleasure, while in grief, survivors may experience these reactions in tandem with occasional positive feelings of relief, peace, and even joy (Zisook & Shear, 2009).

Similar to post-traumatic stress reactions, avoidance of reminders of the death is a common grief reaction experienced by many survivors. Yet grief-related avoidance involves avoidance of thoughts, feelings, or activities that remind the survivor of the permanence of the death (Zisook & Shear, 2009), instead of avoidance of reminders of the death event itself (for example, avoiding cleaning a loved one's room or moving their belongings after the death).

Like post-traumatic stress reactions, grief reactions are normal responses to being suddenly separated from a loved one and are typically most intense in the weeks and months immediately after the death, gradually diminishing in intensity over time. For some survivors, however, grief reactions can persist in intensity over time (like more than one year) and continue to negatively impact overall functioning in ways commonly seen in the first few weeks after a death, developing into a condition known as prolonged grief disorder, or PGD (APA, 2022). Compared to other forms of death and dying, experiencing a traumatic loss can increase the risk for PGD (Djelantik et al., 2017), with prevalence estimates among traumatic loss survivors ranging from 10 to 74 percent across different groups of survivors in the US (Bottomley et al., 2022; Hardt et al., 2020; McDevitt-Murphy et al., 2012; Rheingold & Williams, 2015; Rheingold et al., 2024) and similar rates internationally (Djelantik et al., 2020). It is important for clinicians to note that PGD also commonly co-occurs with PTSD and depression; the majority of survivors with PGD screen positive for at least one co-occurring disorder (Rheingold et al., 2024).

Co-Occurrence of Mental Health Problems After Traumatic Loss

More than two years later, Dave continues to struggle with intrusive, painful memories of finding his son's body following the overdose that took his life. He also has recurrent dreams of walking into his son's room the night of his death and stopping him from doing the drugs that ultimately took his life. He carries a persistent and crippling feeling of guilt for not preventing his son's death, noting that he should have known his son was at risk for relapse after the breakup with his partner since he had been in rehab twice in the past for heroin use. Since his son's death, Dave has become increasingly isolated and withdrawn and often avoids leaving the house except to go to work or to make the twice-weekly trip to the cemetery. Dave has also experienced regular insomnia, sleeping at best four to five hours a night, and has lost a significant amount of weight, which has caused his family to become increasingly worried about him. Although he tries to reassure them that he is okay, he privately admits he often feels like life is now meaningless.

As clinicians, it is important to appreciate the nuanced differences between common responses to traumatic loss to best conceptualize survivors' experiences and plan for intervention strategies that target each response. Further, it is essential to recognize the high rate of co-occurrence between these conditions among traumatic loss survivors. Indeed, recent data from the Bereavement in America study—the largest study to date looking at the prevalence and co-occurrence of bereavement-related mental health problems among a national sample of adults in the US—suggests that the presence of multiple conditions is more common than the presence of any single condition alone among traumatic loss survivors (Rheingold et al., 2024).

Looking specifically at the prevalence of PTSD, depression, and PGD among survivors, for example, over a third of survivors screened positive for two or more of these mental health problems, while nearly 14 percent screened positive for all three conditions—a rate almost twice as high as that observed among individuals grieving natural losses. Given that the presence of multiple conditions is typically associated with greater clinical complexity, clinicians must be mindful of the potential for co-occurring mental health problems when assessing and planning treatment.

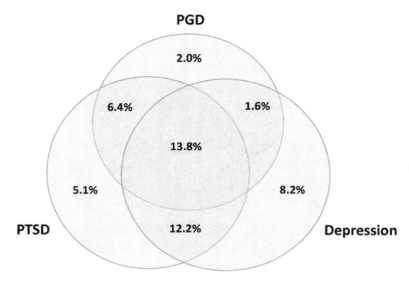

Figure adapted from Rheingold, Williams, & Bottomley (2024)

Conclusion

Traumatic loss poses a significant public health burden in terms of both global mortality rates and the resulting mental health burden on survivors. As many as one in two Americans will experience the traumatic loss of a loved one at some point in their lifetime, placing them at increased risk for persistent post-traumatic stress, depression, and prolonged grief reactions. Major health disparities in the prevalence of traumatic loss further place a disproportionate share of this burden on under-resourced and marginalized communities with limited access to mental health services for bereavement-related mental health problems. Even in resourced communities where services are available, the absence of structured treatments for traumatic loss survivors further limits the availability of care.

Furthermore, though empirically supported, disorder-specific treatments exist for PTSD, depression, and PGD, these treatments are highly differentiated, creating a dilemma for clinicians in terms of treatment selection and sequencing. Moreover, for survivors with significant co-occurring symptoms of PTSD, depression, and PGD, engagement with each of the disorder-specific treatments would present additional time and financial burdens. Our intention with this manual is to help you as a clinician close this gap with your clients. In the next chapter, we will introduce GRIEF Approach—a transdiagnostic intervention for traumatic loss survivors that integrates evidence-based principles in one package to comprehensively address post-traumatic stress, depression, and prolonged grief in a highly individualized and efficient manner.

CHAPTER 2

Introduction to GRIEF Approach

Designed for traumatically bereaved adults, the Grief Recovery with Individualized Evidence-Based Formulation (GRIEF) Approach model combines existing evidence-based strategies into a streamlined, module-based, and comprehensive transdiagnostic treatment that addresses mental health problems commonly associated with sudden and traumatic losses (for example, homicide, suicide, and motor vehicle crashes). GRIEF Approach is informed by research from both the trauma and grief fields over the last few decades showing that traumatic loss survivors are at risk for a variety of co-occurring, bereavement-related mental health problems, which can be addressed using a wide range of evidence-based techniques and interventions. Recognizing this, GRIEF Approach is designed to be a transdiagnostic treatment package that ensures clinicians tailor treatment to the unique needs of each survivor.

Treatment Overview

GRIEF Approach targets symptoms underlying three main mental health difficulties commonly associated with traumatic loss—post-traumatic stress reactions, depression, and prolonged grief—and specifically tailors the content of modules for application with survivors of traumatic loss. This manual, intended for clinicians and providers working directly with traumatic loss survivors, will guide clinicians through each of the steps involved in treatment planning using the GRIEF Approach model, from conducting a thorough assessment of symptoms with a multicultural lens informed by a sociocultural understanding of bereavement to selecting modules for intervention. This intervention was developed to be comprehensive yet flexible to allow for prioritizing and targeting various symptom presentations and needs unique to each survivor.

A concept central to GRIEF Approach is the concept of *approach*. As discussed in chapter 1, avoidance and withdrawal are common after a substantial loss. Although avoidance and withdrawal are understandable coping strategies and can be beneficial for some when used in moderation in the short term, when avoidance and withdrawal are the primary ways survivors cope with the traumatic loss of a loved one, a range of impairing mental health problems can occur. Research from both the trauma and grief fields on existing best practices to foster recovery in the aftermath of a traumatic loss suggests that teaching survivors skills to engage in more approach-based coping can help reduce distress and empower survivors with a greater sense of self-efficacy for managing the primary tasks of psychological adaptation to traumatic loss—managing traumatic distress associated with the death, separation distress associated with the lost relationship, and secondary distress associated with the loss of personal and social resources (e.g., Boelen et al., 2006; Eisma et al., 2013).

To empower survivors in using approach-based coping strategies, these recurrent themes are infused throughout each treatment module: 1) validation of experiences, 2) acceptance of loss, 3) approach of distressing thoughts and emotions, and 4) finding meaning and purpose. Within each module, skills or techniques intended to help survivors enhance approach-based strategies are described and taught so they may be practiced as survivors continue to cope with the pain of traumatic loss. Further, treatment is tailored for each individual based upon an idiographic transdiagnostic formulation of their symptom presentation.

Conceptualization of symptoms and survivor presentation guides the implementation of eight modules provided over twelve to twenty sessions. This treatment package is not designed for modules to be implemented linearly but rather in an overlapping and integrated style that meets the unique needs of each survivor. Each module will be described in detail, containing background information on the theoretical assumptions and evidence-based interventions, recommendations on how to perform the techniques, and associated handouts and worksheets (which can be downloaded online as PDFs at http://www.newharbinger.com/54353).

Rationale

As noted in chapter 1, traumatic loss prevalence is on the rise, and although grief and loss are natural and universal experiences, survivors are at an increased risk for a range of negative mental health problems, including PTSD, depression, and PGD (e.g., Djelantik et al., 2020; van Denderen et al., 2016). Further, there is significant overlap in symptomatology across these disorders (Djelantik et al., 2017), such as a markedly diminished mood or sleep disturbances. Even within each diagnosis, there is a wide range of symptom presentations. For example, the *DSM-5-TR* PTSD criteria allow for significant heterogeneity in symptom presentation among survivors suffering from PTSD (Bryant et al., 2023). Therefore, traumatic loss survivors may present differently from one another and require varied intervention strategies. For instance, while one survivor may experience profoundly distressing recurrent intrusive thoughts of the death notification or the death itself, others may not. The selection and sequence of GRIEF Approach modules will therefore be undertaken differently for each client.

Evidence-based, disorder-specific treatments exist for PTSD, depression, and PGD separately for a variety of populations (Foa et al., 2007; Lejuez et al., 2011; Shear et al.,

2005). However, these treatments have not directly targeted the more prominent themes of traumatic loss, nor do they incorporate intervention strategies within one comprehensive, transdiagnostic package that intentionally addresses the co-occurrence of PTSD, depression, and PGD symptoms. Further, there are limited treatments available that address the symptom complexity of many traumatic loss survivors and most are provided within group-based formats. To date, there are no randomized control trials examining their overall efficacy, only open trials (Rheingold et al., 2015; Saindon et al., 2014).

Further, given their unique mechanisms of action, empirically supported treatments such as prolonged exposure (PE; Foa et al., 2007) and cognitive processing therapy (CPT; Resick et al., 2017) for PTSD, behavioral activation (Lejuez et al., 2011) for depression, and prolonged grief treatment (Shear et al., 2005) for PGD are effective as stand-alone treatments but may be limited in their ability to address the complex co-occurring symptoms that are pervasive among survivors (e.g., Simon et al., 2020). Modular-based, transdiagnostic intervention designs have the advantage of unifying effective mechanisms of evidence-based practice in an idiosyncratic way and "provide innovations in therapy and for the discoverability of the optimal balance of flexibility, prescription, and structure" (Chorpita et al., 2005).

Therefore, the modular design of GRIEF Approach inherently adopts a transdiagnostic, multimechanism framework that addresses a variety of discrete symptoms in one treatment package. In the case of traumatic loss—in which chronic traumatic stress, depressive symptoms, or pathological grief reactions may be primary and may or may not be comorbid with one another—a modular, transdiagnostic, and multimechanistic approach to treatment is ideal to address the unique presentation and needs of each survivor.

Depending on the constellation and primacy of symptoms, GRIEF Approach has the structural advantage of targeting distinct mechanisms of change, such as emotional processing of the trauma (PTSD; Resick et al., 2008), (re)engagement with life and increasing reinforcing activities (depression; Galatzer-Levy & Bonanno, 2012), or finding meaning in the loss and/or revising bonds with a loved one to address separation distress (PGD; Holland & Neimeyer, 2011). Consistent with recommendations for modular-based intervention designs, the delivery of GRIEF Approach is based on a sound conceptualization of the survivor's presenting problems and current needs, which determines the priority and sequence of the treatment modules, all targeting unique mechanisms of change. Of note, similar modular treatment packages have been developed for traumatically bereaved adolescents, such as *Trauma and grief component therapy for adolescents: A modular approach to treating traumatized and bereaved youth* (Saltzman et al., 2017). GRIEF Approach is unique, however, in that it is the first modular treatment package designed for traumatically bereaved adults.

GRIEF Approach also considers research on health disparities in traumatic loss by utilizing a modular, transdiagnostic treatment design that enhances the reach and adoptability of the intervention in a range of clinical settings, including under-resourced community-clinic settings (Gutner et al., 2016; Gutner & Pressau, 2019). Traditional, empirically supported treatments for specific disorders often do not translate well to community-clinic settings, especially in under-resourced areas. Clinics may lack the financial resources to train providers in multiple disorder-specific treatments, especially when high rates of staff turnover may require ongoing investment in training and consultation to ensure sustainability of any given treatment over time.

Because transdiagnostic treatments like GRIEF Approach can address multiple, sometimes co-occurring problems, training staff in transdiagnostic treatments can be more cost-effective over time. Moreover, modular, transdiagnostic approaches to treatment have been associated with improvements in PTSD and other co-occurring symptoms in trauma-exposed youth in under-resourced settings (see Gutner et al., 2016 and Gutner & Pressau, 2019 for review). Therefore, treatments like GRIEF Approach may play an important role in expanding access to mental health care in communities where disparities in mental health problems related to traumatic loss have been largely unaddressed.

Treatment Development

GRIEF Approach is based on a qualitative clinical and research foundation as well as the past decade of ongoing evidence-informed clinical interventions with trauma victims and traumatic loss survivors. The components of GRIEF Approach are not novel but rather an intentional, stream-lined package that represents a comprehensive approach informed from existing literature on trauma- and grief-related mental health problems. Therefore, this treatment package can be viewed as an important resource for clinicians working with adult traumatic loss survivors.

One of the influential works guiding overarching principles to GRIEF Approach is Rynearson's *Retelling Violent Death* (2001), which offers clinicians an integrated treatment approach called restorative retelling (RR) for survivors conducted in group-based formats with intervention components delivered in a prescribed order. Rynearson offers on-point discussion of the unique challenges of traumatic loss, noting that these losses are violent in that they are injurious, violating in that they are transgressive and often forced on the deceased (especially in cases of homicide), and volitional in that they occur as a result of human intention or neglect (Rynearson, 2001). Indeed, RR integrates many practice elements utilized in evidence-based treatments for PTSD, depression, and PGD, including relaxation strategies, cognitive restructuring, behavioral activation, and variants of therapeutic exposures into its group-based protocol.

An important aspect of the early development of GRIEF Approach was to obtain direct feedback from traumatic loss survivors as it relates to intervention development and acceptability to empower the voice of lived experience into treatment conceptualization. As such, we conducted qualitative focus groups with traumatic loss survivors (see Williams, Rheingold et al., 2018) to gather their perceptions on a modular transdiagnostic approach to mental health treatment that would be applicable to a wide range of survivors and gather feedback about specific practice elements that would be included in this treatment. The components of existing evidence-based strategies for symptoms of post-traumatic stress, depression, and prolonged grief were discussed, and the individualized and tailored approach to treatment was reviewed. Survivors were also able to offer thoughts on additional areas of need for consideration in the treatment. For instance, across focus groups, many participants discussed the important role of social support in facilitating adaptation to bereavement. They noted that survivors may move through the grief process with greater resilience by improving social support and connectedness. This is consistent with literature on the recognition of relational needs (Bottomley et al., 2024) for traumatic loss survivors and social support serving as a buffer for development of PTSD in general (e.g., Zalta et al., 2021).

In addition, several modules include not only evidence-based approaches for the treatment of psychopathology but also evidence-informed strategies to facilitate positive growth, or post-traumatic growth, which is an outcome that represents greater postloss functioning relative to preloss functioning in various areas. Furthermore, survivors guided aspects of the intervention that may be essential to traumatic loss treatment, such as psychoeducation and normalization of symptoms, helping all survivors manage trauma and grief cues, and skills to manage strong emotions.

In addition to being developed with direct feedback and input from the survivors themselves, improvements in PTSD, depression, and PGD symptoms before and after receiving treatment using the GRIEF Approach model were observed in a series of clinical case studies with traumatic loss survivors, further supporting the feasibility and acceptability of the model (Rheingold & Williams, 2018). Our goal in developing GRIEF Approach was not to reinvent the wheel or develop a new and novel intervention. Rather, we wanted to synthesize existing theory and evidence-based strategies from different research fields (trauma and grief) that rarely intersect and lean on clinical observations of several decades of work with survivors to create a comprehensive package for clinicians in effectively providing care for this often underserved population.

Overview of Modules and Session Organization

GRIEF Approach is flexible and guided by the conceptualization of your client's symptoms and therapy goals. Therefore, the schematic of GRIEF Approach modules (see below) is the recommended module sequence. The order and presentation of modules should not be considered linear or compulsory but should instead be driven by a sound conceptualization of your client's presenting needs, symptoms, and goals for therapy.

GRIEF Approach Module Summary

Module 1 (Psychoeducation About Grief, Types of Loss, and Traumatic Loss Reactions) occurs in a single session and includes the sharing of information about prevalence of traumatic loss specific to the mode of death, common reactions to and symptoms of traumatic loss, feedback from the assessment session, a description of the tailored GRIEF Approach intervention, and case management, when indicated.

Module 2 (Identifying Emotions and Processing Thoughts) occurs across one to three sessions and includes psychoeducation about emotions, activities to promote emotion identification, exploration of unhelpful thoughts, and the construction of helpful thoughts.

Module 3 (Identifying and Building Strengths) is typically conducted in one session with follow-up across sessions and includes an identification of current effective coping strategies and inherent resilience factors to be leveraged throughout the course of therapy.

Module 4 (Managing Strong Emotions) is conducted in one to three sessions and integrated throughout and includes relaxation, mindfulness, and acceptance-based principles and activities.

Module 5 (Building Healthy Support Networks) is typically one session and helps the survivor map a supportive network and identify relationship roles and strengths. This module can be used for survivors who are withdrawn, lonely, or lacking important resources and may be particularly well suited for losses that are associated with stigmatization (like suicide and overdose).

Module 6 (Meaningful Behavioral Activation) is typically conducted in less than three sessions and includes activity tracking, engagement in *fun, functional*, or *fulfilling* activities, and an exploration of personal values and sense of meaning in daily life that are connected to their loved one.

Module 7 (Revising Bonds) occurs across two to five sessions and includes a more robust introduction to the decedent than was provided at the outset, including a presentation of photos, mementos, and stories, as well as approach-based activities, such as letter writing, therapeutic chair work, or memorialization practices.

Module 8 (Therapeutic Exposure) occurs across five to seven sessions in a consecutive fashion for survivors reporting significant avoidance and intrusive thoughts and death imagery. This module includes approach-based strategies in the form of actions (real-life exposure/approach) and death-imagery (imaginal exposure/approach and retelling of the violent loss).

Prior to commencing GRIEF Approach, you should conduct a thorough assessment of PTSD, depression, and PGD symptoms and related impairment, as these conditions often overlap with one another following traumatic loss (see chapter 3 for further details). Besides a review of your client's goals for treatment, ideally in behavioral terms, the identification of these often co-occurring symptoms will assist you with targeting and prioritizing specific symptom presentations unique to each traumatic loss survivor and, therefore, module selection. In addition, to further inform a strong conceptualization of the case, you should assess your client's strengths, risk and resiliency factors, and cultural and contextual factors relevant to care. You and your client should work collaboratively to ensure that therapeutic exercises and assignments are personally relevant to them. The order of the modules should be survivor-centered, meaning you should consider your client's input when determining the sequence of modules and setting session agendas. In doing so, your client may feel a sense of control and validation in their grief recovery.

GRIEF Approach Module Content and Selection Parameters

Module 1 Psychoeducation About Grief, Types of Loss, and Traumatic Loss Reactions 1 session	• Feedback from assessment • Educate about the prevalence of traumatic loss • Educate about common reactions and symptoms • Overview of GRIEF Approach and discussion of treatment goals • Address secondary stressors (optional)	All survivors, including PTSD, MDD, and PGD
Module 2 Identifying Emotions and Processing Thoughts 1–3 sessions	• Rationale and education • Education about emotions • Introduce the cognitive behavioral triangle • Identification of unhelpful thoughts • Generating helpful thoughts • Practice helpful thoughts	All survivors, including PTSD, MDD, and PGD
Module 3 Identifying and Building Strengths 1 session & incorporated throughout	• Rationale and education • Introduce the concept of resilience • Identify past coping skills • Assign coping skills and address barriers	All survivors, including PTSD, MDD, and PGD

Module 4 Managing Strong Emotions 1-3 sessions & incorporated throughout	• Rationale and education • Deep breathing with practice • PMR with practice • Introduce mindfulness and acceptance • Mindfulness and acceptance activity • Assign practice and address barriers	All survivors, including PTSD, MDD, and PGD
Module 5 Building Healthy Support Networks 1 session & incorporated throughout	• Rationale and education • Introduce social support mapping • Explore supportive relationships and roles • Assign activities	Primary depression (MDD) *Survivors with low social support*
Module 6 Meaningful Behavioral Activation 1-3 sessions & incorporated throughout	• Rationale and education • Introduce the concept of *fun, functional*, and *fulfilling* activities • Activity tracking • Identifying values and values-consistent activities • Assign activities	Primary depression (MDD) *Underengaged survivors*
Module 7 Revising Bonds 2-5 sessions & incorporated throughout	• Rationale and education • Introduction to the decedent • Explore memorialization practices • Correspondence with the decedent • Assign approach-oriented activities	Primary PGD *High-yearning survivors*
Module 8 Therapeutic Exposure 5-7 sessions in succession until PTSD symptom reduction	• Rationale and education • Approach mastery of loss and trauma reminders • Imaginal exposure/approach • Assign approach in action activities and recordings of imaginal exposure/approach • Address barriers and avoidance	Primary PTSD *Avoidant PGD survivors*

Typically, the first four modules are presented to all survivors to provide education and offer core cognitive behavioral skill building to manage trauma-related, depressive, and grief-related distressing emotions and cognitions. The remaining modules can be selected based upon symptomatology and identified goals.

Considerations of Timing of GRIEF Approach

An important consideration for treatment is the timing of when to engage clients in GRIEF Approach. As noted in chapter 1, grief is a normal reaction to loss that naturally diminishes over time for many survivors. As such, you need to be careful to not pathologize all grief responses or assume traumatic loss survivors will have chronic and difficult grief trajectories—indeed, research indicates that many will not. Grief is a personal reaction, and aside from intending to harm oneself or someone else shortly after the loss of a loved one, most feelings, thoughts, and responses are common grief responses. It is a universal experience to feel distress and disorientation and to carry a heavy burden of emotional suffering with having lost someone significant through death. However, grief and bereavement do increase the risk for adverse outcomes, such as physical illness (such as immunological dysfunction or hypertension) and even death. As we have discussed in chapter 1, traumatic loss can also increase the risk for mental health struggles.

Therefore, a thorough assessment is warranted before offering diagnoses and engaging in GRIEF Approach. It is intended for survivors who experience enduring and impairing symptoms or syndromal levels of bereavement-related distress. Moreover, conceptualizing mental health supports for traumatic loss survivors along a continuum of care (Boelen et al., 2019), GRIEF Approach is designed for survivors experiencing diagnosable and impairing mental health problems outside the time frame where such reactions are likely to diminish on their own or with less intensive early intervention.

You should be mindful of the timeline as loss and acute grief responses are common and normal. Thoughts and memories of the deceased or the manner in which the deceased died are prominent early after death. Disbelief, depressed mood, and yearning decline gradually from two to twenty-four months. According to grief research with general bereaved populations, by about six months after the death, acceptance of loss usually increases to where a survivor may demonstrate engaging in productive work, finding meaning and purpose, and becoming capable of experiencing some enjoyment in life (Maciejewski et al., 2007).

Though there is less research on the long-term trajectory of traumatic loss populations, existing literature suggests it may be extended to around one year after the death in such cases (Glad et al., 2022). The dilemma we have as clinicians is the balance of not pathologizing a grief reaction versus neglecting to recognize and treat a clinically impairing constellation of disorders and symptoms. Nevertheless, modules that address PGD may be helpful for those who experienced the death less than a year ago to promote acceptance of the death and prevent PGD development over time.

Timelines and symptom presentations are essential in determining the approach to validating symptoms while guiding skill acquisition. If your client presents in the acute phases of grieving a traumatic loss (the first few weeks to several months after loss), early intervention approaches may be more appropriate to reduce immediate distress and mitigate risk factors for chronic psychological problems. One such early intervention is Skills for Psychological Recovery (SPR; Berkowitz et al., 2010) to assist survivors in regaining a sense of control in their lives after loss and develop competency in managing acute trauma and grief reactions. Preliminary evidence suggests SPR may be adapted and used to facilitate recovery (Williams et al., 2024; Williams & Rheingold, 2020), particularly during the acute phases of grieving a traumatic loss when formal mental health treatment may not be appropriate.

Conclusion

GRIEF Approach is a modular, transdiagnostic treatment for and designed with input from adult survivors of traumatic loss. The model combines evidence-based strategies from existing treatments for PTSD, depression, and PGD into one comprehensive protocol. These strategies are organized into stand-alone modules that can be flexibly tailored to the unique needs of each survivor. In the next chapter, we discuss considerations for diagnosis, planning treatment, and special considerations for using the GRIEF Approach model along with recommendations on how to use this manual in your work with survivors.

CHAPTER 3

Using This Manual: Assessment and Treatment Planning

In the last chapter, we introduced GRIEF Approach, designed so that clinicians can select and tailor modules for each survivor depending on their unique needs, concerns, and diagnostic presentations. In this chapter, we discuss practical considerations for clinical assessment, selecting modules, and planning treatment using the model. However, it is important that you integrate module selection into a more comprehensive clinical interview assessing your client's psychosocial and cultural background, health history, and other information that is likely to be helpful in treatment planning. Next, we will address how to assess different mental health problems commonly associated with traumatic loss. We will also introduce tools to help you select which modules to use based on your client's unique clinical presentation.

Pretreatment Assessment

As underscored throughout this manual, assessment of symptoms as part of a comprehensive conceptualization of your client and their presenting problems is paramount. Therefore, prior to commencing GRIEF Approach, you should conduct a thorough assessment of post-traumatic stress, depression, and prolonged grief symptoms with an eye toward identifying any areas where your client's symptoms are suggestive of a diagnosable mental health problem. The identification of these often co-occurring conditions will assist you with targeting specific symptom presentations unique to each traumatic loss survivor. A core set of treatment modules is recommended for clients who meet criteria for a diagnosable mental health problem in one or more of these domains. As you begin your symptom assessment, we encourage you to first acknowledge the importance of the survivor's relationship with their lost loved one(s) and the way your client experienced the loss. Doing so will allow you to enhance rapport with your client as you prepare to start therapy and give you a more nuanced understanding of the way your client's symptoms are impacting their lives.

Death-Related Circumstances and Characteristics Associated with Traumatic Loss

You may find it helpful to begin the conversation with open-ended questions about the decedent. Not only will this information inform the various steps involved in treatment planning discussed in the remainder of this chapter, but it will likely foster therapeutic rapport building. To begin, consider asking open-ended questions about the decedent such as *Tell me about (loved one). What are some important things you might want me to know about them?*

Next, ask open-ended questions about the circumstances of the death. For instance, how their loved one died (discussed in more detail later in this chapter), whether your client was present at the time of the death or witnessed the death scene, and the extent to which they have access to important details about their loved one's death. The answers can all reveal important sources of distress for survivors. Clients who were present at the time of the death, for example, may recall vivid details of the death event that are mentally replayed in the context of recurrent reexperiencing symptoms. Whereas clients who were not present and lack access to important details about the death (as in cases of unsolved homicide) may experience persistent anger and frustration resulting from the unanswered questions surrounding their loved one's death. They may have reoccurring thoughts and images about what they believe may have happened to their loved one. Open-ended questions can help empathically explore circumstances associated with the death, such as how their loved one died and how they learned about the death.

Lastly, ask open-ended questions about challenges your client has experienced since their loved one's death. This gives clients a chance to express in their own words how their lives have been impacted by traumatic loss and gives you personally relevant examples of ways that different psychological reactions may show up in your client's life. Asking these questions can also serve as a valuable opportunity to begin collaboratively identifying treatment goals with your client.

You can use these questions to segue into a more structured assessment of bereavement-related mental health problems commonly associated with traumatic loss. See clinician handout A.1, "Additional Assessment Questions for Clinicians," as a question guide. Keep in mind that your client's cultural background and other sociocultural factors are likely influencing your client's goals for therapy, views about therapy in general, and the ways your client experiences and expresses their grief. Integrating a framework that facilitates an understanding of your client's identity can enrich your relationship with your client, especially with clients from unrepresented groups, and can help you tailor GRIEF Approach to your client's identity and context.

Using a framework such as the ADDRESSING model (Hays, 2008) can help you understand many facets of clients, including age, developmental disabilities, religion and spirituality, ethnic and racial identity, socioeconomic status, indigenous heritage, national origin, and gender. Also be mindful that persistent trauma and grief reactions that might be considered suggestive of mental health problems in some cultural contexts may be entirely normal in others and thus not appropriate targets for treatment. Using a brief, semistructured interview, like the Cultural Bereavement Interview (Smid et al., 2018), can help you better understand ways that culturally rooted practices and rituals (including religious and spiritual practices) may be influencing your client's adaptation to traumatic loss and any trauma and grief reactions they are experiencing. For example, some questions that may be helpful to understand your client's grief experience in the context of identity and culture may include:

- *Tell me about your views about the afterlife?*

- *What are important mourning rituals that you continue to practice?*

- *How has your faith or spirituality been impacted by your loss and grief experience?*

Next, we review measures available to help assess post-traumatic stress, depression, and prolonged grief reactions.

Post-Traumatic Stress Symptoms

In chapter 1, we reviewed mental health problems commonly associated with traumatic loss, including post-traumatic stress reactions and PTSD. Symptoms of the disorder often include unwanted thoughts of the death, avoidance behavior, shifts in mood and cognitions, and hyperarousal. Given the high prevalence of PTSD symptomatology following traumatic loss, a thorough assessment of PTSD symptoms should be conducted before starting treatment to assess the severity of these symptoms (for instance, does the client meet diagnostic criteria for PTSD?) and their impact on functioning across different life domains. This will help guide the eventual selection and sequencing of GRIEF Approach modules.

Clinician Tip. Selecting which assessment measures to use will likely depend on a number of different factors, including the clinical setting where treatment occurs and clinician and client availability. Although we review clinician-administered interviews and self-report measures of psychological problems commonly associated with traumatic loss, we recognize that not all clinicians will be able to conduct disorder-specific, diagnostic clinical interviews as part of their assessment due to the financial and time burden associated with these interviews. The most important thing is that you use some combination of validated assessment measures to inform diagnosis and treatment planning.

The following clinician-administered and self-report assessment measures can be employed to achieve this goal and most are free and publicly available.

- CAPS-5: The Clinician-Administered PTSD Scale for DSM-5 (CAPS-5; Weathers et al., 2018) is a structured clinical interview designed to help clinicians diagnose PTSD and measure the PTSD symptom severity. It is publicly available, and you can access the interview online at http://www.ptsd.va.gov/professional/assessment /adult-int/caps.asp#obtain.

- PCL-5: The PTSD Checklist for DSM-5 (PCL-5; Blevins et al., 2015) is one of the most widely used self-report instruments to assess PTSD symptoms and screen individuals for PTSD. It is publicly available, and you can access the questionnaire online at http://www.ptsd.va.gov/professional/assessment/adult-sr/ptsd-checklist.asp.

> **Clinician Tip.** There are several advantages to using self-report symptom measures as part of your pretreatment assessment, including their brevity, cost-effectiveness, and ease of administration and interpretation. However, accurate diagnosing requires advanced knowledge of the ways specific symptoms can emerge and are expressed over time. Do not rely on the results of self-report measures alone when making diagnostic decisions. Instead, use these results in combination with information gathered during the clinical interview to make decisions about whether a client's symptoms are consistent with a diagnosis of PTSD or any other condition.

Depression Symptoms

Depressive symptoms are among the most common psychological reactions associated with traumatic loss. Assessing for these symptoms is therefore seen as a requirement prior to commencing treatment using GRIEF Approach. Several commonly used measures for assessing depressive symptoms are discussed here and, as with the previously discussed measures, can be used to identify whether depressive symptoms should be a primary treatment target and to track depression severity over the course of treatment.

- SCID-5: The Structured Clinical Interview for DSM-5 (SCID-5) is a semistructured interview for making major *DSM-5* diagnoses, including major depressive disorder. It has a version for research (SCID-5-RV) and for the clinic (SCID-5-CV; First et al., 2016). The interview is not publicly available. You can find more information here: http://www.appi.org/products/structured-clinical-interview-for -dsm-5-scid-5.

- PHQ-9: The depression module of the Patient Health Questionnaire (PHQ; Kroenke et al., 2001) is a self-administered questionnaire originally developed for administration in primary care settings and, as such, is more parsimonious compared to other self-report instruments. The questionnaire is publicly available, and you can access it here: http://www.apa.org/depression-guideline/patient-health-questionnaire.pdf.

> **Clinician Tip.** Many traumatic loss survivors experiencing depression and other mental health problems will experience some degree of suicidal ideation. A thorough assessment of self-harm and suicidal ideation should be conducted as part of the pretreatment assessment and on a regular basis throughout treatment. Therefore, setting the stage for this at the outset of therapy will pay dividends and may normalize and validate the client's acute emotional pain and suffering while instilling hope. For clients who endorse current suicidal ideation, GRIEF Approach may still be appropriate if there is no imminent plan or intention to harm oneself or others. In such cases, develop a safety plan that can be utilized and revised throughout the course of therapy. If your client endorses intent, articulates a plan, and has the means to carry it out, GRIEF Approach would be contraindicated and a greater level of care should be considered immediately before continuing with treatment.
>
> For more information and resources on conducting a suicide risk screening, the National Institute of Mental Health has an Ask Suicide-Screening Questions (ASQ) Toolkit available for free that can be accessed at http://www.nih.gov.

Prolonged Grief Symptoms

Given the high incidence of PGD following traumatic loss, assessing for PGD symptoms alongside PTSD and depression is warranted. Instruments that assess for PGD symptoms and other grief reactions are presented below. For a thorough review of such instruments, please see Ennis et al. (2023).

- PG-13-R: The Prolonged Grief Disorder 13-Item-Revised (PG-13-R; Prigerson et al., 2021) is a revised version of the PG-13 with items corresponding to PGD symptom criteria as outlined in the DSM-5-TR (2022). It is publicly available, and you can access the questionnaire at http://endoflife.weill.cornell.edu/pg-13.

- BGQ: The Brief Grief Questionnaire (BGQ; Shear et al., 2006) is a clinician-administered screener for complicated grief—the diagnostic precursor of PGD. It is publicly available, and you can access the questionnaire here: http://complicated grief.columbia.edu/wp-content/uploads/2016/05/BGQ.pdf.

Other Clinical Considerations

In addition to post-traumatic stress, depression, and prolonged grief symptoms, clinicians should be aware of the presence of other conditions that may impact the course and outcome of treatment. For instance, research has identified a link between the experience of bereavement and substance use, particularly when the grief experience is protracted and difficult (e.g., Masferrer et al., 2017; Zuckoff et al. 2006). It is important that patterns of substance use are assessed at the outset of treatment. If it is determined that a client meets criteria for a severe substance use disorder that would likely limit their ability to participate in treatment or requires medically supervised withdrawal management, this should be addressed and the appropriate referrals made prior to GRIEF Approach.

It may also be determined that substance use is interfering with their motivation for therapy or that substance use may interfere with the treatment in general. If this is the case, supplementing therapy with motivational interviewing techniques can bolster commitment to the treatment and commitment to refraining from the use of substances before, during, and immediately after GRIEF Approach sessions that serve as a vehicle for emotional avoidance. In fact, in many ways substance use can be seen as an avoidance strategy for survivors, and appropriately naming this and conducting a functional assessment, such as discussing relevant antecedents (like triggers, thoughts, and emotions) and consequences related to substance misuse, may be sufficient to produce some degree of change. Also, psychoeducation about the role of substance use may be beneficial, such as how symptoms may increase when or if survivors begin to decrease use or refrain from substances, in which case you can preemptively help clients plan for how to cope with increased symptoms.

Be aware of the presence of any co-occurring psychotic disorders or other serious mental illnesses that might limit your client's ability to engage in therapy. Generally speaking, the presence of a psychotic disorder or other serious mental illness should not preclude using GRIEF Approach with a client so long as symptoms are currently stable and well managed. If it is determined through the assessment that a client is currently experiencing psychotic symptoms, manic symptoms, or other acute symptoms of a serious mental illness, they should be referred to a higher level of care so that symptoms can be medically stabilized prior to beginning GRIEF Approach.

Treatment Planning

Once you have completed your pretreatment assessment, you are ready to select modules to use in treatment. As we mentioned earlier in this chapter, core sets of treatment modules are recommended for survivors who meet criteria for diagnosable mental health problems, including PTSD, major depression (MDD), or PGD.

As noted in chapter 2, the first four modules are typically recommended for all survivors. Each of the cognitive behavioral skills learned in those modules target transdiagnostic processes thought to underlie PTSD, MDD, and PGD and provide clients with skills that prepare them to engage in some of the presentation-specific modules that typically follow later in treatment. The remaining modules were selected as part of the core set of modules for either PTSD, MDD, or PGD based on existing theory and evidence-based strategies from disorder-specific treatments for these conditions. More detailed discussion regarding the theoretical and empirical basis for each of the different skills and techniques included in this manual is provided in the "Background and Related Literature" section at the beginning of each module.

To illustrate how you might use the core module sets in practice, a clinician working with a survivor presenting with a primary diagnosis of PTSD but not MDD or PGD would select the PTSD core module set, which includes psychoeducation and the cognitive behavioral skill-building activities in modules 1 through 4 in addition to therapeutic exposure exercises presented in module 8. If a client presents with co-occurring PTSD and MDD, but not PGD, both the PTSD and MDD core module sets would be selected. If a client meets criteria for all three conditions, all three core module sets would be selected.

Common Challenges in Assessment and Treatment Planning

What if my client doesn't meet criteria for any mental health problems? As we discussed in chapter 1, post-traumatic stress, depression, and prolonged grief symptoms are common following a traumatic loss, and not all survivors experiencing these reactions will experience them to such a degree that they meet criteria for a formal mental health diagnosis. Survivors experiencing subthreshold symptom levels, however, can still experience significant distress and functional impairment in multiple domains as a result of these symptoms (e.g., Brancu et al., 2016). In such cases, GRIEF Approach can still be useful in addressing persistent mental health reactions associated with traumatic loss.

Rather than selecting core module sets based on diagnostic profiles, consider symptom domains where your client is endorsing the most distress. You can also use specific symptoms reported by your client to guide module selection in these situations. For instance, a client who does not meet diagnostic criteria but still reports specific symptoms (for example, having difficulty reengaging in meaningful activities) may still benefit from psychoeducation to normalize reactions, cognitive skills to help address thoughts and feelings associated with guilt, and meaningful behavioral activation to promote reengagement in positive activities.

Is it too soon to use GRIEF Approach with my client? As we mentioned in chapter 2, GRIEF Approach is intended for survivors who are experiencing enduring and impairing symptoms or syndromal levels of bereavement-related distress that are unlikely to diminish on their own without intervention. Deciding whether your client falls into this category, however, can be a tricky matter. Clinicians familiar with the *DSM-5-TR* criteria for PTSD, MDD, and PGD will recall that both PTSD and MDD can be diagnosed in as little as one month following the traumatic death of a loved one—a time when most survivors are experiencing elevated distress—whereas PGD can only be diagnosed after one year postloss (APA, 2022).

However, studies looking at temporal trajectories of post-traumatic stress, depression, prolonged grief symptoms in bereaved samples suggest that most people experiencing elevated post-traumatic stress and depression symptoms will experience a relatively steep increase followed by a gradual decline in symptoms over the course of the first year after loss (Djelantik et al., 2022; Wen et al., 2023). For these survivors, treatments like GRIEF Approach may be unnecessarily intensive. Although, longitudinal studies of mental health outcomes in the first year of bereavement have also found that, compared to survivors whose symptoms ultimately decrease, individuals who are likely to have chronic and enduring mental health problems tend to endorse elevated post-traumatic stress, depression, and grief symptoms and tend to report more negative beliefs and effortful avoidance as early as six months postloss (Boelen & Lenferink, 2020).

Fortunately, brief, modular early interventions like SPR (see chapter 2), have been developed to target unhelpful beliefs, effortful avoidance, and other psychosocial risk factors for chronic mental health problems among trauma survivors. Recent evidence suggests that SPR is associated with improvements in post-traumatic stress, depression, and prolonged grief symptoms among sudden loss survivors when delivered within the first year postloss (Williams et al., 2024).

So, we encourage you to consider beginning with a less intensive intervention, such as SPR, when working with clients who are less than one year postloss, given the considerable variability in symptoms many survivors will likely experience during the first year after traumatic loss and the availability of promising early interventions for survivors. Only step up to a more intensive treatment like GRIEF Approach if the survivor did not respond to the early intervention. Considering cultural and social norms around grief and bereavement, clients who are more than one year removed from traumatic loss and continue to experience enduring and impairing distress are likely to be appropriate for a more intensive treatment like GRIEF Approach.

Clinician Tip. Psychological reactions to traumatic loss often fluctuate and can be quite variable during the first year after the death. The intensity of trauma and grief reactions during this time tends to ebb and flow, and many clients benefit from practical, skills-focused early interventions aimed at reducing immediate distress and addressing secondary problems related to the loss, as well as fostering recovery. Unless a survivor has a co-occurring condition that requires a higher level of care, we encourage you to consider using less intensive, early interventions as a first step when working with clients who are less than a year postloss.

Free online trainings are available from the National Child Traumatic Stress Network and the National Center for PTSD for clinicians interested in learning more about modular, transdiagnostic early interventions like SPR.

Do I need to deliver core modules in the order they are presented in this manual? An important feature of GRIEF Approach is its flexibility. Every client has their own needs, hopes, and goals for treatment. We designed GRIEF Approach to be survivor-centered so that you can collaboratively determine the order of modules and session agendas. Not only will this help establish a strong working alliance with your client, but it also helps reestablish a sense of control and personal agency over grief recovery. For instance, a client who is experiencing depression and is seeking therapy in hopes of reengaging in positive social activities may benefit more from meaningful behavioral activation during the early stages of therapy before focusing on cognitive restructuring or emotion regulation skill building. Or, as another example, clients reporting multiple health-related social needs may benefit from building positive support networks with an emphasis on connecting them to community and social resources that can help with these needs before advancing to other modules.

That said, you will often find it helpful to begin with psychoeducation around reported symptoms and an overview of the GRIEF Approach model to ensure that you and your client have a shared understanding of treatment aims and goals and to create a common language for your client's experiences. As a final point, skills introduced using specific modules should be integrated throughout the course of treatment, not simply retired after a module is completed. For example, you may introduce processing thoughts early in treatment but find it helpful to use the skill later in treatment when challenging negative beliefs about what is likely to happen during exposure exercises.

Selecting Supplemental Modules and Symptom Measures

You will often find it helpful to assess for the presence of specific symptoms and other concerns that may indicate the need for additional modules when planning treatment. Many symptoms, like effortful avoidance of trauma and grief cues and negative cognitions, are not specific to any one disorder and may interfere with treatment if not properly addressed. Often, information about these transdiagnostic symptoms will naturally emerge in the context of your clinical interview and symptom assessment, so it will not always be necessary to include supplemental symptom measures in your pretreatment assessment. Nevertheless, here are a few examples of supplemental symptom measures that can aid in treatment planning when used alongside other measures of common mental health problems associated with traumatic loss.

- DIS-R: The Dying Imagery Scale-Revised (DIS-R; Williams et al., 2022) is a self-report measure that assesses the frequency with which bereaved individuals experienced death-related imagery over the past month. It is publicly available, and you can view the original article at http://www.tandfonline.com/doi/full/10.1080/0748 1187.2020.1812135.

- GRAQ: The Grief-Related Avoidance Questionnaire (GRAQ; Baker et al., 2016) is a self-report instrument that assesses avoidance behavior related to the death. It is not publicly available. You can find more information here: http://prolongedgrief.columbia.edu/product/graq/.

- GCQ: The Grief Cognitions Questionnaire (GCQ; Boelen & Lensvelt-Mulders, 2005) is a self-report measure that assesses negative grief-related thoughts using nine categories of cognitions related to the death. It is publicly available, and you can access the original article at http://psych.apa.org/record/2005-11045-007.

- YSL: The Yearning in Situations of Loss Scale (YSL)-Bereaved version (O'Connor & Sussman, 2014) is a self-report measure concerning cognitive and emotional symptoms of yearning for a lost loved one commonly experienced during bereavement. The questionnaire is publicly available, and you can access it here: http://maryfrancesoconnor.org/ysl-scale.

- AHC HRSN: The Accountable Health Communities Health-Related Social Needs Screen Tool (AHC HRSN; Centers for Medicare and Medicaid Services, 2023) is a self-report measure assessing health-related social needs that can interfere with recovery after traumatic loss and pose significant barriers to treatment if not properly addressed. Survivors' needs are assessed across ten domains. The measure is publicly available. You can access it at http://www.cms.gov/priorities/innovation/files/worksheets/ahcm-screeningtool.pdf.

Once you have finished your pretreatment assessment and administered any supplemental measures to aid you in treatment planning, you can begin the final process of selecting modules to use in treatment. The following flowchart can aid you in the final stages of selecting modules appropriate to your client's needs as you approach the final stages of treatment planning.

GRIEF Approach Treatment-Planning Flowchart for Clinicians

			Modules
Does your client meet criteria for PTSD?	NO Continue with questions 1a–1b	YES Proceed to question 2	Core PTSD set Modules 1–4, 8
Is your client reporting any of the following as primary concerns?			
1a. Recurrent death imagery or reexperiencing symptoms?	NO	YES	Supplemental module 8
1b. Effortful avoidance of trauma or grief cues?	NO	YES	Supplemental module 8
Does your client meet criteria for MDD?	NO Continue with questions 2a–2c	YES Proceed to question 3	Core MDD set Modules 1–6
Is your client reporting any of the following as primary concerns?			
2a. Significant disruptions in social or recreational activities?	NO	YES	Supplemental module 6
2b. Feelings of being socially isolated?	NO	YES	Supplemental module 5
2c. Multiple health-related social needs?	NO	YES	Supplemental module 5
Does your client meet criteria for PGD?	NO Continue with question 3a	YES	Core PGD set Modules 1–4, 7
Is your client reporting the following as a primary concern?			
3a. Intense yearning for the deceased or proximity-seeking behaviors?	NO	YES	Supplemental module 7

Special Considerations for Treatment Planning with Different Populations

We noted that circumstances associated with the death, including how a survivor's loved one died, can reveal important sources of distress for clients that may need to be considered in treatment planning and as you prepare to begin treatment. While it is beyond the scope of this chapter to review this large body of literature in detail, we feel it is important to highlight some of these special considerations for working with different populations of traumatic loss survivors.

Traumatic Loss from Intentional Injuries

In circumstances of traumatic loss resulting from intentional injuries (such as homicide or suicide), survivors often contend with a number of psychosocial stressors that are likely to come up in treatment. In cases of homicide, for example, where a person(s) is responsible for inflicting violating injuries on the deceased, efforts to get justice for a lost loved one often involve lengthy and emotionally demanding interactions with the legal system, a process that can play out for years after the death and sometimes fails to yield meaningful results for families. Homicide survivors are also confronted with regular reminders of the traumatic circumstances of their loved one's death through media coverage, which can simultaneously increase as cases go to trial. Thus, you should be aware of and anticipate potential exacerbations in trauma and grief reactions resulting from those two stressors and may find it useful to use time in therapy to directly address them.

The perpetrator's relationship to the victim and their family can also affect the available support and how survivors reintegrate into their community. Gang-related homicides, for instance, may necessitate relocation for the surviving family due to ongoing safety concerns, causing linkage to new social supports, whereas police-involved killings may exacerbate cultural mistrust and reluctance to engage with the legal system within one's own community as a source of justice, accountability, and support (Bordere et al., 2021).

Suicide losses can similarly affect available sources of support and how survivors reintegrate into their community. Many suicide survivors experience stigma in the form of being avoided by others in their family or community. They may also experience blame from others, which can be internalized and experienced as negative beliefs related to self-blame for perceptions of failing to prevent the suicide death. These beliefs are often accompanied by strong feelings of guilt and even anger, which can be directed at oneself or the decedent for having caused their own death or "abandoning" the survivor (McGann et al., 2021). Thus, helping clients work with these painful thoughts and feelings will often be an important part of treatment with suicide loss survivors.

That said, attempts at reassuring clients that they were not responsible for or to blame for the death are rarely helpful for survivors in the long term. Instead, we encourage you to help clients critically explore the evidence for and against these thoughts and beliefs (Jordan & McGann, 2017), which often leads to more meaningful and realistic changes in their understanding of the different factors that contributed to their loved one's death (see module 2 for more information).

Traumatic Loss from Unintentional Injuries

Deaths from unintentional injuries (including those resulting from road traffic crashes, falls, drowning, burns, and so forth) can occur under a wide range of circumstances, each of which may have their own implications for treatment. One common feature of this type of death is that they often involve some degree of preventability (for example, a loved one killed in a motor vehicle crash was driving recklessly or not wearing a seat belt; Stewart, 1999). Survivors trying to come to terms with the preventable aspects of unintentional injury deaths may experience anger directed at the deceased or others who were seen as contributing to the actions leading to their loved one's death in ways similar to homicide and suicide survivors.

Deaths from unintentional injuries may also involve mutilating injuries that ultimately affect whether survivors were able to view their loved one's bodies or perform other rituals. In some cases, such as drownings or natural disasters, the deceased's body may have never been recovered, which can exacerbate challenges with acceptance of the death. In addition, under these circumstances, the extent to which families were able to perform important rituals on behalf of the deceased are nonexistent or substantially hampered. These survivors may present with significant guilt that they will want to address in treatment.

Survivors of unintentional injury-related deaths may also experience considerable distress from the uncertainty surrounding the circumstances of their loved one's death (Gamino et al., 2021). Survivors of overdose-related deaths, for example, may struggle with unanswerable questions about whether the overdose was intentional or unintentional, or whether their loved one even knew that they were ingesting a potentially lethal drug. In addition, like survivors of suicide, survivors of overdose-related deaths may contend with high levels of stigmatization for the decedent's drug use, as well as perceptions of self-blame and guilt due to perceived failures in curbing or preventing continued drug use. Further, when drug use was deeply protracted, predeath conflict between the survivor and decedent may produce a sense of relief, which can produce additional feelings of guilt.

Survivors of motor vehicle crash deaths may struggle with questions about whether different safety measures (like guard rails or traffic lights) could have prevented their loved one's death. In the case of unexpected medical complications, survivors may have many questions for medical teams about the course of their loved one's treatment. Helping survivors adopt mindfulness and acceptance-based skills to manage strong emotions tied to the uncertainty posed by these lingering questions will therefore be an important goal of treatment in many situations where unanswerable questions are interfering with the client's coping and recovery.

Conclusion

Selecting modules to use in treatment using the GRIEF Approach model requires a careful assessment of mental health problems commonly associated with traumatic loss. To support clinical decision making, we organized core sets of treatment modules for clients presenting with PTSD, MDD, or PGD, although you can also select supplemental modules based on specific symptoms or concerns that your client hopes to address in treatment. Detailed information about the practice elements embedded in each module, along with recommendations for delivering modules with traumatic loss survivors, is provided in the following chapters. For convenience, each module is presented in a stand-alone chapter that includes a review of background literature on the practice elements, a step-by-step discussion of the module components and tips for implementing these in treatment, and a review of cultural considerations for delivering practice elements. We begin with a core module recommended for all clients that will also typically be the first one used in treatment: module 1, "Psychoeducation about Loss, Types of Loss, and Traumatic Loss."

CHAPTER 4

Module 1: Psychoeducation About Grief, Types of Loss, and Traumatic Loss Reactions

Post-traumatic stress, depression, and prolonged grief reactions can be threatening and overwhelming for survivors who generally receive little information from bereavement care professionals about the prevalence, course, and potential complications that can arise from these reactions. In addition, many survivors' understanding of grief may lean on outdated grief models, such as stage theories of grief, or on prior experiences of grief from natural loss, which is inherently different in its characteristics and potential responses. Therefore, this standard module provides clients with education and information about common psychological reactions to traumatic loss. It also provides an introduction to the strategies, techniques, and structure embedded within GRIEF Approach that can be helpful for survivors in addressing these reactions.

Furthermore, depending on contextual factors, the client may elect to have family members present for this psychoeducation module, or the client can begin to share psychoeducational materials with family and significant others as a between-session assignment. This module can be provided in one session and can be helpful to integrate into initial treatment planning and feedback sessions.

You may need to integrate psychoeducation about common reactions to traumatic loss throughout treatment, especially when transitioning between modules, in preparation for life events that may exacerbate symptoms or when treatment interfering behaviors (such as avoidance of assignments or sessions) occur.

Background and Related Literature

Although the death of a loved one is a common life event for all, the experience of grief can seem distressingly foreign for many. Emotional reactions to loss can drastically vary, from sadness to anger, to guilt, and even relief, often in a bewilderingly rapid fashion. Cognitive, behavioral, and physical reactions (like insomnia, loss of appetite, or nausea) also vary greatly from person to person and sometimes moment to moment. For individuals who experience the traumatic death of a loved one, these reactions may be more intense, protracted, and debilitating. Educating clients on these reactions will help them understand that what they are experiencing is unfortunately common, that they are not "going crazy," and how GRIEF Approach can help. This validates the clients' suffering and sets the stage for hope and recovery.

Psychoeducation is commonly conducted during the outset of most, if not all, evidence-based therapies for a variety of psychiatric conditions. Regardless of the context in which psychoeducation is provided, it generally relies on a number of assumptions. First, if people are provided information on symptoms of psychological disorders, they will likely find these experiences to be less disturbing. Second, psychoeducation involves imparting the message that these experiences are normal given what the person has experienced, which can be reassuring. Third, psychoeducation may increase a sense of hope and the likelihood of adherence to treatment, which is important for those who overly utilize avoidance-based strategies to cope with the loss. Fourth, psychoeducation can introduce corrective information that begins to modify the client's perception of the death, themselves or their perceived role in the death, and the future.

For some time, many clinicians viewed psychoeducation as negligibly helpful at best and, at worst, potentially harmful due to concerns about increasing survivors' views of pathology and dysfunction. However, evidence from decades of research highlights the importance of psychoeducation in a variety of treatment packages for psychological illness, including PTSD (Gould et al., 2007), depression (Tursi et al., 2013), and PGD (Rosner et al., 2011).

Moreover, meta-analyses have revealed that the provision of psychoeducation may reduce psychological symptoms independent of other treatment components (Donker et al., 2009). It should be noted that the effect sizes of these stand-alone psychoeducation interventions were small but suggest that psychoeducation can still contribute positively to treatment outcomes, especially when combined with other treatment components that aim to promote behavioral, cognitive, or affective change in the survivor. Qualitative research with traumatic loss survivors also suggests that psychoeducation is seen as one of the most essential components of treatment with this population in that it can help normalize reactions that commonly occur in the wake of traumatic loss, as well as provide helpful information about the typical course of these reactions (Williams, Rheingold et al., 2018).

Presentation Appropriateness

This module is recommended for all clients.

Agenda for Session

Module 1 first session:

1. Provide an overview of grief and the unique impact of traumatic loss.

2. Review results of pretreatment assessments.

3. Discuss personally relevant examples of symptoms.

4. Review psychoeducational handouts.

5. Clarify treatment goals.

6. Describe GRIEF Approach and how it will address symptoms and client goals.

7. Address secondary stressors (optional).

Module 1 additional sessions:

8. Provide and review additional psychoeducational handouts as appropriate within other modules.

Handouts

Handout 1.1: What Makes Traumatic Loss Different?

Handout 1.2: Dual Process Model of Grief

Handout 1.3: Summary of Post-Traumatic Stress Symptoms

Handout 1.4: Summary of Depression Symptoms

Handout 1.5: Summary of Prolonged Grief Symptoms

Handout 1.6: Overview of GRIEF Approach

Module Components

1. Provide an Overview of Grief and the Unique Impact of Traumatic Loss

Contemporary evidence-based theories of grief should be articulated to clients to correct any assumptions from stage theories of grief or prior experiences that may lead to erroneous beliefs about recovery from traumatic loss. Likewise, time should be devoted to helping clients understand the unique aspects of traumatic loss and why what they are experiencing may be different or more intense, whether based on incomplete theories or prior experiences of bereavement following the natural death of a loved one. Educate clients that a) grief is universal and a natural reaction to the loss of something important to us; b) traumatic loss is different from natural loss; and c) grief is complex and dynamic over the course of our lives.

Grief is universal and a natural reaction to the loss of something important to us. As humans, if we experience love, we will experience grief. This manifests in a wide variety of ways; therefore, different people may grieve differently from one another. There is no "right" way to grieve. All feelings are normal and considered natural responses to the death of a loved one, including thoughts about meaninglessness and suicide. Indeed, explaining that all emotions are understandable following a significant death represents an opportunity to discuss suicidal ideation or intent to harm oneself or someone else. While common, suicidal or homicidal ideation should nevertheless be immediately addressed through a thorough risk assessment with the development of a safety plan when necessary, as noted in chapter 3.

It is helpful to educate clients that grief is not one emotion or experience but rather a reaction to loss that includes a constellation of feelings and emotions, body sensations, and cognitive and spiritual reactions. Feelings and emotions may include yearning, sadness, fear, anger, guilt, anxiety, or relief. The latter may be especially relevant for suicide or fatal drug overdose survivors. Physical or body sensations may include tightness of the chest, rapid breathing, stomach aches and nausea, numbness, headaches, fatigue, and insomnia or hypersomnia. Cognitive symptoms may include confusion, disorientation, poor concentration, poor memory, impaired judgment, hallucinations, and distressing thoughts. Spiritual reactions may include questioning beliefs, anger with God, withdrawal from faith, or comfort by faith. Reviewing these general grief symptoms and reactions early in treatment can normalize client's reactions as you build on this information when discussing bereavement-related mental health problems. Handout 1.1 provides an overview of common grief reactions.

Example introduction to psychoeducation:

Before we review the results of the assessment we did together last session, I thought it may be helpful to talk generally about the impact of grief and traumatic loss, as it may help us better understand what you are currently going through. First, grief is something we as humans will all experience at some point in our lives. Some people say "grief is the price we pay for love"; if we love, we will grieve. It's a natural reaction to the death of someone important to us. All feelings are normal, even if they seem foreign or scary. Despite being natural and common, grief still can impact our health and well-being in many ways.

Let's review some common grief reactions together. These may include emotional, physical, cognitive, and spiritual reactions...

Traumatic loss is different from natural loss. Educating clients on the prevalence of their type of loss and general common reactions associated with that loss can be reassuring in that they are not alone in their experiences. Below is educational information derived from decades of research that may be helpful to discuss.

Traumatic loss in general:

- It includes deaths that are often sudden, intentional or a result from human negligence, and stigmatized. They are also usually violent and can have financial implications.

- It is very common, with 50 percent of adults in the US experiencing the traumatic death of a loved one at some point in their lifetime (Kilpatrick et al., 2013). These rates are even higher among racial minority groups (Keyes et al., 2013).

- Initial reactions to the loss typically include shock, disbelief, and disorientation. Many of these reactions are seen as adaptive, as they help the survivor in the immediate aftermath of a traumatic death.

- Later reactions to the loss can include profound yearning and disbelief, sadness, a sense of meaninglessness, and increased fear for the self or living loved ones.

- Traumatic loss reactions can be more intense than those after a loss to natural circumstances because of the traumatic and sudden nature of how a loved one died.

Additional reactions associated with specific forms of traumatic loss:

- Loss by homicide: stigma, justice system involvement, feelings of anger toward the perpetrator, potential desire for revenge, media involvement, and feelings of guilt.

- Loss by suicide or drug overdose: self- and social stigma, mixed emotions toward loved one or their death, feelings of guilt, feelings of anger at others (such as providers, associates, and family members).

Example dialogue about how traumatic loss is unique (descriptions will differ based upon characteristics of the death and your client's reactions):

Clinician: Traumatic loss is unique to other types of loss. Have you ever experienced the death of a loved one before?

Client: Yes, my sister died of breast cancer six years ago.

Clinician: And how would you describe how your grief from the death of your son is different from the loss of your sister?

Module 1: Psychoeducation About Grief, Types of Loss, and Traumatic Loss Reactions

Client: My son's death was so sudden. I mean, I wasn't expecting my sister to die either, but given she was sick, I understood why she died. I just keep thinking about why my son was killed. It doesn't make sense to me. It has affected everything. And I can't stop crying. It just feels so intense. I just do not know how I will ever live my life again.

Clinician: Exactly. The suddenness, the violent nature of your son's death, the lack of meaning and understanding of the loss, and the intensity of your emotions makes your grief to this traumatic loss different from other types of loss. Your reactions make sense given the type of loss you've experienced. Others who have experienced the murder of a loved one report similar feelings and reactions, including anger at the person who killed their loved one or a desire to seek revenge, anger or disappointment at the criminal justice system, or frustration with the media...

Grief is complex and dynamic over the course of our lives. Given many survivors lean on the stages of grief model to understand their reactions, you may find it helpful to provide a brief overview of other more contemporary and evidence-based models of traumatic loss response. This will assist clients in recognizing that grief is complex and nonlinear, will continue over the course of our lives in different ways, and that leaning into or approaching grief in everyday life experiences may be useful to help us live a full and meaningful life. For instance, you can describe the basics of the DPM of grief: that grief includes both loss-oriented stressors (such as grief work, intrusions of grief and denial, or avoidance of restoration changes) and restoration-oriented stressors (such as attending to life changes, doing new things, denial or avoidance of grief, or new roles or relationships) and that adaptation to grief inherently requires oscillating between the two during everyday life and over time. It should be made clear that grief is not linear or stage-based but rather an ongoing process throughout the lifespan. Handout 1.2 can be used to guide discussion.

Example dialogue:

Clinician: Have you heard of the stages of grief?

Client: Yes, and since my son died, I've felt so sad. My family keeps telling me I need to feel anger, but I just don't know how.

Clinician: Many people think we need to grieve in stages. However, we know from more recent research that this is not really the case. Grief actually is more complex. Yes, we carry grief over the course of our lives, but our grief experience will morph and change. It will not always be the same.

             Grief includes both loss-oriented stressors and restoration-oriented stressors. Loss-oriented stressors are the meat of grief work; it also includes

45

intrusions of grief, yearning for our loved one, and denial or avoidance of new aspects of life. Now, restoration-oriented stressors include things like attending to life changes, doing new things, adopting new roles or relationships and, perhaps, denial or avoidance of grief. We ping back and forth between loss-oriented and restoration-oriented reactions and stressors in our everyday life.

Sometimes people struggle with one or both of these types of stressors and may find themselves experiencing one at the exclusion of the other. We sometimes experience problems when we're grieving when we're not able to move back and forth between these poles. However, when we approach and lean into both loss- and restoration-oriented grief responses and stressors and allow ourselves to move freely between the two, we can begin to adapt and live a life with hope and meaning.

2. Review Results of Pretreatment Assessments

An important step in providing effective psychoeducation is gathering information about the kinds of reactions that feature most prominently in each client's unique presentation. Prior to beginning therapy, conduct a thorough intake assessment to gather information about the client's background, the circumstances surrounding the loss, and presenting symptoms and their impact on functioning. We also recommend using one or more of the standardized screening tools that assess post-traumatic stress, depression, and prolonged grief symptom severity from the previous chapter. Reviewing the results of these measures prior to starting treatment with a client can help identify areas that may be important for additional discussion or inquiry during initial treatment planning. Feedback should be given based on objective and subjective reports of symptoms (see below).

3. Discuss Personally Relevant Examples of Symptoms

It is essential to provide psychoeducation in a collaborative way that reflects each client's unique experiences to ensure that the information helps clients better understand something about the nature and course of their own reactions. Moreover, soliciting reactions and feedback from the assessment and its interpretation illustrates to the client that they are an active partner in the therapeutic journey and that they are the ultimate experts on their experience. To facilitate this assessment discussion, you may choose to go over the symptom measures completed during the initial intake with your client.

Example of introducing assessment feedback:

Thank you for filling out these questionnaires last time. These questions will be useful for us as we come up with a treatment plan that will be most helpful for you and meet your goals for therapy. One of the reasons I asked you to complete these specific question-naires is that these questions ask about several common experiences that many people who have experienced a traumatic loss may have at some point in their grief. As you completed these questionnaires, what kinds of reactions really resonated with you and your experiences since (loved one) died? Which reactions have been most difficult for you? How have they affected your life? You reported that you experience meaningless-ness nearly every day since (loved one)'s death. Tell me more about that...

Allowing clients the opportunity to more fully describe the information provided on the assessment measures is often helpful for clients who may not have had the opportunity to share more detailed information about these experiences with others. You should also gather information about ways that specific reactions occur in your client's life, which can then be used to inform treatment planning.

At this point, as part of the psychoeducation phase, you may start to normalize the reactions and symptoms that clients are reporting. This often provides clients with an immediate sense of relief by reminding them that they are not "going crazy" and can further reassure them that treatment may be helpful given the success of many clients with GRIEF Approach. Providing examples of postloss behavioral avoidance or other common reactions after the traumatic death may be particularly helpful. An illustration of how a clinician might normalize symptoms for a client following the traumatic death of their son (Michael) can be found below.

Example:

Client: I keep trying so hard not to think about Michael's death because I just feel like I'm going to break down every time I do. So, I've pretty much stopped talking to everyone because every time I go out or I pick up the phone, someone asks me about him or how I've been doing since he died. I've just pretty much stopped going out or answering the phone or anything.

Clinician: It's really scary thinking that you'll break down every time Michael's death crosses your mind. If we can pause here for just a moment, one thing that I'd like for you to know is that what you're describing is a really natural response to losing someone like this. In fact, many other survivors of sudden and violent losses that I have talked with have told me they've had similar experiences. If you think about it, it kind of makes sense that we try to avoid doing things or being around people that might remind us of the circumstances of the death given how painful it is to think about. It's kind of like avoiding those things gives us a bit of space to breathe.

Client: Yeah, exactly. It's good to know other people experience this, too, because my husband and my sister keep telling me I need to start going out more.

Clinician:	It almost seems like others can't see how overwhelming all of this is. You know, even though avoiding doing things or being around certain people can be helpful in the short term, why might it make some of these reactions (gestures toward questionnaires) worse or keep them from getting better in the long run?
Client:	I just feel awful all of the time.
Clinician:	That's right! Actually, relying only on avoidance as a means of coping may keep us stuck and make accepting and integrating the harsh reality of Michael's death that much more difficult over time.

In many circumstances, clients will report a sense of validation and connection with other survivors when clinicians normalize reactions, as is illustrated in the example above. This may be especially true for losses that are fraught with stigma, both social and self-imposed, such as deaths due to suicide or fatal overdose. Note, however, that the clinician also invites the client to join in a discussion about the potentially problematic aspects of intense behavioral avoidance while joining with the client's experience of the avoidance as something that provides temporary relief.

Clinician Tip. In normalizing symptoms and reactions, be mindful of acknowledging both the helpful and problematic aspects of reactions when appropriate.

4. Review Psychoeducational Handouts

After discussing personally relevant examples of symptoms, provide the client with psychoeducational handouts that explain how their symptoms fit within the broader context of common bereavement-related mental health problems. Handouts 1.3–1.5 provided online as part of this module include information about post-traumatic stress, depression, and prolonged grief reactions. Review the information in the handouts that apply to the unique symptom presentation of your client with them and give them the opportunity to ask questions.

Example for a client who suffers from post-traumatic stress, depression, and prolonged grief:

The toll of traumatic loss tends to emerge for survivors in three important ways: post-traumatic stress, depression, and grief reactions. While they might all sound similar, there are some important differences between them that are important for us to consider as we think about what treatment might look like for you. First, post-traumatic stress symptoms are just that—stress reactions brought on by how your loved one died. For example, you might feel constantly keyed up and keep thinking about the death or having nightmares about the death even when you try not to, which can lead you to try really hard to avoid things or people that remind you of the loss.

While post-traumatic stress symptoms are usually centered on the death itself, depression is different in that it usually involves a deep sadness, loss of interest in things that you usually enjoy, and even hopelessness about life more generally. Then there are grief reactions that are more specific to the relationship we had with our loved one and the pain we might feel about the lost relationship itself. Grief reactions might include things like intense yearning for your loved one or frequently seeking out places or things that make you feel more connected to your loved one, even when doing so might negatively impact other parts of your life. Other grief reactions may be a profound sense of disbelief about the death, meaninglessness in life without them, or a feeling as though a part of you died with your loved one.

What questions or reactions come up for you as we talk about these different types of reactions? How might these reactions be reflected in your own journey? Which of these reactions make living the life you want most difficult?

It can also be helpful to ask clients how they see their own reactions fitting into these different categories and, if your client is endorsing symptoms across multiple symptom categories, ask them which symptoms they think are most important to address first in therapy. This collaborative approach encourages active participation from your client and helps you build a strong working alliance with them. After reviewing the key handouts with your client, encourage them to read the handouts between sessions.

> **Clinician Tip.** After conducting the initial psychoeducation session, follow up with clients about any questions or new insights they had about any of the information shared. Once clients understand the nature of common psychological reactions to traumatic loss, they may begin to recognize new ways that these reactions occur for them in daily life that can be helpful to focus on in session.

5. Clarify Treatment Goals

After reviewing general grief responses, traumatic loss characteristics, and the client-specific clinical profile, a brief discussion of treatment goals will help you and your client work together toward a common direction and assist you in prioritizing modules to focus on first. You can open the discussion of goals by asking your client what they would like to accomplish in therapy. Of note, many clients may indicate that they do not know what their goals are or cannot envision life without their loved one. This is a common response that is worthy of validation. If this comes up with your client, note that this experience is entirely understandable and then offer up some suggestions based on assessment results to generate discussion of potential therapy goals. Generating several behaviorally specific goals may also be useful to guide assessment of treatment goals. For instance, if a client indicates they want to find joy again, you might ask how they might know when they're finding joy or what others might observe them doing if they found joy again.

Example:

> Now that we've talked about some of the difficult reactions and symptoms you've been facing after (loved one)'s death, let's talk about our goals in treatment together. You've heard of the saying "time heals." Actually, time itself doesn't really heal. It's what we do with the time that matters. Right now, you may just be living or surviving, and we want you to get to the point of not just living but having a full life; not just surviving but thriving. Our goal is not to get rid of grief because you'll always grieve since you will always love (loved one). Our goal may be to learn how to carry the grief and loss lighter. Our goal may be to honor their life or create meaning from the loss. To perhaps sit in loss-oriented work more or lean into restoration-oriented work. What are some goals you want to achieve together in therapy?

6. Describe GRIEF Approach and How It Will Address Symptoms and Client Goals

You and your client may find it helpful to begin conceptualizing their current difficulties given the improved understanding of how symptoms manifest in their life. In addition, reiterating or clarifying treatment goals and how GRIEF Approach can uniquely address these specific goals and reported symptoms can help to build motivation for treatment. You can introduce the treatment package and a brief overview of its components and use handout 1.6 as a guide. Doing so will help draw your client's attention to how GRIEF Approach can address their distressing reactions and therapy goals.

In addition, you should describe the general format of treatment and expectations. This includes sharing information about the number of sessions and typical session length and the role of between-session assignments to assist clients with skill acquisition. Inquire with your client about their reactions, including any concerns that may be addressed before scheduling the next session.

The following is an example of how you might preview the remainder of the treatment. It is recommended that you incorporate client-relevant examples of ways that treatment can help them achieve therapy goals when possible (for example, "The cognitive exercises that we'll do in the next few weeks will help you to gather other possible perspectives or outcomes related to you meeting with family and friends, so that these situations don't always feel so stressful").

Module 1: Psychoeducation About Grief, Types of Loss, and Traumatic Loss Reactions

Example:

Let's talk about what to expect from our working together in approaching your grief, if that is okay with you? This treatment involves a number of different components that address the challenges we've talked about thus far, as well as help you to achieve your goals for therapy. This treatment is intended to be tailored specifically to you, so we'll need to put our heads together as a team to decide which components are most important for your goals. I may be the expert on this therapy, but you're the expert on your life, so it's important we work together to make sure we're consistently on target with your goals.

To give you a sense of what we'll be doing, you can expect this treatment to help you recognize emotions and how to cope with them. We'll acknowledge your strengths and discuss things that have helped you cope with powerful emotions in the past to see if it might make sense to do those things more regularly. It might make sense to learn new strategies, such as mindfulness, relaxation, or reviewing our ways of thinking, that will help you to cope when emotions are very strong. This treatment will also include discussions about the important people in your life or people who can provide support when you need it the most. You can also expect this treatment to really help you with the things you want to do more often, such as activities that are fun, serve a particular function, or are personally fulfilling to you.

When you feel ready, and ideally after some coping skills are identified and utilized regularly, we will discuss ways that you can maintain a relationship with your loved one despite their physical absence. Another important component of this therapy addresses that thing called avoidance that we discussed earlier. For example, perhaps you've found yourself avoiding things that really matter to you because the emotional pain feels like too much to bear. This therapy will help us approach these things in a way that makes sense to you and allows you to feel empowered and in control.

Ideally, we'll meet once per week for about fifty to sixty minutes. You can also expect me to ask you to complete those questionnaires again so that we can track your progress and identify any changes we may need to make along the way. Because we'll be tracking your progress, it's hard to say exactly how many sessions will be needed, but we've found that successful treatment can be completed within twelve to twenty sessions. One other thing—I'll ask you to complete between-session assignments so you can practice some of the skills we discuss in here.

What concerns do you have about what I've said thus far? What are some of your reactions to what I've shared?

> **Clinician Tip.** In cases where you are providing sessions via telehealth, it is important to share additional information about and discuss special considerations related to confidentiality using online platforms, privacy (especially if conducting home-based telehealth where others in the home may be present), and safety planning for clinical emergencies.

7. Address Secondary Stressors (Optional)

A number of survivors, as a result of the death, may have significant secondary stressors including safety, financial, housing, childcare, new caregiving responsibilities, or health stressors. For instance, for homicide loss survivors, concerns about safety for oneself or others may be relevant. Financial insecurity, which can lead to other stressors, may be relevant for survivors who experience the death of a primary income earner. Likewise, widows and widowers who have dependent children may experience an abrupt shift in parental responsibilities.

It is important to keep in mind that secondary stressors may not only impact the emotional response of survivors but also interfere with their ability to engage in treatment. As such, survivors may have significant social services and case management needs that warrant assistance. Conducting a brief needs assessment may be useful to assist survivors in connecting with resources within their community that can help address these needs that often interfere with treatment and produce less-than-ideal outcomes.

8. Provide and Review Additional Psychoeducational Handouts

As you continue with treatment and introduce new modules, you will often find it helpful to review and refer to the psychoeducational handouts. Occasionally reviewing this information when your client has questions about their experiences or how treatment works will provide a common thread across sessions, reminding clients of how treatment works and giving them an overall roadmap for what to expect in the sessions ahead.

Cultural Considerations

Survivors will have different concepts of distress depending on their cultural background, and you should listen for and consider using the terms and expressions that your client uses and are familiar with when discussing common reactions. Consider the impact of culture and intersecting identities in determining whether a particular behavior (such as a coping strategy or memorialization practice) is adaptive relative to their broader context by engaging clients in direct discussions about ways that their lived experiences and identities are related to their symptoms and expectancies regarding treatment. This will also help you promote engagement in therapy by validating clients with marginalized identities (Graham et al., 2013). Making connections with local community leaders who are familiar with cultural practices and attitudes related to trauma and loss, as well as mourning practices in local communities, can be an important way for you to learn ways that trauma and grief reactions are culturally shaped, especially when you are working with clients who hold different sociocultural identities from you.

Cultural factors may also shape the way symptoms are expressed, which may affect the extent to which clients see their reactions as fitting within certain symptom categories. For example, somatic complaints regarding mood or anxiety symptoms are more prominently featured among Latinx individuals compared to European Americans (e.g., Varela & Hensley-Maloney, 2009). You should also be sure that psychoeducational materials are available in alternative formats for clients unable to read handouts, such as materials provided in the client's native language or utilizing more imagery for clients with limited written literacy.

Conclusion

Providing psychoeducation about common reactions to traumatic loss, including post-traumatic stress, depression, and prolonged grief reactions, is an important first step in treatment. It can help clients understand their reactions in new ways, offer a sense of reassurance, and increase motivation and engagement in treatment. Psychoeducation can also move clients to take a more realistic and compassionate view toward themselves, their own personal value, and in some cases, their perceived role in their loved one's death. For more detailed information on psychoeducation concepts see Walsh (2010) and Whitworth (2016).

The next module—module 2—includes additional skills for helping clients continue working with and processing unhelpful and painful beliefs about themselves and the world that may have developed after their loved one's death.

CHAPTER 5

Module 2: Identifying Emotions and Processing Thoughts

Many survivors have difficulty identifying the various feelings and emotions associated with grief and some develop unhelpful beliefs about grief, loss, and the future that can inhibit recovery and restoration (for example, *I need to grieve to be close with my loved one, My life will always be meaningless without my loved one*).

This standard module offers education, discussion, and monitoring of common grief emotions and relevant symptoms, as well as identification and possible modification of grief-related thoughts and beliefs that may be associated with emotional responses that interfere with daily living. This module can be provided within one to three sessions.

Background and Related Literature

Emotion identification and cognitive restructuring are core components of common cognitive therapy strategies for depression and anxiety. Cognitive (or cognitive behavioral) therapy is based upon the premise that mental health difficulties and distress are often maintained by maladaptive cognitive factors. In an effort to normalize the panoply of grief cognitions that may be experienced by individuals affected by traumatic loss, language in this module related to cognitions focuses on *unhelpful* and *helpful* thoughts rather than whether thoughts are maladaptive, distorted, or rational; terms that may be used in more traditional cognitive therapy approaches.

According to Beck's model (1970), maladaptive cognitions include thoughts and beliefs about oneself, others, and the world that influence one's emotions and behavior. Treatment, therefore, focuses on identification of emotions and thoughts, evaluation of thoughts, and the development of more adaptive thoughts and beliefs when appropriate. In doing so, changing thoughts and beliefs leads to changes in emotions and distress, as well as behaviors.

Concepts for this module are based upon existing cognitive behavioral theories and cognitive therapy strategies. Over 260 meta-analyses support the efficacy of cognitive behavioral therapies for a number of mental health problems (Hofmann et al., 2012), including problems commonly associated with traumatic loss, like depression (*Cognitive Therapy of Depression* by Beck et al., 1979) and PTSD (using CPT; Resick et al., 2017).

Research suggests that traumatic loss survivors are significantly more likely to experience negative thoughts about themselves, life generally, and the future, as well as misinterpretations of personal grief reactions relative to people who experience other types of losses (Boelen et al., 2015). Moreover, research has demonstrated that individuals who experience negative cognitions about the self, the future, or their own personal grief reactions are at greater risk for postloss mental health problems relative to individuals experiencing minimal negative cognitions (e.g., Boelen et al., 2015; Boelen et al., 2016; Mancini et al., 2011). Recent studies have also found that cognitive behavioral interventions designed to target these negative cognitions can be useful in addressing a range of bereavement-related mental health problems among traumatic loss survivors (Lenferink et al., 2023; Soydas et al., 2019).

This module provides basic recommendations and strategies for using common cognitive processing interventions and techniques from cognitive behavioral therapies with survivors, as well as special considerations when working with this population.

Presentation Appropriateness

This module can be useful for all clients suffering from grief and trauma-related difficulties to set the stage for emotion awareness, transformation of unhelpful thoughts, strategies that promote psychological distancing (defusion) from thoughts and feelings related to grief (such as sadness, anxiety, anger, or guilt) and trauma-related symptoms.

Agendas for Sessions

This module is designed to be flexibly delivered in one to three sessions. Deciding how many sessions to dedicate to core module components will depend on several factors, including clients' prior experiences with and knowledge of cognitive behavioral concepts, presenting problems and goals for therapy, and how quickly they are able to apply skills developed across each component.

If a client has prior experience with cognitive behavioral techniques from past therapy, for example, or is not reporting primary concerns related to unhelpful or painful beliefs related to their loved one's death, you may be able to review the rationale for the module, the impact thoughts and emotions have on each other, and steps for processing unhelpful thoughts in as few as one or two sessions. When these concepts are new to clients or they are especially bothered by unhelpful thoughts, more sessions may be indicated. A session-by-session agenda outlining how to cover core module components is provided below.

Module 2 first session:

1. Provide rationale for identifying emotions and processing thoughts.

2. Provide education about emotions.

3. Assign mood tracking.

Module 2 second session:

4. Educate about the cognitive behavioral triangle.

5. Educate about unhelpful thoughts.

6. Assist client in unhelpful thought identification.

7. Assign mood and thought tracking.

Module 2 third session:

8. Provide education about helpful thoughts.

9. Review the client's unhelpful thoughts and identify helpful responses.

10. Assign mood and thought tracking with helpful thought identification.

Module 2 ongoing sessions:

11. Assign mood and thought tracking with helpful thought identification as needed for rehearsal.

Handouts

Handout 2.1: Emotion Education

Handout 2.2: Emotion Identification

Handout 2.3: Mood Log

Handout 2.4: Cognitive Behavioral Triangle and Thought Identification

Handout 2.5: Mood and Thought Tracking with Helpful Thought Identification

Module Components

1. Provide Rationale for Identifying Emotions and Processing Thoughts

Grief, particularly as a result of the traumatic loss of a loved one or close other, can include an array of emotions that vary in magnitude and sequence. For instance, individuals bereaved by a traumatic loss may experience profound sadness over the absence of a close attachment figure while experiencing other difficult emotions, such as anger, guilt, shame, and confusion. Given the common complexity of emotions among traumatic loss survivors, understanding these emotions and the conditions in which they emerge is imperative for your client and a prerequisite for techniques that may provide a means to change, reduce, or accept their emotional reactions.

The identifying emotions and processing thoughts module will assist clients in identifying their emotional and physiological experiences (body sensations) to set the stage for learning strategies for dealing with strong emotions in the moment. Understanding the relationship between emotions and thoughts can improve clients' insight into grief emotions, allow them to identify where they get stuck in moving through emotions or thoughts, and provide a framework for carrying strong loss-related emotions while still engaging in life.

Below is a brief script of the rationale for this module.

As we discussed before, the traumatic death of someone close to us can bring about many emotions, some of which may be quite distressing and interfere with your life and ability to adapt to this loss. Over the next few weeks, we're going learn about how we feel—both our emotions and body sensations. In addition, we're going to pay attention to our thoughts: what they are saying and how they impact how we feel. By being more aware of our thoughts and feelings, we can better manage strong emotions in the moment. Does that sound okay with you?

2. Provide Education About Emotions

Educate your client about the myriad types of emotions and feelings that compose grief, particularly when occurring in the context of a traumatic death. Helping clients identify and clarify specific emotions and feelings they are experiencing allows them to verbalize their experience and provide critical information regarding how to tailor strategies to manage such emotions. Often, clients report feeling overwhelmed, bad, or filled with grief, but they have a difficult time clarifying the complex individual emotions they may be having in any given moment. Clarifying these different emotions can assist clients with feeling less overwhelmed by them all, becoming more aware how each emotion may influence behaviors and engagement in life, and offering a sense of mastery or confidence in handling difficult or strong emotions when they are experienced.

Below is an example of how to educate clients about grief emotions:

Grief itself is not an emotion but rather a constellation of emotions. It can include sadness, anxiety, guilt, horror, helplessness, hopelessness, relief, fear, longing, and many more. Emotions related to grief can feel overwhelming at times, like you're being washed over by a great big wave, and it sometimes feels like the wave will never end. However, grief emotions do ebb and flow over time. Sometimes, especially earlier on, these waves seem very big and hit us nonstop, and we often feel like we're drowning in them. But over time, we can learn that these waves may change—they may come less frequent, they may not be as big at times, and there are times we can predict when they may come. Paying more attention to these waves of emotion can help us better prepare for them and learn other ways to manage them, perhaps learning ways to float instead of getting swept away. Don't worry—I will be here with you on this journey to help you.

Emotions are more than just feelings; they involve physical changes in how your body feels and may impact your thoughts. Emotions also influence what we want to do and what we end up doing. For example, if you feel angry, this may involve the thought that Person X is blocking my goal, along with an increased heart rate, muscle tension, increased energy, and wider eyes. As such, it may be difficult to "slow down", and you may be less likely to hesitate and think through consequences to your actions leading to more impulsive or unhelpful actions.

In addition, emotions are often cued or triggered (be mindful of this word as it could be a cue for survivors to gun violence loss) *by a situation, something in our environment, a reminder of your loved one or a reminder of their death, or even something internal, like a thought or body sensation. We'll discuss this a bit more later in our session.*

Primary and secondary emotions. It is important that you discuss primary and secondary emotions as both types have unique origins and, thus, warrant different intervention approaches. Primary emotions are innate reactions to a situation. These instinctual emotions have existed throughout the history and evolution of humankind and hold numerous functional and adaptive properties across cultures. They include joy or happiness, fear, anxiety, sadness, anger, and disgust. Each of these emotions can help someone behave effectively in a given situation. For instance, fear is a natural emotional response to a dangerous situation, and it is this emotional reaction and the corresponding physiological responses that helps us make decisive actions to preserve our safety. Similarly, sadness following the loss of an important attachment figure may help signal the need for emotional support from others and initiate proximity-seeking behaviors to address the deceased attachment figure. Primary emotions occur often in the absence of cognitions—they occur innately within a given situation.

In contrast, secondary emotions are *reactions* to primary emotions, thoughts, or behaviors. For example, if someone feels shame about their sadness, the shame is a secondary emotion, and sadness is primary. Secondary emotions include shame, guilt, and regret, among others. They are often brought about through one's cognitive processes, such as thoughts that one ought to feel differently than they do. This may be driven by inaccurate beliefs about what other people think about one's emotions (for example, *They think I am weak if I cry* or *I am crazy if I look anxious*) or beliefs about the appropriateness of specific emotions (for example, *I should be sad that my loved one is dead*).

Secondary emotions may also be generated following unhelpful thoughts or appraisals of a situation, such as *I should have seen the red flags*, producing the emotion of guilt. Further, a person may be afraid of an emotion because they are having trouble identifying or understanding it (for example, *Because I am feeling this way it means I'm going crazy* or *It will last forever*). Secondary emotions of this kind may make someone want to avoid situations that cue or trigger the uncomfortable emotions. Therefore, secondary emotions may not be helpful in many cases; however, it is important to recognize that they are normal.

You can illustrate this during the discussion by drawing a circle on a whiteboard or blank piece of paper and writing *primary emotion* inside the circle. Then draw a bigger circle around the smaller one and label this *secondary emotions*. You can then include the primary and secondary emotions that the client has reported. Another visual example of this concept is to hold up your hand as a fist—explain that your fist is core pain or (primary) emotion, move the other hand around the fist about one or two inches away and indicate this extra layer around core pain can be extra suffering (secondary emotions).

Interestingly, the emotion of anger in the context of grief and trauma can be both a primary emotion and a secondary emotion. Recognizing the function of the emotion can sometimes help identify whether it is a primary or secondary emotion. For example, a client may focus intensely on anger feelings about an interaction with a victim service professional when discussing the days after the death notification but reports having a hard time expressing other feelings from those days. Anger in this situation may be a distraction from other primary emotions related to the emotional pain of the loss in the initial days (such as sadness and disbelief). It is sometimes "easier" to feel anger directed at something or someone than it is to sit with or acknowledge feelings of sadness, longing, or fear, and this may be particularly true depending on cultural or social scripts and personal identities. Gently pointing this out may assist clients in their willingness to recognize primary emotions they may be having. You can provide handout 2.1 to accompany the conversation.

Many emotions are cued by either internal or external cues. Assisting clients to become more aware of these can not only help them better clarify emotions but also understand what situations, experiences, or reminders may cue and be associated with a given emotion.

This allows clients to better anticipate or predict strong emotions as they arise, leading to improvements in their overall sense of self-efficacy and control.

For clients that have elevated post-traumatic stress and grief symptoms, helping tease apart trauma (cues related to the actual death and how their loved one died) and grief cues or reminders (cues related to life without their loved one physically present) may be an important part of treatment. Trauma reminders often cue fear-related symptoms, including intrusive thoughts about the death, nightmares, and increased distress when reminded of how their loved one died. Trauma cues can be external cues, such as situations, people, objects, words, smells, and sounds. For example, someone whose loved one died by car crash on a highway may feel increased distress when driving on highways as it is a reminder of how their loved one died. Trauma cues can be internal cues, as well, such as a racing heart rate and intrusive thoughts of the death.

Grief reminders often cue longing and yearning emotions. Grief cues can be external and internal cues. External grief cues can be situations, people, objects, words, smells, and sounds. For example, sitting down at the dinner table and looking at an empty chair or smelling a loved one's favorite dessert can cue longing and yearning feelings or other grief emotions, such as sadness, anger, or loneliness. Internal grief cues could be dreams about or memories of a loved one. Helping clients who have both trauma and grief cues tease apart these differing cues can be useful as different coping strategies may be utilized depending on the type of cue. Further, just noticing and putting a name to such cues can allow clients to anticipate and prepare for them and feel more in control of managing them when they arise, as they inevitably will.

Activity. Give the client handout 2.2 and encourage your client to think about the past week and generate a list of emotions they experienced related to their grief. In addition, help your client identify the cue (such as situations, reminders, or thoughts) associated with that emotion (for instance, memory of loved one → sadness; court or legal proceeding → anger; *I failed my loved one* → guilt).

Clinician Tip. When noticing primary and secondary emotions, validate all emotions, so as to not inadvertently dismiss or judge an emotion a client may be experiencing.

Below is a sample dialogue related to noticing cues and primary and secondary emotions.

Clinician: During this past week, let's see if we can identify some of those grief emotions you may have had and what or if there were any cues that brought about those emotions. Tell me about a strong grief emotion you noticed that you had since we last met.

Module 2: Identifying Emotions and Processing Thoughts

Client:	Yesterday, I just couldn't stop crying because I was missing my son so much.
Clinician:	Sounds like yesterday was a difficult day. What emotion was related to your crying?
Client:	I just felt yearning and sadness. I just wished my son was here with me.
Clinician:	Okay. You were having the emotions of yearning and sadness. Anything else?
Client:	I was feeling guilty because the day before I went to a party for a cousin. I felt like I was dishonoring my son by going to a happy event.

Note: Here, there may be a desire to explore the client's thoughts associated with her feelings of guilt. However, this can be done in a later session when helpful and unhelpful thoughts are presented. Currently, the goal is to help clients be more aware of their emotions and what cues them.

Clinician:	Sounds like thinking about the party the day before was a cue for your feelings of guilt. Would you say the party the day the before was also a cue for your sadness and yearning yesterday?
Client:	I'm not sure; I just get filled with so much emotion. I don't know where it comes from sometimes, and it's all-encompassing. But I guess I was thinking about the party, which then made me think about missing my son.
Clinician:	Okay, so sounds like perhaps yesterday thinking about the party cued sadness and yearning, as well as feelings of guilt. I think, in this case, your feelings of sadness and yearning are primary emotions and the feelings of guilt are secondary emotions. We'll talk more about why that is and what we can do with these emotions. For now, let's just write all of this down together so we can better understand each of your different emotions as they come.

3. Assign Mood Tracking

To assist with becoming adept at identifying emotions and the context in which they often occur, have clients start to observe and track their mood on a daily basis using handout 2.3, so they can have a better understanding of the types and intensity of emotions (for example, using a scale of 0–10), which serves as valuable clinical information for subsequent modules. Further, tracking mood provides an opportunity for clients to begin distancing themselves from their emotions and disentangling themselves as a person from their emotions (and soon thoughts). You may want to share how clients are not their emotions—emotions are felt in the moment with waning intensity over time (for instance, *I am feeling sad* versus *I am a sad person*). If your client is having both trauma and grief-related symptoms, further clarifying if emotions are tied to grief and loss (the missing of their loved one) or trauma (the way their loved one died) can also help to separate the different types of emotions and symptoms commonly associated with traumatic loss.

A sample description includes:

> *Over the course of the next week, I would like you to track your mood and feelings each day to notice what kinds of emotions you are having, how intense these feelings are, perhaps using a scale, like zero to ten, and what situations bring them on. I want us to better understand the waves of emotion you experience.*

In following sessions, review completed mood logs and explore your client's knowledge and awareness of situations that may cue grief and trauma emotions and clarify between the different types of grief and trauma emotions they may be experiencing.

4. Educate About the Cognitive Behavioral Triangle

After your client can better recognize different grief and trauma emotions, educate them on the relationship between feelings or emotions (what we feel), thoughts (what we think), and behaviors (what we do). Likewise, you should note that there are also three components of grief: what we feel, what we think, and what we do.

> **Clinician Tip.** Use a visual aid, such as a whiteboard or blank piece of paper, with a triangle and the labels "Feeling," "Thought," and "Behavior" above each point of the triangle. Later, you can utilize real-world examples from your client's life to assist with understanding.

For instance, you could say:

> *As we discussed, what we feel is often cued or brought about by something outside of us or inside of us. How we feel can be affected by what we think and what we do. In this sense, emotions, thoughts, and behaviors are all intimately linked and affected by each other. Let me give you an example: As a child, Jack was bitten by a dog, and now he becomes anxious and fearful when he is around other dogs. When Jack sees a dog, his heart starts to race, he begins sweating, and he feels really jittery and shaky. Jack thinks that the dog may bite him if he goes near it, which increases his fear. Instead, to avoid the perceived danger and the feeling of fear, Jack walks in the opposite direction to stay away from the dog. So, in this example, how are thoughts, emotions, and behaviors*

linked? Right—when Jack sees a dog, he has the thought that it may bite him if he goes near, which creates the emotion of fear, which then influences his behavior to avoid dogs.

To further illustrate the cognitive behavioral triangle and how emotions, thoughts, and behaviors influence each other, you can ask your client to identify each component of the triangle, using a whiteboard or paper, during the sharing of examples (like the one provided above): what we feel (feeling or emotions), what we think (thoughts), and what we do (behavior). You should work with your client to solicit examples, particularly those that may reflect areas of difficulty or grief- or trauma-related symptoms. You may also provide additional relevant examples and suggestions to assist with client apprehension.

Feelings. This can include both emotions and body sensations, such as heart palpitations, shortness of breath, nausea, sweating, feeling shaky or jittery, feelings of choking, numbing or tingling sensation, and light-headedness or dizziness.

Thoughts. Thinking about your loved one, oneself, others, the world, the future, the nature of the loss, and the impact the loss has on your life.

Behavior. Substance misuse and avoiding people, reminders of the loss, or aspects of a situation.

Note to your client that each component contributes to a grief response. At this point, emphasize that our thoughts may play a significant role in how we feel emotionally (not just physically), which can also affect what we do (behaviors). You are advised to utilize the triangle illustration to convey the relationship between feelings, thoughts, and behaviors. Then, ideally using grief-related examples provided by your client, demonstrate how they are related, once again using the visual aid.

> **Clinical Tip**. Take a developmental approach, such that you solicit examples from clients in an increasing fashion as the module progresses. Having clients explain their understanding of the relationship between feelings, thoughts, and behavior in their own words and using appropriate examples can serve as a marker of proficiency in understanding the concept.

Below is an example:

Losing a loved one can change how we think about the world and ourselves. It can shift our beliefs. Maybe we see the world as a dangerous place now. Maybe we have negative views about ourselves or our ability to cope. Maybe we have different views about God or a higher power. This is all normal and typical with grief, especially traumatic grief.

Sometimes our thoughts and beliefs about the world change in ways that help us move forward, but we can also have a number of thoughts about the loss and life now that aren't helpful and may keep us stuck, or worse. Sometimes we hold on to these thoughts because we feel connected to our loved one by having them, because we accept the thoughts as truth and see no end in sight, or to make sense of the loss.

Our role now is to identify these thoughts, to see how they impact your feelings and emotions, and to see how they're connected to your behaviors. Just like we talked about before. So, in essence, we may ask: Are these thoughts helpful? Are they accurate? Maybe they're not accurate. Or maybe they are, but they're not helpful. Perhaps, gently shifting these thoughts to more helpful thinking may ease the burden or pain you're experiencing. To clarify, we aren't trying to create positive thinking—that's not the goal—but rather develop more helpful thoughts that still reflect the truth of your experience.

For example, after a loved one's death, we can start to feel so overwhelmed by things that we might think to ourselves, I'll never really be happy again, which can cause feelings of sadness and despair. In turn, these feelings can increase the likelihood that we withdraw and isolate from others. Now, let's say you tell yourself, Even though I'm feeling really overwhelmed right now, maybe I can still find moments of happiness in the future. *How are the emotions associated with that thought and that possibility different?*

(Client responds with "less upsetting" or "reassured.")

Yeah! And if you're experiencing a sense of reassurance as opposed to despair, how might your behavior be different?

(Client suggests staying more engaged with others and feeling more motivated to attend to day-to-day life tasks.)

Yes, you got it. So, you can see that by gently shifting our thoughts to ones that are more helpful, we often start to feel better and can better choose the behavior we want in any given situation. How else do you think this might relate to the experience of losing a loved one? Can you think of any examples in your own life in which thoughts played a big role in how you felt and what you did? What about thoughts you may have related to (loved one)'s death or its impact on your life and future?

Clinician Tip. If clients have trouble identifying examples in which grief-related thoughts affected their feelings (emotions and physiological reactions) and subsequent behavior, encourage them to think back to a time in which they recently experienced a powerful, distressing emotion or feeling. Once an emotion is identified and labeled, assist the client with identifying the thoughts (or behaviors) that preceded the emotion, as well as their behavioral reactions. If difficulty persists, consider additional easy-to-follow examples (such as seeing a friend on a walk who doesn't wave *hello*) to foster understanding.

5. Educate About Unhelpful Thoughts

After you determine your client has a sufficient understanding of the relationship between thoughts (particularly unhelpful thoughts) and feelings and behaviors, you should assist them with identifying current thoughts about their loss. To start, work with your client to identify all grief- or trauma-related thoughts, not just unhelpful thoughts. Together with your client, draft a list of the various thoughts related to the death that your client is having by writing them down on a piece of paper or whiteboard.

At first, you should not try to challenge or comment too much on the thoughts being named but rather restate them out loud with "You are having the thought..." to confirm content and meaning. Offer praise to your client for noticing all thoughts and writing them down. The initial goal is simply to identify thoughts without judgment. Moreover, you may want to emphasize that stating, *I am having the thought...* and writing thoughts down on paper is a cognitive distancing (defusion) technique that helps to further drive the point that these are simply thoughts—they are not us, they are something we have and are carrying. We are distinct from these thoughts. Follow-up questions such as, *And what does that thought mean to you?* or *If this thought were true, what would it say about you?* can help further identify additional related thoughts and beliefs that may have not been identified by your client.

Common unhelpful thoughts that survivors of traumatic loss report include thoughts related to:

- helplessness and control (*Things will never be the same*)

- blame (*She should have gotten help before*)

- injustice (*It's not fair that he was killed*)

- guilt and survival guilt (*I should have been there for her; I should have died*)

- coping (*If I stop grieving, I will forget my loved one*)

- fear (*Something bad will happen to me or my family*)

- shame (*Because he took his own life, the world looks down on our family*)

- stigmatization (*People don't want to hear about him—he was just an addict*)

- interpretations about grief (*Feeling joy means I am dishonoring the loss*)

In particular those who experience a traumatic loss will have cognitions similar to those who have experienced other potentially traumatic events, such as guilt and a strong sense of personal responsibility for not having been able to prevent a loved one's death.

> **Clinician Tip.** At this point, you should not try to challenge cognitions or beliefs. The initial goal is to just become more aware of thoughts and their relationship to emotions and behaviors.

6. Assist Client in Unhelpful Thought Identification

You should help your client recognize that unhelpful thoughts are a part of grief and are common after exposure to traumatic events. In addition, provide education about how focusing on unhelpful thoughts can maintain grief and negatively affect mood and in particular that unhelpful thoughts can keep us from moving through grief and keep us stuck. Alongside your client, review examples of unhelpful thoughts identified in session and assist them with noticing relationships between their thoughts, feelings, and behaviors. Questions to explore include but are not limited to: *Does or did that thought help you do or not do certain behaviors or activities? How does or did that thought make you feel?*

7. Assign Mood and Thought Tracking

After spending time in session identifying thoughts related to grief and trauma, assign homework for the following week. Clients should continue to write down grief and trauma-related thoughts that they may be having between sessions. In addition, to help clients become more aware of the connection between their thoughts and feelings, mood tracking should be included as part of the between-session homework. Use handout 2.4 to assign homework of tracking feelings, thoughts, and behaviors. You should take time at the beginning of the next session to review client's thoughts, emotions, and behaviors from the prior week using the handout.

In addition, discuss with your client what it was like to observe and notice thoughts and feelings over the course of the week. Praising effort rather than content is advised and can help mitigate challenges and barriers associated with noticing and writing down thoughts and feelings. If clients did not do their homework of tracking thoughts and emotions or they found it too challenging, acknowledge this challenge without judgment and spend time in session reviewing the week and writing down situations that may have cued thoughts and feelings with your client. Doing so will help underscore how homework is essential while curbing any avoidance behaviors.

8. Provide Education About Helpful Thoughts

Once you conduct a review of homework from the previous week, the potential usefulness of developing more helpful thoughts to cope with and manage grief and trauma-related thoughts and emotions should be discussed. If appropriate, you can begin gently challenging unhelpful thoughts using Socratic dialogue and related techniques. It is important that the client fully understands that the goal of identifying helpful thoughts is not the same as "the power of positive thinking" or trying to paint a rosier view of the world or their experience. Instead, the aim is to gently direct attention to thoughts that may be helpful, more balanced, or encouraging during such a difficult time in their lives.

Be careful in the aftermath of a traumatic loss not to minimize the reality of the trauma and loss by negating or criticizing the client's reported thoughts and beliefs. Validating a client's thoughts as understandable in the context of their experience is important. You should make clear that the goal is to assist clients with focusing less on unhelpful thoughts and more on helpful ones, as doing so will help them move forward in their grief journey.

Below are several examples of common unhelpful and helpful thoughts related to grief.

	Unhelpful Thought	Helpful Thought
Helplessness and control	*Life will never be the same again.*	*Some very important aspects of life will definitely be different now, and I can still live a meaningful life carrying this loss.*
	It's all up to me to make sure nothing bad happens to anyone else I love.	*I can't stop everything bad from happening, but I can try my best to make sure the people I love are taken care of.*
Blame and injustice	*I could have prevented this from happening.*	*I had no way of knowing they were about to die—I couldn't prevent something I didn't know was coming so quickly.*
	Their death has shown me that the world is an unjust place.	*What happened to my loved one was unfair, but maybe their story can bring about change and hope in others.*
Guilt and survival guilt	*I should have done something differently.*	*At the time, I did the best that I could with the knowledge I had.*
	I should have died—not him.	*Neither of us deserved to die.*
Coping	*I should be coping better. I'm not coping well; that must mean something's wrong with me.*	*My reaction reflects how bad this event was and how much this person meant to me. Most people have reactions like this when they experience the death of someone close.*
	Nothing will ever make this better.	*Nothing will ever fully take my grief away, but maybe there are things I can do to help make each day more fulfilling.*

	Unhelpful Thought	**Helpful Thought**
Interpretations about grief	*If I feel joy again, that means I have forgotten the loss.*	*I will never forget my loved one. Feeling joy means I can live life while carrying this loss.*
	I need to keep busy, or I will fall apart.	*Difficult emotions are okay to have. I can ride the wave.*

Clinician Tip. Be mindful to not enter a debate with clients about whether their thoughts are justified or accurate but rather help them test out the effect those thoughts have on their feelings and behaviors.

9. Review the Client's Unhelpful Thoughts and Identify Helpful Responses

Take some time to review your client's recently tracked unhelpful thoughts and assist them with reframing or restating the thought from a more helpful angle. It is important to allow clients to develop helpful thoughts on their own as opposed to you providing the thought for them. Example questions could include:

- *What could you say that may be kinder to yourself?*

- *What could be more helpful to help you in that moment?*

- *What would you say to a close friend who had that same thought?*

To aid in developing competency with this skill, you can encourage clients to write down the original unhelpful thought with a helpful thought next to it.

If there are one or two unhelpful thoughts that seem to be global or particularly upsetting, have the client write the helpful thought on an index card they can tape somewhere in their house, such as on the refrigerator or bathroom mirror, to read regularly. Alternatively, to promote the integration of more helpful thoughts, it may be beneficial for clients to write unhelpful thoughts on one side of the index card with the client-driven helpful thought on the other. Such cards can be easily referenced when unhelpful thoughts are experienced throughout the day. You could also have the client write the helpful thought using an application on their phone to help them carry the helpful thought with them.

10. Assign Mood and Thought Tracking with Helpful Thought Identification

For homework, assign mood and thought tracking with the addition of helpful thought identification using handout 2.5.

> **Clinician Tip.** Language is important here when addressing helpful thoughts. Try to avoid words like "restructure," or "challenge," or "distortion," which are often used in traditional cognitive strategies. Instead, consider using phrases such as, *Learning to carry the loss lightly, What words can help you lean into life just a little bit,* or *Let's take a look at that thought and its impact, and see if we can lighten this.* Such phrasing can validate the grief experience while encouraging clients to explore helpful thoughts and approach both their grief and current life.

11. Continue Assigning Mood and Thought Tracking with Helpful Thought Identification

The goal of rehearsing or practicing helpful thoughts is to encourage clients to spend more time on helpful thoughts that mobilize and energize them to engage in life's activities, as well as shift beliefs from grief-oriented to restoration-oriented content, or, for some clients, to allow them to be willing to experience avoided difficult emotions. As such, you should assign clients to practice helpful thoughts as needed. In addition, as treatment progresses, additional unhelpful thoughts may emerge. Encourage clients to continue practicing this skill: notice thoughts, test them out, identify if any are unhelpful, and identify helpful thoughts. Over time, this process becomes more integrated in day-to-day life. As such, continued practice is heavily emphasized.

Cultural Considerations

In some cultural traditions, the belief in a higher power may significantly influence thinking, behavior, and feelings, particularly in the context of grief. While these religious or spiritual beliefs may serve as a protective factor for recovery for some, they can also produce negative reactions for others, especially for traumatic losses where the victim may have played a role in their death (for example, a homicide victim engaging in illegal activity or a suicide). As such, a client's religious or cultural beliefs may be associated with shame or guilt. Depending on your client's cultural background and religious or spiritual practice, you should ask them how these beliefs contribute to or influence their feelings, behaviors, and thoughts. You may need to do additional research to better acquaint yourself with the cultural or religious considerations of your client. For further exploration of several religious contexts on traumatic loss, see Janice Lord's (2008) *Spiritually Sensitive Caregiving: A Multifaith Handbook*.

Furthermore, survivors from marginalized, minoritized, or racialized communities may also experience significant distress associated with beliefs about the role race, ethnicity, or other aspects of identity played in their loved one's death or their adjustment since the death. In such circumstances, be mindful not to dismiss or carelessly challenge clients' beliefs about the role of racism or discrimination in their bereavement experiences as this can ultimately be experienced as a microaggression by your client. This would negatively affect the therapeutic relationship and their willingness to discuss these important considerations in the future.

Conclusion

The painful emotions that often accompany traumatic loss are frequently coupled with thoughts and beliefs that amplify those painful emotions. Many survivors experience negative beliefs associated with a sense of helplessness, guilt, shame, and stigma. Learning to recognize when these thoughts are occurring and how they affect our behaviors and feelings is a critical step in learning to challenge unhelpful thoughts. In this chapter, you learned tips for helping clients construct more helpful thoughts and beliefs, which can ultimately contribute to resilience. In the next chapter, we introduce the third standard module in the GRIEF Approach model to further enhance clients' coping strategies and promote resilience.

For more detailed information on cognitive behavioral therapy concepts, see Beck (1970), Beck (2020), and Resick et al. (2017).

CHAPTER 6

Module 3: Identifying and Building Strengths

All people have the capacity to manage and cope with adversity, including the traumatic loss of a loved one or close other. Although traumatic loss survivors present to treatment under significant distress, they often have strengths and coping strategies that they have used during past adversities that could be identified and reinforced to manage current grief and trauma symptoms. Therefore, this standard module focuses on the survivor's strengths and resourcefulness to foster independence, resilience, and the ability to make adaptive choices that enhance their well-being.

Importantly, enhancing one's self-efficacy (a belief in one's ability to organize and execute behaviors that will produce desired outcomes) will assist the survivor as they continue carrying their grief throughout treatment and beyond. Additional coping strategies and techniques that promote resilience that are not yet familiar to the survivor will be introduced during subsequent sessions. This module can be provided within one session with follow-up integrated across other sessions.

Background and Related Literature

A strengths-based approach posits that individuals inherently have both protective and risk factors that can respectively help or hinder one's response to adversity. Protective factors can be fostered to buffer against the negative impact of adversities; this is often referred to as resilience (Bonanno, 2005).

Research indicates that there are many ways in which an individual may demonstrate resiliency. Iacoviello and Charney (2014) have identified six psychosocial factors that promote resilience in individuals: 1) optimism, 2) cognitive flexibility, 3) active coping skills, 4) maintaining a supportive social network, 5) attending to one's physical well-being, and 6) embracing a personal moral compass. Typically, survivors are engaged in activities or utilize coping skills that fall into these domains, and they should be acknowledged for such efforts. In turn, this can bolster one's sense of self-efficacy—an important factor in adaptation to traumatic loss (e.g., Smith et al., 2015; Titlestad et al., 2022).

Targeting resilience in treatment now, by incorporating resilience-focused elements, can also increase the positive impact of the intervention overall. Keep in mind that the goal of resilience-focused strategies is not necessarily to remove or prevent the individual from experiencing distress, as one may foster resilience and feel distressed at the same time. Rather, the goal is to harness competency in coping while managing distress in the present moment and the future.

Presentation Appropriateness

This standard module can be useful for all clients in approaching the initial stages of treatment from the perspective of highlighting client strengths in managing adversities to fostering resilience and self-efficacy.

Agenda for Session

Module 3 first session:

1. Provide education on resilience.

2. Assess strengths.

3. Identify past coping strategies.

4. Assign resiliency strategies for practice.

Module 3 additional sessions:

5. Review the use of resiliency strategies and problem-solve potential barriers.

6. Assign resiliency strategies for practice.

Handouts

Handout 3.1: List of Commonly Noted Strengths and Coping Strategies

Handout 3.2: My Strengths

Module Components

Often grief and trauma responses are viewed by survivors as signs of weakness, shortcomings, or failures. Encouraging clients to acknowledge and build upon personal and cultural strengths engages clients in their grief journey, challenges these beliefs of weakness and failure, and builds a sense of competency in managing and approaching difficult emotions to achieve desired outcomes. Three concepts of strength-based resilience include: 1) everyone has the capacity to foster resilience—these are skills that can be honed, 2) strengths and solutions will not be the same for everyone—identifying individualized strengths and tailored plans is necessary, and 3) community strength is just as important as individual strength—therefore, this module may be combined with module 5.

1. Provide Education on Resilience

Begin the discussion of resilience with the question, *What does resilience mean to you?* to gather an understanding of your client's perspective on resilience. Often a client may define resilience as strength in coping with stressors. To further explore the potential meaning of resilience, ask your client to identify someone either in their own life or in history who demonstrated resiliency during stressors or adversity. Then ask, *What behaviors did that person display during those stressors?* Write down the behaviors that person displayed on a piece of paper or a whiteboard and repeat them out loud.

Provide a definition of resilience and rationale for fostering resilience.

Here is a sample definition and rationale you can use when working with clients:

Resilience is defined as being able to adapt to adversity and trauma in a manner that allows reengaging in life. It is not bouncing back or returning to how you once were, as you are forever changed. It also is not necessarily without distress. So, someone can foster resilience and feel distressed at the same time—someone can feel distressed and still do what is most meaningful to them. It is building on your personal strengths, which all humans have, to help you through your grief journey.

We are born with the tools to be resilient, and we can learn and practice additional tools. It isn't a simple matter of either you are or you aren't resilient. Resilience involves behaviors, thoughts, and actions that can be learned and developed by anyone. Often, how we are coping with grief and trauma is viewed as signs of weakness or failures. They are not failures. In fact, we can build upon your strengths to help you through your grief journey, to challenge these unhelpful beliefs of weakness and failure, and to build a sense of competency in managing and approaching your difficult emotions related to your loss.

2. Assess Strengths

You should note to clients that before they learn new coping strategies, the first step is to build upon their own reservoir of resilience and personal strengths. Open a discussion with clients around qualities and characteristics they would consider strengths. See handout 3.1 for commonly noted strengths. This could include a) character strengths, b) spiritual or faith-based strengths, c) cultural connections, d) thinking approaches, e) behaviors or activities, or f) community-related strengths. You should aim to encourage a range of activities and strategies that can be employed if a situation limits your client's resiliency repertoire (for example, strategies that can be used in public settings versus private spaces). Use handout 3.2 to write down a list of client-specific strengths, and update it throughout treatment as often as necessary.

3. Identify Past Coping Strategies

You can help your client brainstorm how they have coped with adversities in the past and what the impact of such strategies was. Coping strategies can include a wide range of activities, such as journaling, exercising, talking to others, going to church or reading spiritual passages, baking, gardening, helping others, self-care (like taking a bath), sitting on a porch with a cup of tea, or being around children, to name a few. Other commonly used coping strategies are listed to help generate ideas in handout 3.1.

Clinician Tip. Besides exploring ways clients have coped with past adversities, facilitate discussions about ways they may knowingly or unknowingly draw on cultural resiliency to navigate traumatic loss (Tyler et al., 2023). Discussing ways that a client's family and culture shaped their understanding of healing and healing practices may serve to strengthen their personal sense of cultural pride and resilience (see chapter 3 for more detailed discussion on assessment of cultural considerations in grief and loss).

Clinician Tip. When introducing resiliency concepts, sometimes clients will note that nothing they have done before works now. It is important to validate that managing traumatic grief can be challenging. Perhaps reviewing together what they have used in the past may bring up new ideas or an opportunity to see how they could be tweaked to provide some brief moments of respite now and to reconnect with their own strengths. Alternatively, suggestions can be made to the client and couched as an experiment to maintain motivation for treatment if specific components fail to initially produce desired outcomes.

4. Assign Resiliency Strategies for Practice

After a thorough discussion, work with your client to collaboratively identify several resiliency strategies or strengths from their generated list that they could engage in within the next week. Validate that the goal of these strategies is not necessarily to make all distress go away but rather to build their sense of mastery to manage distress by reconnecting with their strengths. Write down and schedule what strategies your client will commit to use this week. To increase the likelihood of completing this assignment, you are advised to indicate when these strategies will be used (for instance, a day and time or when distress is high).

Of note, during the discussion, it is common for clients to comment that some of the coping strategies they may have used to manage adversities in the past are current reminders of their loved one. For example, talking to their loved one for support or doing an activity they would have done with or for their loved one (such as baking their loved one's favorite dessert or going fishing). Future modules will integrate activities that remind your client of their loved one or encourage them to do activities in honor of their loved one. At this point in treatment, gently encourage your client to simply try the identified coping activity as a source of resiliency if they can and want to do so.

However, if it seems unlikely your client will engage, other coping strategies should be identified as the focus of the upcoming week. The purpose of this module is not yet to target avoidance but to build in regular engagement in coping strategies that will assist clients in managing distress. This will foster their connection with their strengths and promote self-efficacy. Avoidance-related behaviors will be addressed and targeted beginning in module 4, when learning ways to manage distress.

Below is a sample clinician-client dialogue related to identifying strengths and coping strategies from a prior adversity.

Clinician: Let's start to build your own reservoir of resilience. What may be some strengths of yours that you identify with now or from the past in how you have coped with adversities?

Client: Well, I don't know. I just don't think I have any strengths anymore without my husband. He was my everything.

Clinician: He was such an important part of your life. And he sounds like a strong support for you. I wonder if we can look back to the past when you struggled with something big, all the ways you managed to cope, including leaning on your husband. Can you think of a time in your past that was a challenge?

Client: My sister was diagnosed with breast cancer five years ago. She is fine now, but I remember a time when I was so worried and upset. I was living in a different state, so I couldn't be with her during her treatments.

Clinician: Sounds like a difficult time in your life. Think back to that time. What were some strengths that you leaned on to help yourself?

Client:	I talked to my husband. He was there for me throughout. I just miss having him here.
Clinician:	Your husband sounds like he helped to keep you grounded. In addition to your husband's support, what other personal strengths or coping strategies did you use when your sister had breast cancer?
Client:	I prayed a lot. And I would try to focus on the things around me in my daily life that I was grateful for, as you just never know what's going to happen next.
Clinician:	Okay, great. Anything else?
Client:	I used to find comfort in singing too.
Clinician:	How did these strengths impact you at the time?
Client:	They helped me get through each day. I guess. Especially days when my sister had doctor's appointments.
Clinician:	So, it sounds like, in addition to the support of your husband, prayer, gratitude practice, and singing are strengths of yours that helped you in the past. Let's write those down as we continue to generate a list of your personal strengths. I would also like to hear more about each of these. For instance, tell me more about your gratitude practice...

5. Review Use of Resiliency Strategies and Problem-Solve Barriers

During follow-up sessions, check in with your client about the use of resiliency strategies. It is important to praise clients for their efforts, even if they were not always successful. Adequate time should be dedicated to problem-solving either challenges or barriers to using identified resiliency or coping strategies. Common barriers include not remembering to do the activity, avoidance of reminders of the loss, and no access to materials or other resources. Other barriers may include a perceived inability to engage in strategies because of distress. You may want to encourage clients to lean into such challenges as potential opportunities to continue to practice using their strengths in the face of emotional difficulties; therefore, supporting the concept that we can foster resilience while carrying distress.

6. Assign Resiliency Strategies for Practice

You will continue to review and assign resiliency strategies to engage in as treatment continues, and specific strategies may change depending on the content of the therapy module. Prior strengths and resiliency strategies will be augmented with the addition of new coping strategies during module 4 and module 5.

Cultural Considerations

For some clients, spirituality and religion may be identified as a prior strength and source of resilience. However, other clients may be in conflict with these areas of strength since the loss. It is common after traumatic loss to question or develop conflicting beliefs and feelings toward their belief in God, spirituality, or religious or cultural traditions. Referred to as *complicated spiritual grief*, a sense of discord, conflict, and distance from God or a higher power, and at times members of one's spiritual community can have a deleterious impact on the survivor (e.g., Burke & Neimeyer, 2014). You should acknowledge that this conflict is common among traumatic loss survivors when appropriate. This theme can be revisited with clients during module 7, if it is a source of distress or concern.

Furthermore, clients may identify sources of cultural resiliency and strength during session but also vary considerably in the degree to which they identify with their culture of origin. Be sure to consider the extent to which clients identify with and engage in resilience practices common in their cultures of origin.

Conclusion

Enhancing personal strengths and engaging in activities that strengthen one's community fosters resilience. Using the skills and tools presented in this module gives you an opportunity to help survivors of traumatic loss recognize and draw on personal and community strengths that can help them move forward in healthy ways. Clients can also draw on personal strengths discussed in this module throughout treatment to promote engagement in activities and exercises discussed throughout this manual.

An important coping skill that can also promote resilience is the ability to manage strong emotions as they occur in our day-to-day life. In the next chapter, we present a standard module for teaching clients effective ways of managing strong emotions as they come up, module 4.

CHAPTER 7

Module 4: Managing Strong Emotions

Often, grief symptoms and other reactions to loss, such as depression and anxiety, are avoided because of the emotional suffering and pain associated with these experiences. Research suggests that avoiding such emotions may help to soothe the survivor in the short term but likely has negative consequences in the longer term, such as an exacerbation of grief-related symptoms. Mindfulness and relaxation-based strategies may assist a survivor across a range of negative emotions and distressing reactions to better accept and cope with their grief experiences.

Some key elements in fostering recovery after traumatic loss include emotional awareness, the ability to accept and manage strong reactions that often follow traumatic loss, a belief in one's ability to cope, and self-compassion. Mindfulness is one way to strengthen these abilities. In addition, specific relaxation skills can offer assistance in regulating stress responses (such as difficulty falling asleep) and provide tools to encourage confidence in approaching difficult situations. Several present-focused mindfulness and relaxation strategies are incorporated into this module, which is one to three sessions in length and can be incorporated across other integrated sessions.

Background and Related Literature

The ability to tolerate and manage strong emotions is important in our day-to-day lives. Emotion regulation, or the ability to recognize, evaluate, and modify emotional reactions (Berking et al., 2008), is central to this process, though overreliance on some emotion regulation strategies can undermine an individual's ability to manage strong emotions and increase risk for mental health problems in the long run. For example, experiential avoidance, or efforts to avoid upsetting thoughts and feelings (Hayes et al., 1996), and repetitive rumination about the causes and impact of negative emotion are emotion regulation strategies that have been associated with the development and maintenance of several mental health problems, including PTSD (e.g., Orcutt et al., 2020), depression (e.g., Cribb et al., 2006), and prolonged grief (e.g., Eisma & Stroebe, 2021). Many cognitive behavioral treatments for these disorders now aim to teach clients emotion regulation and other skills to help them feel more confident in managing and accepting strong emotions rather than avoiding them.

Research suggests that practicing various relaxation exercises may assist individuals in reducing distress and improve overall well-being. One such relaxation tool, breathing practice, has been shown to be an effective tool for decreasing distress and anxiety (Chandla et al., 2013; Chen et al., 2017; Fincham et al., 2023). However, it is important to note that breathing may not be helpful for the direct treatment of panic symptoms (Pompoli et al., 2018). As such, clinicians need to be thoughtful in the approach and rationale for introducing deep breathing, as the goal is to provide a tool to help *manage* stress, not necessarily make high levels of distress go away.

Another type of relaxation tool is progressive muscle relaxation (PMR), initially developed by Edmund Jacobson in the 1920s and revised over the years, which has been shown to reduce stress and foster states of relaxation (Carlson & Hoyle, 1993; Conrad & Roth, 2007; Toussaint et al., 2021). PMR is often included in comprehensive cognitive behavioral interventions for anger management (DiGiuseppe & Tafrate, 2003) and insomnia, also with comorbid diagnoses (Taylor & Pruiksma, 2014), demonstrating improvement in sleep quality and emotion regulation (Sun et al., 2013).

Mindfulness concepts have received significant attention in the literature over the past two decades with a growing body of evidence for the positive effects of mindfulness on both well-being and psychological stress (Goyal et al., 2014; Keng et al., 2011). It has been integrated in a number of evidence-based treatments, including mindfulness-based cognitive therapy (MBCT; Ferguson et al., 2021), acceptance and commitment therapy (ACT; Hayes et al., 2012), mindfulness-based stress reduction (MBSR; Kabat-Zinn, 2003), and dialectical behavior therapy (DBT; Linehan, 2015).

Mindfulness-based strategies have been shown to be useful adjunctive approaches for PTSD to target symptoms of avoidance, negative cognitions, self-blame, and guilt (Banks et al., 2015; Lang et al., 2012). Mindfulness is thought to reduce the symptoms by promoting nonjudgmental acceptance of trauma-related cognitions, increasing self-compassion, and reducing self-blame, as well as increasing openness to experiences and the willingness to approach fearful stimuli and, therefore, reducing avoidance (Boyd et al., 2018). Further, mindfulness-based interventions have been shown to reduce depression symptoms in bereaved samples (O'Connor et al., 2014), further supporting the use of mindfulness-based techniques in helping survivors manage a wide range of strong emotions.

Presentation Appropriateness

This standard module can be useful for all clients to help foster approach and acceptance strategies to manage strong emotions, which are often avoided after traumatic loss and lead to additional suffering. Relaxation exercises, such as PMR, may be useful for clients who struggle with grief-related anger or sleep difficulties, such as trouble falling asleep.

Agenda for Sessions

This module is designed to be flexibly delivered in one to three sessions depending on a number of factors, such as your client's prior experiences with and current use of emotion-focused coping and relaxation skills and their treatment goals. If your client is already well-versed in mindfulness meditation or similar practices, for example, you may be able to deliver this module in as little as one session with follow-up across other sessions. For clients who do not report using these kinds of strategies or for whom these concepts and skills are largely new, you may need to use all three sessions to deliver this module to ensure that skills are properly translated to your client. Clients with more severe emotion regulation difficulties may also need at least three sessions dedicated to this module, with follow-up on skills across other sessions.

Module 4 first session:

1. Provide education on relaxation.

2. Introduce and practice deep breathing.

3. Assign deep breathing for practice.

Module 4 second session:

4. Provide education on and practice progressive muscle relaxation.

5. Assign progressive muscle relaxation for practice.

Module 4 third session:

6. Problem-solve barriers to utilizing relaxation skills.

7. Provide education on mindfulness.

8. Practice mindfulness.

9. Provide education on mindfulness in daily living.

10. Assign mindfulness exercises for practice.

11. Additional mindfulness practice.

Module 4 additional sessions:

12. Introduce the concept of acceptance.

13. Assign mindfulness exercises for practice.

14. Start future sessions with brief mindfulness exercises.

Handouts

Handout 4.1: Instructions for Deep Breathing

Handout 4.2: Deep Breathing Recording Form

Handout 4.3: Instructions for Progressive Muscle Relaxation (PMR)

Handout 4.4: Progressive Muscle Relaxation (PMR) Recording Form

Handout 4.5: Instructions for Mindfulness

Handout 4.6: Mindfulness Recording Form

Scripts for Clinicians

Clinician Script 4.1 Progressive Muscle Relaxation

Clinician Script 4.2 Leaves on a Stream Mindfulness

Module Components

1. Provide Education on Relaxation

Anxiety, anger, and sleep difficulties like insomnia are all common grief reactions. Relaxation strategies, such as deep breathing and PMR, may be useful tools for clients to manage sleep and daily grief-related distress. You can present to clients the potential benefits of learning and practicing relaxation strategies to assist in calming the body when they are engaging in activities or situations that may be stressful or when they experience intense grief-related anger or other emotions. Additionally, relaxation strategies can be presented to help clients settle down at night to fall asleep when this is a goal of treatment. It is important, however, to note that relaxation strategies alone will not remove all anxiety or distress. These feelings, including anger, are normal reactions to traumatic loss and, therefore, are not bad or something clients have to eliminate. However, relaxation strategies can improve confidence in managing these emotions and promote self-efficacy when engaging in activities that may cause distress.

A simple rationale to present to clients is noting that the body cannot be stressed and relaxed at the same time; therefore, several skills may help them calm their body during difficult activities or situations. It should be noted to clients that relaxation is not a panacea or "fix it" skill but rather one of many tools they can use to calm their body or approach difficult situations.

Here is an example rationale when introducing relaxation strategies:

Using techniques to relax your body can help you manage distressing emotions. Often, when we feel anxious or angry, our breathing increases, our heart races, and our muscles tense. Our body senses a threat and breathes faster to get more oxygen into the body as the heart beats faster, and the muscles tense to prepare the body to respond to danger. However, if we can relax our body by slowing down our breathing or reducing muscle tension, we can reduce our levels of physical arousal. We are going to practice two different relaxation techniques that will help slow the arousal down and relax the body.

2. Introduce and Practice Deep Breathing

Guide clients through a five- to ten-minute deep breathing exercise. Ask them to get in a comfortable position, gently close their eyes if they are willing (if not, invite them to fix their gaze on a fixed object, like a spot on the floor), and guide them through an intentional deep breathing activity. You may find it helpful to test the utility of the activity by asking your client to provide pre- and post- activity anxiety or stress scores.

Below is a script that can explain deep breathing along with brief instructions for a square breathing activity:

By slowing down our breathing, we can help the body relax. Today we're going to practice a straightforward four-count square-breathing strategy. We are going to use four seconds to breathe in, then hold the breath for four seconds, exhale for four seconds, and then rest for four seconds. You can imagine breathing in a square-like pattern. I'm going to walk you through this for two to three cycles and then have you try two to three on your own. Before we begin, what is your current anxiety or stress on a scale from 0 to 10 with 10 being the worst anxiety or stress and 0 being none at all?

Now, gently close your eyes if you are willing. If not, just focus your gaze on a focal point in front of you. Now slowly take a deep breath in two...three...four, and hold two...three... four, and out two...three...four, rest two...three...four. (Repeat one or two times.)

Now, take several even, slow breaths now at your own pace. (Pause for several breaths.) As you continue to breathe, bring your attention back into the room...and when you are ready, you can open your eyes.

At the conclusion of the practice, you should process the activity with your client. Reassess their anxiety or stress rating and use the decrease in these ratings as validation for use in everyday practice. If the rating did not decrease, you can discuss how new skills often require practice before mastery or seeing results. For a small number of trauma-exposed individuals, relaxation strategies can increase anxiety, as being vulnerable to releasing body tension can be a trauma cue. If this occurs for your client, that is okay. Just note that and consider adding these types of exercises on their in vivo hierarchy as an exposure-based exercise instead (see module 8).

Also, inquire with your client about their general impressions of the activity, including any difficulties they experienced or what they noticed from a physiological standpoint. It may also be helpful for you to discuss situations in which square breathing may be beneficial, including any barriers to engaging in the activity. Furthermore, processing the experience (as well as other strategies outlined in this module) may reveal unhelpful or inaccurate thoughts related to relaxation. You can guide clients to consider some of the cognitive strategies discussed in module 2 to help address these thoughts, if relevant.

> **Clinician Tip.** For some clients, especially those with extensive trauma histories, feelings of relaxation may have a countereffect and increase physical arousal, as a sense of calm may cue feelings of vulnerability. If this reaction occurs, you may want to shift to a more mindfulness- and acceptance-based strategy to welcome all experiences or consider adding these types of exercises on their in vivo hierarchy as an exposure-based exercise (module 8).

3. Assign Deep Breathing for Practice

Provide instructions for deep breathing (handout 4.1) and assign homework to practice deep breathing daily; it is encouraged that clients track this practice and their pre- and post- activity anxiety or stress levels on a recording form (handout 4.2).

4. Provide Education on and Practice Progressive Muscle Relaxation

PMR is another relaxation technique that involves briefly tightening and then relaxing different muscles to help clients become more aware of muscle tension and the sensation of its opposite—relaxation. Building an awareness of the physiological difference between these can help your client intentionally release muscle tension when it is recognized. Once a client is well-versed and competent in basic PMR skills, you can expand on this foundation to maximize its overall effect and utility. For example, a longer version of PMR can systematically target muscles across the entire body to promote relaxation. This comprehensive exercise can be used regularly to help clients fall asleep and increase general relaxation daily. Furthermore, rather than systematically tensing and relaxing specific muscle groups, you can lead your client through an internal body scan to detect tense muscles and then intentionally relax the specific muscles that were noticed as being tense.

It is recommended that PMR is practiced in session before any at-home assignments are given so you can guide and observe clients during practice and problem-solve issues that may arise. There are a number of online resources that can guide you and your clients through PMR exercises. Like other relaxation activities, it is helpful to assess pre- and post-activity levels of anxiety or stress to gauge the effectiveness of the activity. Below is an example rationale for PMR. See script 4.1 for a sample script you can use to guide clients through the first PMR activity in session.

Example rationale of PMR:

> Progressive muscle relaxation, or PMR, is another relaxation technique that involves briefly tightening and then relaxing different muscles. It is helpful to purposely tighten a muscle group first to notice the sensation and be aware of the body's feelings before we, with intention, relax that same muscle. It is like swinging a pendulum from tension to relaxation. Noticing the feeling of tension, the feeling of relaxed muscles, and the difference between the two, will help you better manage muscle tension during difficult situations or activities (and help you with falling asleep).

> We will take some time to practice this together so you can feel comfortable using it yourself. There is no need to tense muscles to the point that it causes pain or that you hurt yourself, so be careful in how much you flex each muscle. Also, there is no magic formula in terms of which muscle groups should be targeted. I am going to guide you through this today focusing on your hands, shoulders, jaw, forehead, and toes. I will do it alongside you, so if you are not sure what I am asking you to do, you can open your eyes to see how I am doing it.

> Before we begin, what is your current anxiety or stress on a scale from 0 to10, with 10 being the worst anxiety or stress and 0 being none at all?

5. Assign Progressive Muscle Relaxation for Practice

Provide instructions for PMR (handout 4.3) and assign client homework to practice PMR daily; it is encouraged that clients track this practice, as well as their pre- and post-activity anxiety or stress levels, on a recording form (handout 4.4).

6. Problem-Solve Barriers to Utilizing Relaxation Skills

During follow-up sessions, review the use of deep breathing and PMR skills. Alongside your client, review the completed deep breathing or PMR recording form. It is important that you praise clients for their efforts, even if they were not always successful in completing daily practice or did not notice changes in anxiety or distress. If they did not complete the assigned practice during the previous week, you should spend some time problem-solving barriers to using deep breathing and PMR skills. Barriers most often include remembering to do the activity. You can assist clients in planning when they can practice and have them add it to their schedule or set a reminder on their phone or watch. In addition, clients may comment that deep breathing or PMR did not achieve the desired degree of relaxation. You should closely examine the recording form or inquire with your client about the amount of time spent conducting each activity. Like all skills, continued practice is essential to develop a sense of mastery, and this may particularly be important for a new skill, such as PMR.

7. Provide Education on Mindfulness

Helping clients understand the basic concepts of mindfulness can assist in managing, approaching, and accepting difficult emotions that come along with grief. Mindfulness has been described by Jon Kabat-Zinn (founder of UMass Stress-Reduction Clinic and Center for Mindfulness) as "paying attention in a particular way, on purpose, in the present moment and non-judgmentally" (Kabat-Zinn, 1994, p. 4).

When clients are in the present moment, resting in the here and now, they are fully engaged with whatever they are doing. Often, clients are not in the present moment—they may be reliving past conversations or experiences or they are worrying about or planning for the future. Further, they sometimes are on *autopilot*, going through the motions of their days and relationships and, thus, often missing out on what is happening in the here and the now.

Here is a sample script introducing mindfulness concepts:

One approach to assist with both managing strong grief emotions and engaging in life is mindfulness. Mindfulness is paying attention in a particular way, on purpose, in the present moment and nonjudgmentally. Consider driving, for example. Have you ever driven home and not remembered the drive? You probably didn't run any red lights, as your mind and body were on complete autopilot. Perhaps you were thinking about an event that occurred earlier that day, or maybe you were thinking about the things you need to do once you arrive back home. Either way, your mind was not truly present. That is the opposite of mindfulness! In simplest terms, mindfulness is being awake.

Mindfulness is brought about by focusing one's awareness on the world around us or inside of us while calmly acknowledging and accepting one's feelings, thoughts, and bodily sensations. This can lead to a greater awareness of our surroundings and inner (emotional and cognitive) world. An example of mindfulness is deliberately pausing to become aware of the colors and sounds in our immediate environment, leaning on the senses of sight and

85

sound. An example of physical mindfulness is to take a moment to feel our toes and notice the warmth, cool, or pressure on a part of the foot, without judging it as good or bad—just noticing it as it is, in the present moment. By pausing and observing the mind (our thoughts), clients can resist getting drawn into a spiral of negative thinking and become less reactive. Psychologists and other cognitive scientists have noted the benefits of mindfulness by increasing our attention to the present, which can potentially quiet distress.

Below are the three components of mindfulness in more detail:

- *Mindfulness is purposeful*: focusing on a particular thing, gently redirecting attention back if the mind wanders. Doing one thing with intention.

- *Mindfulness is nonjudgmental*: not labeling experiences as "good" or "bad." Simply notice them as they are.

- *Mindfulness is present centered*: focusing on the present experience rather than past events or future possibilities.

> **Clinician Tip.** Some clients may wonder if mindfulness is a spiritual or religious practice, feel ambivalent about its use, or think it is only about meditation. Share that mindfulness is just learning to be awake and fully engaged in life—with all sensations, experiences, feelings, and thoughts. Meditation is a form of mindfulness, but one does not have to engage in formal meditation to practice and benefit from mindfulness.

Mindfulness takes practice as we tend to automatically compare and judge the world, ourselves, and others. Learning to be mindful can help to develop acceptance and understanding of the way our body feels. It can help clients become more aware of thoughts without the need to push them away, accepting them as they are—simply thoughts (words or images, nothing more). Further, mindfulness can help clients face the present moment with curiosity rather than escaping it. Mindfulness is like being a curious internal scientist—observing, learning about the present experience objectively, without trying to change it.

Clients may have difficulty grasping the concept of mindfulness when first introduced. It can be helpful to provide metaphors to illustrate the rationale and process of mindfulness.

For example, consider the following metaphor:

So right now, you may feel like you're barely keeping afloat trying to doggie paddle, fighting waves in a big stormy ocean of grief, and perhaps you aren't even aware of where you are in the ocean. Mindfulness is learning to notice the waves, observe them, watch them come and go without fighting them, and allowing yourself to float instead of struggle with the waves of grief. By doing so, if we allow the ocean to be, the intensity of the waves may quiet. Regardless, when we allow the ocean to be, we are not adding additional suffering by fighting the waves, and we can devote more energy and attention to activities that are meaningful to us.

8. Practice Mindfulness

You can introduce your client to a brief mindful breathing exercise to introduce the concept of mindfulness during the session. You will want to underscore to your client that mindful breathing is different from deep breathing to achieve relaxation, as our intention is not to change the breath or calm our body but rather to just notice and observe, without judgment. Ask your client if they are willing to close their eyes and adopt a comfortable posture with feet flat on the ground.

You can then follow the mindful breathing exercise using a soft and slow tone of voice:

If you are willing, gently close your eyes with your feet grounded. Settle in your seat. And just take a few moments to focus on your breath… Just observe and be present with your breath… Perhaps notice the cool air with each inhale and warm air with each exhale… Perhaps notice your chest rising and falling with each in- and out-breath… Just simply notice, with curiosity, your breath. Our goal is not to change your breath, but maybe you notice your breath changing…this is okay—don't judge this, just be present with your body as it breathes… (Pause.) And your mind might wander; that's okay, too, no judgment, just notice it wandering. You could even say to yourself, "Ah, there's my mind wandering," and gently return your attention to your breath… (Allow a bit of silence.) Our breath grounds us… Our breath sustains us… Our breath gives us life. We can be mindful in the present moment by just focusing on our breath…. And when you are ready, you can slowly open your eyes and reengage with the room.

Like all in-session practice, you should process the experience with clients with questions such as, *What changes did you notice in your body? Did you notice that your mind wandered? If your mind wandered, what did you do?* Validate that the mind will wander, which is normal and universal. Convey this and encourage your client to simply notice the mind wandering and to gently return their attention back to the exercise. You can also remind clients that one component of mindfulness is being nonjudgmental. Additional metaphors, such as the mind as a "problem-solving machine" or an untrained puppy that is always distracted and requires redirection of attention, can be helpful.

You should also inquire about emotions that came up and were attended to by your client, particularly when your client finds they are pulled away by their thoughts. Questions that may be useful include: *What did you notice in your body when you found yourself distracted? Did you notice your stomach tightening and your muscles tensing? Did you notice judgmental thoughts directed toward yourself for being distracted?* Physiological sensations are part of our present experience—they occur in the here and now—and mindfulness can help clients notice them with self-compassion and acceptance.

9. Provide Education on Mindfulness in Daily Living

It may be important for you to convey to clients that mindfulness can be practiced and integrated in day-to-day life. This may be particularly essential for clients with limited time to complete between-session assignments. Clients will have many opportunities to be present, in the moment, doing just *one* activity (watch out for multitasking!), with purpose and without judgment throughout their day. Clients do not necessarily have to carve out additional time to practice mindfulness (although this may be especially beneficial). Engaging with the present moment can assist clients in restoration-oriented daily-life activities. Several areas clients can consider incorporating mindfulness into everyday life include:

- listening to music

- making a cup of tea or coffee

- exercising

- brief three-minute mindful breathing

- taking a shower

- doing the dishes or other chores

- walking to car

- eating mindfully

- stepping outside for several minutes and just *be* with the outdoors or nature

- listening and reflecting in conversation with someone else

Example script to explain how to practice mindfulness throughout daily activities:

Although structured practice, like practicing mindful breathing, can help you develop this skill, there will be opportunities throughout the day in which you could also practice mindfulness. Taking a shower, for example. We all usually take showers or baths, so this doesn't take extra time. Next time you take a shower, do it with intention. Focus your attention on just the shower. Let your thoughts and emotions in other areas from your past or your future gently go as you tend to just your shower. Smell your soup or shampoo before using it. Notice the water as it hits your back. Is it cold? Is it hot? Try not to judge, just notice and describe. Notice the sensations when you rub your shampoo in your hair. Close your eyes. Does that change the experience any? Just be in this shower. Again, we aren't creating an experience but rather being present and awake in an activity that we often do on autopilot. How does showering mindfully change the experience? If done daily, you may notice a deeper sense of groundedness and calm.

10. Assign Mindfulness Exercises for Practice

Like the previous relaxation exercises, clients should be encouraged to practice mindfulness daily. Handout 4.5 provides a summary of mindfulness information reviewed in session. Handout 4.6 allows for tracking. Regular and consistent practice is critical, as many clients are less familiar with mindfulness compared to relaxation. Moreover, given the prominent role of the mind and its natural (and strong) tendency to ruminate on the past or think about the future, the ability to develop mindfulness skills may take substantial time and effort. For this reason, it is advised that clients begin with regular (daily) but brief practice of mindful breathing, as well as integrating mindfulness into daily-life activities. Once clients become more familiar with mindfulness and begin to develop that skill, you can introduce longer and more sophisticated mindfulness exercises.

11. Additional Mindfulness Practice

Continue to expand the presentation and practice of different mindfulness exercises in sessions to allow clients to explore using mindfulness not only to engage with present-day life, fostering connection with restoration-oriented daily living, but also to start to engage with and approach loss-oriented grief content. Once your client has a baseline level of knowledge regarding the rationale and process of mindfulness, you can incorporate longer and more immersive mindfulness exercises. For example, the guided meditation *Leaves on a Stream* (LeJeune, 2012) is a common mindfulness exercise that may allow clients to better observe thoughts without getting caught up in them. It guides clients to notice thoughts and let them go—to be an observing mind. In doing so, clients may feel less emotionally tied to thoughts and will be better able to tolerate distressing thoughts.

Rationale for noticing thoughts mindfully:

Mindfulness can be helpful for learning to allow space for all thoughts to just be. It can allow us to approach our thoughts with curiosity rather than disappointment and shame. Grief can involve difficult thoughts, and we sometimes cope by pushing them away or even grip them tightly. Learning to notice these difficult grief thoughts can allow you to notice your thoughts without trying to force them to be or not to be, freeing up emotional effort and attention to help you do the things that are most important to you.

You can then engage your client in an in-session guided *Leaves on a Stream* mindfulness exercise (LeJeune, 2012). See script 4.2 for a sample script.

12. Introduce the Concept of Acceptance

After developing a basic understanding of the rationale and process of mindfulness, clients are likely to have a better framework for understanding the concept of acceptance. It may be helpful to highlight or review the key components of mindfulness: paying attention on purpose, nonjudgmentally, and in the present moment. You should explain that mindfulness enables us to be less judgmental about our experiences. This allows us to approach the present moment with acceptance.

Acceptance is being open to all experiences without judging them as good or bad. It is acknowledging thoughts, emotions, and experiences for what they are, embracing the whole situation, even the parts that may be uncomfortable. It is about moving through life on a steady course, like a ship that cuts through the ups and downs of life's waves. The ship cannot avoid the downs because the waves are inevitable—a part of being in the ocean. With acceptance, survivors can hold their grief thoughts and emotions more lightly. Clients may know these thoughts and feelings are there, but they are not gripping them too tightly or trying to push them away, allowing your client to engage with the world around them, in the present moment. Clients can learn to encounter emotions, such as grief, sadness, anxiety, anger, and to accept them for what they are—not trying to change or get rid of them. Interestingly, acceptance allows us to appreciate feelings, such as joy, peacefulness, and happiness, which often go by unacknowledged, particularly when someone is feeling intense grief.

Acceptance does not mean resigning to what is happening in a passive way. It simply means actively acknowledging that what is happening, is happening. Acceptance does not tell us what to do. What we choose to do comes out of understanding the moment fully, not just a reaction to the moment while gently carrying our grief. Analogies and metaphors can be a helpful way to understand or explain the concept of acceptance. The following tug-of-war analogy is adapted from ACT (Hayes et al., 2012).

> *Imagine you are in a tug-of-war with a monster. Between you is a reeking pit of mud. No matter how hard you pull, it seems like you can't win. The harder you pull, the closer you're pulled to that pit of mud. What can you do?*
>
> *You can let go of the rope. That is acceptance. In this analogy, the monster is like your grief emotions and thoughts. Acceptance ends the process of trying to fight them. Rather than losing the battle to control them again and again, you simply let them be.*

Mindfulness and acceptance are difficult concepts for many clients to initially understand as they are novel approaches to managing thoughts and emotions that are not typically taught in life. Acknowledge that these are difficult concepts, which may not be grasped quickly or easily. After all, society often encourages us to seek comfort or to avoid what is perceived as negative—the concept of experiential avoidance that we referred to earlier in this chapter—rather than to take a stance of acceptance, so this process may be especially difficult to cultivate. Encourage clients to notice critical thoughts or judgments that come with the difficult process of mindfulness and acceptance. They get easier and become more effective with practice—just like any skill in athletics, music, or cooking. Once learned, this skill is always with you.

> **Clinician Tip.** Some clients may report that accepting positive emotions feels unfaithful or disrespectful to their loved one. You may want to gently encourage your client to consider the possibility of being able to hold both grief and positive emotions. Grief does not have to be mutually exclusive to feelings of joy or contentment.

13. Assign Mindfulness Exercises for Practice

Practice mindfulness daily and track on handout 4.6. You are encouraged to take a developmental approach when assigning practice. For example, it may be advantageous to have clients begin with practicing mindful breathing daily before moving on to incorporating mindfulness in daily activities or practicing longer, more elaborate exercises (such as *Leaves on a Stream*, LeJeune, 2012).

14. Start Future Sessions with Brief Mindfulness Exercises

After teaching your client mindfulness concepts, you can start each subsequent session with a three-minute guided mindfulness exercise to continue to reinforce the importance of using mindfulness in daily practice to assist with managing strong emotions.

Cultural Considerations

An advantage of mindfulness is its ability to validate difficult emotions, including discrimination, stigmatizing attitudes, and oppression, while promoting action and self-advocacy. That said, in addition to discrimination experiences, individuals from underserved and -resourced backgrounds have a higher probability of enduring multiple life stressors beyond the traumatic loss of a loved one. As such, accepting or "inviting in" painful or distressing thoughts and emotions may seem foreign and counterintuitive. In such cases, you should be prepared to acknowledge how avoidance of painful thoughts and feelings has been both helpful and unhelpful for your client. It may have helped blunt the pain of past experiences of discrimination or loss, for instance; it may also have limited awareness of the ways a client has choices in their life, including how to respond to painful thoughts and feelings evoked by these experiences (Sobczak & West, 2013).

Another consideration when it comes to grief and mindfulness is that, while it may be true that painful grief surrounding the traumatic death of a loved one serves a function (to communicate the loss of an extremely meaningful relationship), it may be difficult for your client to see how these emotions can still be part of an enriching life. In such moments, you can validate your client's anguish and their understandable desire to avoid such pain by helping them see that this pain reflects the deep love they have for their deceased loved one and how avoiding such pain may actually make life (and the process of grieving) more difficult. Survivors from cultures where emotion and the outward display of emotion is generally viewed as a weakness may also be reluctant to engage in activities that involve greater acceptance of painful feelings, in which case it may be more helpful for you as clinician to recommend using mindfulness as a means of gaining greater personal insight into the consequences of accepting versus avoiding emotions (Sobczak & West, 2013).

Some individuals, when first learning about mindfulness, have concerns that it is religious or spiritual in nature. It is important to stress that mindfulness is not based on any specific religion. The practice is truly just learning how to be present in life and how to relate to the internal experiences that all humans have. Alternatively, survivors of faith may be concerned that mindfulness is inconsistent with their religious orientation. However, the clinician can draw parallels between the process of mindfulness and religious practices (like prayer) and can collaborate with the client on how to embed mindfulness within their faith-based activities (for example, being mindful while at a religious service). Indeed, mindfulness may actually enhance one's religious practice.

Conclusion

Managing the strong emotions that come with grief, and especially traumatic loss, can sometimes seem like an overwhelming, if not impossible, task. Relaxation skills, like deep breathing and PMR, can empower clients to feel more confident in managing strong emotions by reducing some of the physical sensations associated with strong emotions like sadness, fear, and anger. Similarly, mindfulness exercises can limit experiential avoidance of strong emotions and empower survivors by showing them they can approach painful feelings without being taken over by them. If you are interested in learning more about mindfulness skills and ways to incorporate mindfulness skills in your work with clients, consider the helpful resources at the end of this chapter.

Each of the four modules covered up to this point are considered standard modules you would use with any client. The remaining modules are optional ones recommended for clients based on their unique symptoms and presenting concerns. In the next chapter, we cover module 5, which you will use with clients with limited social support and those presenting with depression.

Books on Mindfulness

Harris, R. (2021). *When life hits hard: How to transcend grief, crisis, and loss with acceptance and commitment therapy*. New Harbinger Publications.

Kabat-Zinn, J. (2005). *Wherever you go, there you are: Mindfulness meditation in everyday life* (10th ed.). Hachette Books.

Kabat-Zinn, J. (2012). *Mindfulness for beginners: Reclaiming the present moment—and your life*. Sounds True.

Kumar, S. M. (2005). *Grieving mindfully: A compassionate and spiritual guide to coping with loss*. New Harbinger Publications.

Naht Hahn, T. (1996). *The miracle of mindfulness: An introduction to the practice of meditation*. Beacon Press.

Naht Hahn, T. (2010). *You are here: Discovering the magic of the present moment*. Shambhala.

Websites

Headspace: http://www.headspace.com/meditation/meditation-for-beginners

UCLA Mindful Awareness Research Center: http://www.uclahealth.org/marc

UC San Diego Center for Mindfulness: http://www.mindfulness.ucsd.edu

Mobile Apps

Apps are another good way to learn and practice mindfulness. Several good mobile apps (some require subscription) are *Headspace*, *Calm*, and *Insight Timer*. For traumatic loss related to mass violence incidents, *Transcend NMVC* is a comprehensive self-help app.

CHAPTER 8

Module 5: Building Healthy Support Networks

Surviving the traumatic loss of a loved one can be a highly stigmatizing experience, leaving survivors feeling isolated or even different from others. For many survivors, it may seem at times as though no one else can comprehend the depth of their emotional pain. This sense of isolation and disconnection can be especially overwhelming when the deceased was a primary source of support for the survivor—someone who could be relied on to offer reassurance, advice, and practical assistance when needed. This optional module helps clients identify and build healthy social support networks with the goal of helping clients establish and maintain meaningful, supportive relationships with friends, family, and their broader community. This module can be delivered in one session and can be integrated with other modules that involve behavioral techniques or assignments, such as positive activity scheduling (module 6) or activities that serve to memorialize or maintain a connection with the decedent (module 7).

Background and Related Literature

Social support broadly refers to social bonds and relationships that serve to provide individuals with emotional, instrumental, and informational assistance (House et al., 1988; Turner & Brown, 2010). A large body of research spanning several decades has consistently shown that perceived social support is associated with health and overall well-being (e.g., Cohen, 2004), in part because social support acts as a buffer against the adverse effects of stress and adversity on psychological well-being (Cohen & Willis, 1985). Social support can also help ensure that individuals have access to resources that are needed to maintain a sense of psychological well-being (Hobfoll et al., 1990), especially in the context of extremely stressful events like the traumatic loss of a loved one.

A number of studies have demonstrated that greater perceived social support can serve as a protective factor against chronic post-traumatic stress (Wang et al., 2021) and depression symptoms (Gariépy et al., 2016). Several recent studies have also documented an association between perceived social support and prolonged grief reactions (e.g., Mason et al., 2020), including among samples of traumatic loss survivors. For example, available social support has been associated with lower post-traumatic stress, depression, and prolonged grief reactions among homicide survivors (Burke et al., 2010; Rheingold & Williams, 2015), while less perceived social support was associated with PTSD and co-occurring PTSD and PGD among internally displaced individuals grieving conflict-related traumatic losses (Heeke et al., 2017). Likewise, social isolation and loneliness have shown to exacerbate PGD symptoms over time (Harrop et al., 2023).

So, while helping clients build healthy support networks may in and of itself help ameliorate bereavement-related distress, building healthy support networks may also enhance treatment outcomes. Research among individuals receiving treatment for PTSD, for example, has shown that treatment outcomes were better among individuals with greater social support (Price et al., 2018; Thrasher et al., 2010), perhaps because this helps individuals manage stress associated with completing other intervention components and increases the likelihood that individuals can complete different homework assignments (e.g., Tarrier & Humphreys, 2004). Further, building social support networks has been included in evidence-informed early interventions for trauma and disaster, such as SPR (Berkowitz et al., 2010). The following sections discuss recommendations and strategies for helping traumatic loss clients build healthy social support networks.

Presentation Appropriateness

This module is recommended for clients with elevated depression symptoms and may be appropriate for clients experiencing post-traumatic stress or prolonged grief reactions who lack socio-emotional resources.

Agenda for Session

Module 5 first session:

1. Provide rationale for building a healthy support network.

2. Provide education about different kinds of social support.

3. Introduce social support mapping and explore supportive relationships.

4. Create a social support engagement plan.

Module 5 additional sessions:

5. Continue engaging supports and address communication challenges.

Handouts

Handout 5.1: Types of Social Support

Handout 5.2: Social Support Map

Handout 5.3: Social Support Engagement Plan

Module Components

1. Provide Rationale for Building a Healthy Support Network

Following the traumatic loss of a loved one, clients can suddenly find themselves feeling isolated, even from those closest to them. This sense of isolation may happen suddenly or gradually. Often, it comes from feeling unseen, unheard, or misunderstood by others around them. In the months and years after a death, clients' attempts at sharing their grief with others may be met with indifference or invalidation as when people casually encourage them to let go or move on. Other times, they may be confronted with painful silence from those closest to them who now seem to avoid conversations with them because they themselves don't know what to say or how to sit with the raw anguish that often accompanies life after traumatic loss. Still, other times, isolation may be self-imposed—even when they know they have others who will listen and support them in their grief, they can be reluctant to do so out of concern for being a burden on others. Isolation and loneliness may be especially prominent among those who have experienced a particularly stigmatizing loss, such as in the case of suicide or accidental fatal drug overdose.

When the deceased was a primary source of support and companionship, isolation may also be rooted in real changes in day-to-day routines and lifestyle brought about by the death. Clients who relied on the deceased for transportation, childcare, or other practical needs, for example, may suddenly feel overwhelmed by the challenges of managing these new tasks on their own and, in the absence of supportive others able to provide some practical assistance, can begin to feel alone in their struggles. Feelings of loneliness and isolation can be further compounded by a lack of information about resources that can help clients navigate these new challenges.

The goal of building a healthy support network is to help clients identify and connect with supportive friends, family, and others in their broader community. Specifically, you want to help clients identify others who can provide them with emotional security through acceptance of painful and difficult emotions, help clients problem-solve ways to cope with painful emotions and new challenges, and help clients engage in new life opportunities that support long-term recovery (Feeney & Collins, 2015).

Below is a sample clinician-client dialogue related to discussing the rationale for building a healthy support network:

Clinician: How have your relationships with others changed since Nathan died?

Client: I lost a lot of friends after Nathan died. Even some of my so-called family aren't welcome at my house anymore. Right after he died, a lot of people would come by and check on us and ask us what we needed, but slowly, week after week, they stopped showing up. Then when they did show up, they'd act uncomfortable if me or my wife started talking about Nathan or about how it was time to "move on." I told more than one person who told me that to get out of my house and never come back. You lose a child and don't "move on" from it, you know?

Clinician: It's almost like everyone else went back to their own lives, and they didn't allow space for this grief, like they wanted to put it all behind them.

Client: That's right. I think my wife even tries to forget sometimes because it all just gets to be too much. So sometimes I try not to even talk to her about Nathan and how much all of this still just hurts. (Begins to cry.)

Clinician: Sometimes you try to hide all of this grief and pain from her because it's like you want to protect her.

Client: Yeah, she's going through a lot herself, and I don't want her to worry more about me. But then when I don't talk to anyone about this stuff, and I hold it all in, it all just builds up until I feel like I'm going to explode, and that just makes everything worse for both of us. So, yeah, I don't know what to do or who to talk to really.

Clinician: What do you think it would be like to have others in your life you could trust to turn to when you need to let things out or just want to share something about Nathan that makes you happy?

Client: That'd be great, but I don't know who that would be.

Clinician: Yeah, we all need people close to us that we can trust to turn to at different points in our lives. Let's see if we can spend some time today thinking about the different kinds of support that might be available from the people you know, who you might trust to give you that support, and brainstorm ways to find different kinds of support that might be missing.

2. Provide Education About Different Kinds of Social Support

An important part of building a healthy support network is helping clients identify potential sources of social support; people who can provide different kinds of support as needed at different times throughout the lifespan. Generally speaking, these include *emotional, instrumental, informational,* and *appraisal* support (House, 1983). Utilize handout 5.1 with client to explore different kinds of social support.

See Cacciatore et al. (2021) for a more detailed discussion regarding these and other expressions of social support relevant to traumatic loss survivors.

> **Clinician Tip.** Research with traumatic loss survivors (Cacciatore et al., 2021) has found that, of all the expressions of emotional support they valued most, hearing someone else speak their loved one's name was among the most deeply appreciated. When given permission by clients to do so, clinicians are encouraged to use the deceased's name(s) as a direct expression of emotional support.

3. Introduce Social Support Mapping and Explore Supportive Relationships

An important step in helping clients build healthy support networks is identifying social resources and supports already available to the client that are either underutilized or could be utilized in new ways. This might include acquaintances, friends, family, and other community members. Visually displaying available social resources using a social support map like the one in handout 5.1 can be a useful way to help clients feel more connected to existing social resources.

Start by asking clients to identify people (and even pets) that are important to them or play an important part in their life. Encourage clients to brainstorm as many people as possible, listing family, friends, neighbors, people from work, school, faith-based organizations, and even helping professionals (Tracy & Whittaker, 1990). Doing so during this initial step of social support mapping can increase the likelihood that clients will be able to identify at least one person who can provide needed support across each different domain (emotional, instrumental, informational, appraisal) and also help them identify potential sources of support they might not have otherwise considered. Further, visualizing possible sources this manner may help to counter any negative thoughts about the perceived availability of support. When possible, try to help clients identify at least eight to ten people or supports that are important in their life. Utilize handout 5.2 to create a written map.

> **Clinician Tip.** When brainstorming and identifying people important to the client, encourage clients to consider people that are important to them, even if they do not see or even talk to them regularly. Reminding clients that these important people are available can facilitate reconnection with important others.

Once clients have generated a map of potentially important people, help clients consider who on the map might be available to provide different types of support for them. You can engage clients in this process by asking questions, such as *Looking at the people we have on your map so far, who could you go to for emotional support? Who do you provide instrumental support to? Who could you go to for advice on ways to cope with grief?*

Note here that clients may identify individuals who are able to provide them with multiple kinds of support. Clients may also find that, of the important individuals listed at the beginning of the activity, there is no one that they perceive as being available to provide them with certain kinds of support, such as instrumental or appraisal support. In these cases, be prepared to make recommendations and referrals to possible sources of support available in the client's community, which could include social service agencies that can help them with instrumental support needs or grief-specific support groups to help with emotional or appraisal support.

To ensure that recommendations and referrals are as successful and helpful as possible, make sure to stay up-to-date on different community resources available to clients across different community agencies and keep updated contact information for those resources and supports. In addition, there are a number of national organizations that keep loss-type-specific resources for peer support, such as the American Foundation for Suicide Prevention (AFSP) and Parents of Murdered Children (POMC), to name a few.

As clients build their social support map, they can draw arrows between themselves and their support people to demonstrate the direction of support (do they receive support or do they provide support?). Clients could also draw thicker lines to indicate the strength of the support connection. This allows for the ability to review the depth and directionality of their connections with others. For example, if a client has a lot of people that they provide various types of support to but little in receiving support, increasing receiving support may be helpful. Also, if a client has a lot of thin lines and not many close relationships (thicker lines), a focus on strengthening relationships could be of value.

It is important to note that a client's deceased loved one may be important to include on their social support map, as some people find support and connection from their loved one, even if they are not physically present. This may dovetail into module 7. If the deceased loved one is included on the map, make sure the focus is on how the loved one provides support now, as opposed to when they were living.

Clinician Tip. While reviewing the social support map, be sure to ask clients if there are important individuals they have identified who are negative supports. In the same way that the goal of this activity is to identify and encourage connection with potential social resources and supports, explicitly recognizing and discussing potential sources of negative support can be important when making decisions about who the clients will try to connect with in the coming weeks and months.

Below is an example of a completed social support map:

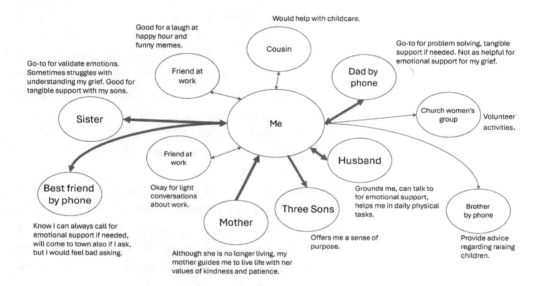

4. Create a Social Support Engagement Plan

After identifying potentially supportive relationships, help clients identify social support domains where they are in greatest need and make plans to engage at least one person who can potentially provide that support in the upcoming week. Use handout 5.3 to guide discussion and write down the engagement plan. In creating the plan, try to create one that is as concrete as possible in terms of how and when clients will engage potential supports, including steps needed and when the specific steps will be accomplished. Greater specificity in planning can increase the likelihood that clients will follow through in reaching out to potential supports.

Additionally, discuss any anticipated barriers to and facilitators of engagement, including resources clients may need to engage specific supports. In the event clients identify a lack of tangible resources, like transportation or time off work, as potential barriers, help them brainstorm ways to mitigate these when possible. This may include helping clients directly connect with and engage community-based supports that can provide them with instrumental support as part of their engagement plan.

> **Clinician Tip.** Some clients who identify emotional or appraisal support as their greatest area of need may be reluctant to ask others for support but may feel more comfortable providing support to others by initiating positive, mutually supportive social interactions. In these circumstances, clinicians may want to help clients identify individuals from their social map who both want and need similar kinds of support and discuss a plan for providing that support to others.

5. Addressing Communication Challenges

Over the coming weeks, encourage clients to continue engaging in social supports and problem-solve any challenges that arise. One common challenge is effectively communicating needs to others within the survivor's network. For some clients, communicating needs may be challenging and can be impacted by intense emotions. For others, finding the right words to seek support may be difficult. And other clients find being assertive about needs while protecting the relationship a struggle. Clients may need to plan or practice communication when seeking healthy social support, as well as potentially manage unwanted social support from well-meaning people.

Discussing assertiveness skills may prove useful to assist clients in mastering engagement with their social support network in a healthy way. For instance, teaching a basic assertiveness framework such as *I understand... I feel... I need...* may provide structure that can be practiced in session to assist with expressing emotions and needs.

Below is an example of this framework for a client seeking additional emotional support from a friend.

> **I understand** *you do not know what to say when I talk about my son.* **I feel** *sad and lonely at times. Talking about him helps me feel connected to him. When I talk about him with you,* **I just need** *you to listen. You do not need to say anything. Will that be okay?*

For others, working through standard phrases when managing questions from well-meaning people at inopportune times can be helpful. Below are two examples of such example phrases.

> *I don't want to go there right now, but thank you for caring.*

Or

> *Thank you for your concern, but this is difficult to talk about at this time.*

Cultural Considerations

As a clinician helping clients identify potentially supportive relationships, you should be mindful of cultural differences in who in a social support map might be considered an appropriate provider of different kinds of support. For instance, cultural background may influence the extent to which clients are willing to seek emotional or other kinds of support from family members (such as spouses or parents) over friends and others in their extended network, as in cultural contexts where clients see themselves as being responsible for providing various forms of social support to others within their family unit. Inappropriately encouraging clients to seek support from a family member in such cases can ultimately create more stress for the client and negatively impact treatment. Therefore, working closely with the client to explore their available support, including the alignment of potential support with cultural practices and the client's identity and maintaining a genuinely curious stance without judgment, is part of culturally responsive care. This is particularly important when the clinician and client have distinct cultural backgrounds and identities.

Moreover, be mindful of how different community-based agencies (and professionals capable of providing different kinds of support who are housed within those agencies) are viewed by local communities, especially when you work with clients in minoritized and under-resourced communities. Some agencies, for example, that may be identified by either the client or clinician as potential sources of support may have negative reputations for discriminatory practices and microaggressions against minoritized clients. In staying up-to-date on social resources available to clients in their broader communities, seek to understand how different agencies are perceived by the communities they serve and try to avoid encouraging clients to engage with these agencies as part of their social support engagement plan.

Conclusion

Surviving a traumatic loss can at times feel like an isolating experience. Helping survivors engage with trusted, supportive others in their family and community can begin to reduce this sense of isolation. Engaging healthy support networks provides survivors with a sense of connection, of being cared for and caring for others, and in some cases, much-needed assistance with activities of daily living. Survivors experiencing severe depression symptoms can also draw on support networks to help them start reengaging in meaningful, restoration-oriented activities, a topic that is covered in the next chapter on module 6. For more detailed information on enhancing social support in clinical practice see Cacciatore et al. (2021) and Tracy and Whittaker (1990).

CHAPTER 9

Module 6: Meaningful Behavioral Activation

In coping with traumatic loss, survivors often find that many aspects of their day-to-day lives drastically change. For instance, survivors may suddenly lack financial or other resources needed to do many of the things they previously enjoyed, or they may find that attending to family and other responsibilities after the loss affords them few opportunities to do many of the things that used to bring them pleasure and meaning before the death. In addition, due to the pain of the loss, the physical absence of the deceased, or a sense of meaningless in life, survivors may experience a lack of interest in activities that were once enjoyable prior to the death. This optional module helps survivors identify and engage in values-based activities across multiple domains with the goal of helping grievers reengage in activities that promote a greater sense of personal pleasure, purpose, or accomplishment. It can be delivered in one to three sessions and can be integrated with other modules that involve behavioral techniques or assignments, such as activities that serve to memorialize or maintain a connection with the decedent (module 7).

Background and Related Literature

Behavioral activation generally refers to a set of behavioral interventions that aim to help individuals increase engagement in positive, rewarding activities. It is rooted in behavioral models of depression (e.g., Lewinsohn et al., 1980), which generally assume that depression is at least partially a result of external circumstances where opportunities to engage in positive experiences are reduced or severely limited. Most behavioral activation interventions involve common elements of self-monitoring behavior and activity scheduling with the goal of increasing the frequency of behaviors that have the potential to lead to positive, meaningful experiences (Stein et al., 2021).

Over the last three decades, behavioral activation has emerged as one of the most effective frontline treatments for MDD (Ciharova et al., 2021; Ekers et al., 2014). Studies have also shown that it can be beneficial in reducing anxiety and improving overall activity levels (Stein et al., 2021). Additionally, behavioral activation can be helpful in addressing prolonged grief reactions. These often have a negative impact on multiple aspects of a survivor's day-to-day life, from social contacts with family and friends to eating, sleeping, and attending to other personal care needs (Monk et al., 2006), which can greatly reduce opportunities for survivors to engage in activities that are perceived as having positive outcomes. Behavioral activation interventions directly focus on helping survivors build these and other new activities back into their daily lives, creating new opportunities for social reengagement and activities that might lead to a renewed sense of identity, meaning, and purpose.

Studies have shown that behavioral activation can be helpful as a standalone intervention or in combination with other techniques in reducing both depression and prolonged grief reactions in a number of different bereaved populations. As a standalone intervention, behavioral activation has been associated with improvements in depression, prolonged grief, and post-traumatic stress reactions in adults who met diagnostic criteria for PGD (Papa, Rummel et al., 2013; Papa, Sewell et al., 2013). Similar outcomes among survivors living with PGD have been observed when behavioral activation is combined with therapeutic exposures (discussed in more detail in module 8) in both older adult and veteran samples (Acierno et al., 2021; Acierno et al., 2012). The following sections discuss recommendations and strategies for using behavioral activation with traumatic loss survivors, as well as special considerations when working with survivors.

Presentation Appropriateness

This module is recommended for survivors with elevated depression symptoms and may be appropriate for survivors experiencing prolonged grief reactions who are underengaged in personally meaningful or other functional activities beyond those associated with commemorating or seeking proximity to their deceased loved one.

Agenda for Sessions

This module is designed to be flexibly delivered in one to three sessions depending on a number of factors such as your client's prior experience with behavioral therapies, their ability to engage in valued activities outside of sessions, and how quickly they are able to identify and articulate personal values. If your client intuitively understands the rationale for behavioral activation, can articulate personal values across multiple domains, and can readily identify activities that reflect those values, you may be able to deliver this module in one session with follow-up across sessions thereafter. Often, discussing and identifying values-based actions requires more effortful thought than can be accomplished in a single session, so you may need to spend up to three sessions delivering this module, especially with more severely depressed clients.

Module 6 first session:

1. Provide rationale for meaningful behavioral activation.

2. Provide education about different kinds of activities.

3. Assign activity-tracking worksheet.

Module 6 second session:

4. Review activity-tracking assignment and problem-solve barriers.

5. Discuss personal values across life domains.

6. Identify values-consistent activities.

7. Select values-based activities for homework.

Module 6 third session:

8. Review and reassign activity tracking and problem-solve barriers.

9. Continue discussing personal values and values-consistent activities.

Module 6 additional sessions:

10. Continue assigning activity tracking with scheduled activities as needed.

Handouts

Handout 6.1: Types of Behavioral Activities

Handout 6.2: Activity Schedule

Handout 6.3: Valued Activities

Handout 6.4: Activities Calendar

Module Components

1. Provide Rationale for Meaningful Behavioral Activation

Our lives often change drastically after someone close to us dies. Things that survivors used to do or enjoy may seem to hold little meaning, or they may suddenly lack the resources or time needed to engage in activities. Painful emotions related to the loss, like sadness, fear, or anger, can also lead survivors to withdraw from others, limiting opportunities to engage in pleasurable and meaningful activities that might otherwise enhance mood and overall functioning. However, withdrawal and isolation often trigger new negative events and stressors that contribute to the maintenance or worsening of painful emotions related to the loss, essentially creating a vicious cycle of depressive symptoms. Using a diagram (like the one below) can help clients understand the connection between the loss, their emotions, and their behavioral actions, and perhaps more importantly, the rationale for behavioral activation.

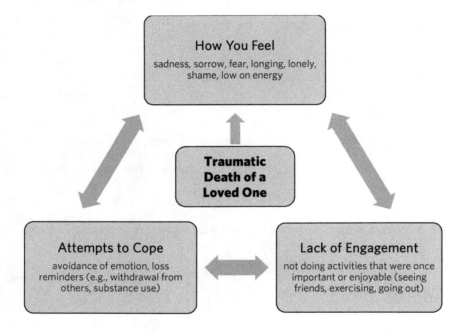

The goal of behavioral activation is to help clients identify and engage in activities that enhance positive emotions, increase a sense of competence or meaning, and improve overall functioning. In other words, the more we do things that are personally enjoyable and meaningful, the better we will feel.

Below is a script to explain the rationale for behavioral activation:

Sometimes when we're already feeling so overwhelmed with our grief, it can seem like doing anything, even something we might really want to do, especially when our loved one is no longer here physically, is a struggle. And to protect ourselves from more struggle and pain associated with our loss, we can start to withdraw from people and things we used to do, especially if they remind us of our loved one. Even though you're just trying to take care of yourself, you still find yourself struggling. It can almost start to feel like a cycle. (Draw a diagram to illustrate the connections between feelings, lack of engagement, and attempts to cope, using client examples. Once this is clear, continue.) *What we do affects how we feel, and the more you do things in different areas of your life that at least give you the opportunity to feel good again, the better you'll likely start to feel over time, even through this loss. And it's important to keep in mind that if we wait around to feel better before we start doing things again, we may be waiting a long time and making our situation worse. It's usually best to begin doing things, little by little, to help us feel better on our journey through loss.*

2. Provide Education About Different Kinds of Activities

An important goal of behavioral activation is helping clients identify and engage in activities that are meaningful and support one's personal values across multiple life areas. Generally speaking, these activities include *fun*, *functional*, and *fulfilling* activities (Acierno et al., 2012). Utilize handout 6.1 to provide information about types of behavioral activities to your client. Of note, activities that were once perceived as fun or fulfilling before the death may no longer be enjoyable. Therefore, have conversations with clients about the potential of engaging in fun and fulfilling activities they once found pleasurable and identifying new activities that may be pleasurable.

See module 7 for additional details on building in fulfilling activities in daily life that may provide a sense of connection to loved ones.

3. Assign Activity-Tracking Worksheet

An important step in meaningful behavioral activation is to ask clients to track their activities throughout the day. This will help them better understand a) what kinds of activities help them feel better or are otherwise missing from their lives and b) times throughout the week when they may be able to add more fun, functional, and fulfilling activities. Using a calendar like the one in handout 6.2 is a useful way to help clients monitor their daily activities.

In addition to tracking and monitoring activities, clients should rate their mood while completing each activity (Lejuez et al., 2011). Doing so can be useful in identifying the extent to which any given activity is fun, functional, or fulfilling and also helps clients directly connect the idea that what they do affects their mood. Mood ratings can be assigned on a 0–10 scale, where higher scores indicate better mood. Encourage clients to track and rate daily activities on the day they occurred to ensure that important activities are not missed and that mood ratings are as accurate as possible. Completing activity tracking worksheets should be assigned weekly for homework throughout the duration of the module.

4. Review Activity-Tracking Assignment and Problem-Solve Barriers

During the next session, review the activity-tracking worksheet with your client, reinforcing and acknowledging their effort and attempts to do so. Use this as an opportunity to have a discussion with your client about any connections they may have noticed between their mood and daily activities. Some clients may report feeling surprised at how much time they found themselves spending on activities that were, in hindsight, not pleasurable or meaningful. Here, it can be useful to point out that our behaviors—what we do—can contribute to feeling more depressed, just like they can contribute to feeling better. Take note of any activities that were associated with higher mood ratings and consider whether these are activities that your client may want to and can do more of in the future.

If your client had difficulty completing the worksheet, problem-solve barriers that came up. Some clients may have difficulty remembering what they did at different points throughout the day, especially if they try to retrospectively complete worksheets at the end of the day or several days later. Encourage clients to write down what they are doing frequently throughout the day and to leave the worksheet somewhere they are likely to see it.

Clinician Tip. When reviewing homework with clients, be sure to reinforce any initial efforts to monitor activities. If they did not complete their homework, spend time in session reviewing several days during their week and complete the monitoring worksheet together in session.

5. Discuss Personal Values Across Life Domains

As clients get used to the idea of tracking their activities throughout the day, discuss how these activities map onto different life areas and help them articulate what their personal values are in each of these. Explain to your client that understanding their personal values is an important part of behavioral activation since arbitrarily selected fun and functional activities are less likely to hold meaning and improve how we feel compared to those that help us live our values (fulfilling activities). Life domains discussed with clients might include relationships (including family, friends, and romantic relationships), education or career, recreation or leisure, health (physical, psychological, and spiritual), and daily responsibilities (Lejuez et al., 2011).

Across each of these different life domains, help your client begin to identify and articulate what their personal values are. Lejuez et al. (2011) define values as "an ideal, quality, or strong belief in a certain way of living." In other words, values are our inner life compass—they help to point out the direction we want to go in life (what is important to us) and how we want the journey to look like (desired qualities of ongoing action; Hayes et al., 2006). It may be useful to share with your client that values are our heart's deepest desires for how we want to behave in any given moment, describe what we want to stand for in life, what sort of person we want to be, or the strengths and qualities we want to continue developing. As such, make clear to your client that values are *not* goals, although they can help us to achieve specific goals.

6. Identify Values-Consistent Activities

Values can provide guidance, help one stay on track, or more importantly, help one find their way again when they go off track. You can facilitate discussions with your client about their values across numerous life domains by asking open-ended questions about aspirational roles and behavior qualities across each of these different areas. Then, work with your client to identify activities consistent with each of these different values. In other words, help your client identify actions that help them live the values important to them in different parts of their lives. Work collaboratively with your client to write down important values and associated activities using handout 6.3.

Clinician Tip. When helping clients identify values associated with personal relationships, be open to discussing how they might also want to commemorate and remember their loved one.

7. Assign Values-Based Activities for Homework

Using the activities generated on handout 6.3, select one to three activities to schedule for the upcoming week and include these on the activity-tracking worksheets (an example activities calendar is included in handout 6.4). It is important that selected activities are not too difficult in the beginning as this can increase the possibility that your client will not be able to complete the activity, potentially leading to negative impacts on your client's mood. It is also important to include a combination of fun, functional, and fulfilling activities, as fun activities are most likely to have the most immediate impact on mood.

Clinician Tip. Initial efforts to engage in activities may not lead to substantial changes in mood. Be encouraging and remind your client that it takes time and to stick with it.

At times, survivors may be substantially depressed, with limited engagement in functional activities (such as hygiene or eating). In such cases, it may be advantageous to prioritize functional activities, with fun and fulfilling activities embedded once some momentum with completing activities is established.

8. Review and Reassign Activity Tracking and Problem-Solve Barriers

As with the previous session, review the activity-tracking worksheet with your client and check with them to see how the assigned values-based activities went during the previous week. Praise any attempts your client made to track their activities and initiate new values-based activities. Also note any barriers to completion that came up during the week. If a scheduled activity turned out to be too complex or required resources unavailable to the client, consider whether activities need to be broken down into simpler, actionable steps that can be completed over the course of a week or multiple weeks (for instance, planning a trip or an event or applying for a job).

Continue assigning new activities throughout the remaining sessions. Also consider what resources, information, or equipment your client might need to complete certain activities in the future. Occasionally, this will mean helping clients think about whether others should be invited to participate in scheduled activities (and even inviting others to participate in specific activities can be identified as a behavioral activation activity to be assigned that week).

> **Clinician Tip.** Clients may select activities that honor or create a sense of connection with their loved ones. For example, if their loved one enjoyed playing or listening to music, gardening, or other similar activities, some clients may choose to engage in those activities both for fun and as a way of maintaining connection with their loved one.

9. Continue Discussing Personal Values and Values-Consistent Activities

Articulating the sometimes-unspoken personal values that guide our actions across different aspects of our lives can seem new and challenging for some clients. You will likely need to spend more than one session with many clients on this important topic, allowing space for them to explore the values that are most important to them in terms of how they approach their relationships, work, recreation, daily responsibilities, and health and well-being.

Similarly, your client may discover or get ideas about new values-consistent activities from the previous week's homework. Continue to generate new ideas about values-based activities that your client can and wants to engage in over the coming weeks. Remember that the more options a client has available to them, the more likely they are to find at least a few personally meaningful activities they can engage in on a regular basis.

10. Continue Assigning Activity Tracking with Scheduled Activities

Over the coming weeks, continue assigning values-consistent activities intended to improve mood along with weekly activity tracking. Regularly engaging in values-based activities can help create a healthier balance of grief-oriented and restoration-oriented activities. Over time, these fun, functional, and fulfilling activities will become more integrated into daily life, which can further improve mood, reduce depression symptoms, and strengthen your client's overall self-efficacy.

Cultural Considerations

Although behavioral activation is an idiographic and contextual approach that takes into account personal and cultural values, a consideration of your client's intersecting cultural identities in exploring values and assigning activities is advised. Depending on your client's cultural background, it may be considered inappropriate or disrespectful to engage in fun activities or activities in some life domains within a certain period following the loss. So, you should inquire directly around unique cultural perspectives on grief.

In addition, seek consultation from community leaders or others familiar with the survivor's culture to better understand norms and expectancies regarding grief and loss when working with clients whose cultural background is different from your own. Specific values may not easily translate from English to other languages. Therefore, when applicable, consider the survivor's native language when mutually exploring values and values-based activities. Also, for many survivors, religion may play a prominent role in their adaptation to loss. As such, religion and spirituality should be assessed, and religious or spiritually-based activities should be explored when relevant.

You should also recognize that secondary losses and resource losses that might have occurred as a result of a loved one's death can limit the range of activities available to clients. If your client relied on their loved one for transportation or income, for example, the added hardship of losing these resources will likely undermine efforts to engage in desired activities. In these circumstances, it can often be helpful to problem-solve ways to mitigate these barriers, which may include connecting clients to community resources that can assist with unmet social needs.

Clients living in under-resourced and disadvantaged neighborhoods where violent crime rates may be disproportionately higher may also encounter significant safety concerns associated with leaving home to engage in scheduled activities, and you should be careful not to confuse such concerns with avoidance or noncompliance with treatment. Similarly, be prepared to brainstorm low-cost or free activities with your clients, especially those with limited economic resources (Vergara-Lopez & Roberts, 2015).

Conclusion

Meaningful behavioral activation is an effortful process of identifying and engaging in personally relevant, valued activities that can be especially helpful for survivors experiencing more severe depression symptoms. Traumatic loss often disrupts daily routines and can lead to increased isolation and withdrawal, which gradually maintains depression over time. The skills and tools discussed in this chapter can help clients restore and create new routines that also honor their loved one's memory and role in their life. For more detailed information on behavioral activation concepts see Acierno (2015) and Lejuez et al. (2011).

Because some clients may have difficulty shifting away from more grief-oriented thoughts and actions, especially clients experiencing more severe prolonged grief reactions, the next module (module 7) is designed for clients with severe prolonged grief reactions and those with significant separation distress. It is focused on helping your client maintain a sense of connection with the deceased while integrating the reality of the loss.

CHAPTER 10

Module 7: Revising Bonds

Adjusting to a world without the deceased is the chief challenge for many traumatic loss survivors. When deaths are sudden, violent, or caused by human (in)action, the relational void can be even more challenging. For instance, the suddenness of traumatic loss inherently precludes the possibility for final goodbyes, addressing unfinished business, or the ability to prepare for life without the deceased (for example, financial planning). Some of the earliest theories of adaptation to bereavement, such as Freud's grief work hypothesis (Freud, 1917), erroneously perpetuated the belief that successful adaptation requires a relinquishing of the relationship with the person who died. Instead, research and phenomenological wisdom suggest that, instead, successful adaptation may hinge on the ability of the bereaved to revise the bond between them and the deceased.

This optional module aims to assist survivors through the process of revising the bond with the person who died in a manner that reconfigures the attachment and the nature of the ongoing relationship in personally meaningful ways while paying tribute to their loved one's life and legacy. In addition, revising bonds with the person who died may help counter the urge to avoid distressing emotions related to the reality of the death. This module can be provided in two to five sessions and can be integrated with other modules that involve discussions or activities related to your client's relationship with the deceased or memorialization practices, such as module 6.

Background and Related Literature

Humans are hardwired for attachment—we instinctively seek close attachments with primary caregivers shortly after birth and strive to maintain these and other attachments throughout our lives. For instance, after birth, humans seek the literal (Harlow & Zimmermann, 1959) and figurative comfort of a caregiver, such as a mother, as doing so ensures a sense of safety and helps to improve the odds of survival (Bretherton, 1992). Humans never outgrow this need for supportive and nurturing relationships.

Throughout the lifespan, the experience of *felt security*, or a deep sense of safety in our convictions that a close other is physically and psychologically available when needed, is provided through the attachment bond with others (Waters & Cummings, 2000).

Therefore, when a loved one dies, the regulating function of the attachment bond, which once fulfilled a panoply of relational needs, is no longer available.

Accommodating the loss requires the reorganization or relocation of the relationship in the physical absence of the close attachment figure. Often, this process of reconfiguration requires a shift from the physical relationship to one that is purely at the level of mental representation—the active construction of a symbolic connection through imagination and memory (Field, 2006). If this is achieved, attachment functions of the predeath relationship can be preserved and aid adaptation to a loved one's absence, albeit manifesting in dramatically different ways. In this manner, the revised bond may continue to serve as a safe haven to provide comfort in times of great stress or a secure base to help orient the bereaved toward constructing a new life (Field, 2006). In addition, the revised bond may involve identification with values that were held in high regard for the deceased. They serve as a source of guidance or inspiration for the bereaved or as an internalization of caregiving functions, such as increasing capacities of self-compassion.

The nature of the attachment bond with the deceased and its relation to adaptation to their death has been theorized for centuries. Empirical examination of this association, however, is relatively new. Though there is complexity to the findings of this body of research, literature suggests that revising and, possibly, maintaining a figurative bond with the deceased can be adaptive and facilitates postloss adjustment. This seems to be particularly true among those at risk for PGD (e.g., Neimeyer et al., 2006), which is chiefly characterized by a profound and protracted yearning for the deceased that causes significant emotional distress or impairment. Indeed, disorder-specific interventions aimed at ameliorating the distress and impairment associated with PGD among the general bereaved population incorporate revising bonds as a signature component of treatment (see Shear et al., 2005).

It should be noted, however, that revising and maintaining a connection to the deceased may not be uniformly beneficial for all, as in cases where the relationship between the survivor and their loved one was especially troubled or conflicted, and this may be particularly relevant for survivors of traumatic loss. Relationships that were marred by interpersonal discord may involve unresolved conflict, which research suggests increases the risk for PGD (Holland, Plant et al., 2020; Holland, Klingspon et al., 2020) and, therefore, may require rectifying in session before discussions of an ongoing connection commence.

For relationships that were riddled by substantial abuse or neglect, maintaining a bond may not be indicated, and a process toward relinquishing the relationship, whether in part or in whole, should unfold in session. Given the suddenness of traumatic loss, unfinished business with the deceased is also a common theme among survivors and requires careful clinical attention. As such, thoughtfully identifying which aspects of the relationship should be maintained, revised, or relinquished is a core component of this module, and clinicians and clients collaborate to identify these targets in session.

Presentation Appropriateness

This module is primarily recommended for survivors with elevated PGD symptoms who contend with distressing and debilitating yearning for the deceased, but may also be important for any client experiencing elevated yearning or separation distress. This module may also be useful for clients experiencing distress related to unfinished business or unresolved conflict with the deceased.

Agenda for Sessions

This module is designed to be flexibly delivered in two to five sessions depending on a number of factors, such as PGD symptom severity and, especially, the severity of yearning and separation distress and your client's goals and preferences for maintaining a revised bond with their loved one. Clients experiencing elevated yearning and separation distress but who do not meet criteria for PGD, for instance, may find that they are able to begin revising bonds in healthy ways through a discussion of commemorative-imagery strategies and exercises like the life imprint activity over the course of two or three sessions. Clients presenting with more severe yearning in the context of PGD, however, will likely need more sessions.

Module 7 first session:

1. Provide a rationale for revising bonds.

2. Introduce commemorative-imagery strategies.

Module 7 second session:

3. Review commemorative-imagery strategies.

4. Discuss to-be-maintained or relinquished aspects of the relationship.

5. Introduce and assign the "hello again" letter.

Module 7 third session:

6. Review the "hello again" letter.

7. Introduce and assign the response letter (if indicated).

Module 7 fourth session:

8. Review the response letter.

9. Revise connections.

10. Assign activities for revising connections.

Module 7 additional session:

11. Continue reviewing and assigning new activities.

Handouts

Handout 7.1: Life Imprint Activity

Handout 7.2: "Hello Again" Letter Activity

Handout 7.3: Response Letter Activity

Handout 7.4: Revising Connections

Module Components

1. Provide a Rationale for Revising Bonds

As mentioned previously, emotional distress often accompanies the lost attachment figure resulting from death. Many of the previous treatment modules focus heavily on the death and its impact. This module can help your client turn their attention toward how the deceased's *life* has had an impact, and how to move forward with a revised connection to the deceased that acknowledges the reality of the loss while providing comparable core attachment functions (for example, a safe haven, a secure base, or identification or internalization).

Many clients you work with will have *no doubt* heard from family, friends, or others that they need to move on from their grief or let go of their loved ones—messages that are more often than not perceived as invalidating, hurtful, and offensive. Accordingly, some clients may feel a sense of validation, or even relief, upon discussing the rationale for revising bonds—that is even when important relationships change suddenly under the most heartbreaking of circumstances, not all aspects of that relationship that brought us strength and comfort need to be let go of or left behind in a forgotten past.

When introducing the rationale for revising bonds, be mindful of and acknowledge that an important relationship in your client's life—their relationship with the deceased—has fundamentally changed and will not look the same as it once did. However, compassionately and gently explore with your client ways that their loved one continues to impact their life and other's lives, as well as aspects of the bond that may be helpful and unhelpful to their journey ahead. Finding tangible ways to "introduce" or commemorate their loved one in session with you as a therapist can help your client explore what aspects of the relationship they may want to cultivate and sustain over time, as well as aspects they may want to relinquish.

2. Introduce Commemorative-Imagery Strategies

Encouraging your client to (re)introduce their loved one will help to begin the process of revising the bond and set the stage for an ongoing connection, if indicated. You can begin by asking survivors to bring photos, mementos, songs, or other meaningful items that best represent the life of their loved one. In addition, you can encourage a) the sharing of comforting stories of the loved one, b) descriptions of characteristics of the loved one, or c) what their perceived purpose in life was. All of those options serve to maintain an ongoing connection and to approximate the core attachment functions that the loved one once served. You can then work together to determine ways that the connection can be maintained outside the therapy room, leaning heavily on ideas first offered by your client.

Below is a sample clinician-client dialogue related to introducing commemorative-imagery strategies as a tangible way to stay connected to their loved one:

Clinician:	Up to this point in therapy, we have focused a lot on how Tony's death impacted you. I wonder if we can shift a bit today and instead discuss ways in which Tony's *life* impacted you. How does that sound to you?
Client:	Sure. That sounds nice.
Clinician:	You have told me that you have some pictures of Tony on your phone. Can you pull one of those photos up? (Client opens their phone and selects a picture). I have come to know Tony to some extent through our work together, but if you were to introduce him to someone using this picture, what would you say? What would you like them to know about Tony? What kind of person was he?
Client:	(after a long pause and a deep breath) Well, Tony was an amazing human. He was a dedicated and loving father. He grew up very poor, but he was always so determined to succeed and give back. He even started a fundraiser at work for the local Boys and Girls Club. I never truly realized how much he meant to so many people. I guess I didn't realize how much that rubbed off on me too. (Client begins to cry.)
Clinician:	M-hm. Stay there for a moment—tell me more about how that part of him rubbed off on you.
Client:	I know I'm someone who is pretty persistent and determined. And those qualities have gotten me really far in life. It just never dawned on me how much of that is because of Tony.
Clinician:	Right. And as you sit here acknowledging that, what is coming up for you?

Client: Just so bittersweet... It's comforting to think about that, the things that he passed on to me. He really used to give me such great advice when I needed it too. He truly was my rock, my guide, at the most difficult moments in life. So, on that other side of comfort is so much pain and fear without him.

Clinician: So, on the one hand, while you reflect on who Tony was and what he meant to you, you can see how much your life together shaped who you are, like modeling and instilling hard work and determination, or serving as a wise companion in life...and that brings you a sense of comfort.

Client: Yeah. Absolutely. When I talk about him in that way, thinking back about his life and how it brought so much color to ours, it is comforting...like it helps me feel like a part of him is still with me.

Clinician: M-hm. A part of him is still with you, and that brings you comfort.

Client: But I know that when we finish today, the fear and absolute pain of not having him around will sink in like it has before. All those great things about Tony are gone... Just completely lost.

Clinician: Yeah. So, while thinking about Tony in this way—sharing stories, pictures—brings you comfort because it helps you feel like you can carry a part of him with you, there is also that deep sense that all that has been lost.

Client: Yep.

Clinician: I wonder what it would be like to try out ways of carrying him with you, knowing that your relationship with Tony will never be the same, but not losing those aspects of your relationship that brought you comfort and guidance.

Client: I have tried so hard not to talk about Tony. But talking about him and feeling connected to him was really comforting, so I'd be willing to try it.

Clinician: We will work together to figure out some ways to still feel connected to Tony despite his death. So even though he is not physically here with you, you will always have a relationship with him. What are some ways that you think you can stay connected with Tony as you continue to move forward?

Client: Oh, I don't know. At some point, I want to get involved in the fundraiser he started, but I don't think I'm ready for that. Maybe I can start writing down more of these things I told you today, like in a journal or something?

> *Clinician:* That's understandable. I know that working with the fundraiser is one of your goals, and we will get you there. But I think journaling about his impact is a fantastic place to start.

If a client has difficulty identifying ways in which their loved one left an impression on them or others or expresses a desire to continue identifying these qualities, clinicians can assign a life-imprint activity (Neimeyer, 2012). This is a semistructured exercise that promotes reflection on ways that a deceased loved one influenced one's personal characteristics and qualities. This activity can help the survivor shift their attention from what was *lost* to what was *gained* through their relationship with their loved one and set the stage for work more directly pertaining to the ongoing connection (see handout 7.1).

> **Clinician Tip.** When working with clients with prolonged, severe grief reactions, you may need to incorporate a discussion about the changed nature of the relationship and what is possible in the future given their loved one is no longer physically present. Moreover, using commemorative imagery may reinforce intense yearning and proximity-seeking.

3. Review Commemorative-Imagery Strategies

At the outset of the next session, you should allot adequate time for processing commemorative activities engaged in outside of session, including the life-imprint activity, if introduced in the previous session. Process insights gained or emotions experienced from engaging in commemorative activities. Such a review will assist your client in their movement toward acceptance of the death while excavating and acknowledging the aspects of the loved one that may persist past their physical absence; thereby, creating one form of maintained connection.

4. Discuss To-Be-Maintained or Relinquished Aspects of the Relationship

Reviewing commemorative-imagery strategies, including the life-imprint activity, may afford you and your client a lens with which to identify aspects of the relational bond they may want to affirm as they move forward in their bereavement journey. Or, on the contrary, such a review may permit the identification of aspects of the relationship they may wish to relinquish.

Some survivors of traumatic loss may identify multiple aspects of the relationship that were problematic. Given the often suddenness of traumatic loss, survivors are precluded from opportunities to address these relational strains. As such, you are advised to consider ways your client may wish to relinquish aspects of the attachment bond or address unfinished business as the inability to do so may have prevented acceptance and integration of the loss.

For instance, for suicide- or overdose-loss survivors, predeath relational strain may have manifested through consistent, yet futile, efforts to support the deceased in their sobriety or mental health struggles up to the point of the loved one's death. Similarly, for these populations, guilt may be prevalent and profoundly distressing among those that perceive themselves to be culpable for the death, either directly (for example, providing drugs or following an argument or breakup) or indirectly (for example, not being present at the time of overdose or failing to see warning signs of suicide). In these instances, one's ability to adapt to the loss is substantially hampered, and treatment should therefore include techniques to rectify these relational perceptions.

> **Clinician Tip.** For clients who experience perceptions of responsibility for the death, cognitive strategies outlined in module 2 may be used independently or in tandem with relational techniques to assist the survivor with gathering a full picture of the death that more accurately assesses responsibility. Doing so will assist your client with making sense of the loss and efforts to accept its finality and implications.

5. Introduce and Assign the "Hello Again" Letter

After setting the stage for reconfiguring the relationship in a manner that maintains an ongoing symbolic relationship with the deceased, you can introduce the "hello again" letter (White, 1988), which builds on the commemorative imagery in more tangible ways. This is not a goodbye letter, as this implies an ending to a relationship, but rather a letter to set the stage for reimagining a different type of connection or relationship with their loved one. In the "hello again" letter, survivors write a letter directly to their deceased loved one using prompts outlined in handout 7.2.

Below is a sample dialogue that illustrates introducing the "hello again" letter with a suicide loss survivor:

Clinician: As you describe your emotional reaction to the homework, I can see how Steph's death left a deep mark on your life in pretty profound ways. What, if anything, stood out to you?

Client: Well, what stood out to me because it kind of caught me off guard, was just how much Steph brought out the best in me. Since he shot himself, I've

Module 7: Revising Bonds

just had such a hard time getting past the self-blame. And so, I sort of felt like the qualities he brought out would never come back and that's what I deserve. We had such a bad fight a few days before he died.

Clinician: Yeah, like there are all these great things that Steph brought into your life, and you hope to carry those with you, but the guilt sort of obscures your view, which would be an understandable reason why moving forward is so hard.

Client: (sighs) It's a terrible mix, really. And I've been trying to shut it all out—the good stuff, the guilt. It's honestly all too overwhelming to sit with.

Clinician: Overwhelming... Yeah. I wonder how it might be for you to sift through those mixed feelings and, since we've been discussing ways to reconfigure the relationship with Steph since his death, how it might be for you to put this in a letter addressed to Steph? I wonder if you might experience some surprising insights like before...

Client: Oh God! I don't think I can do that... I'll totally fall apart, I think.

Clinician: It will be difficult, no doubt. And I want you to lean into that—to tell Steph in the letter just how difficult it is to write to him about these thoughts.

Client: Okay. I can try that... After all, I did say something similar when you asked me to do the last assignment.

Encourage your client to speak to both the positive and negative aspects of the relationship as they respond to prompts. It is important to use prompts as opposed to an open-ended letter when approaching this activity, as prompts can assist survivors in moving through aspects of their grief constructively as opposed to getting stuck in difficult thoughts and emotions. If your client is struggling to complete the "hello again" letter for homework, create time in session to complete the writing assignment.

> **Clinician Tip.** "Hello again" letters are not intended to be used exclusively with clients to address predeath relational strains. They are also indicated for clients who have avoided explorations of a revised or continued bond and therefore would benefit from the comfort of this imaginal dialogue.

> **Clinician Tip.** Given the emotional toll this assignment may have for some clients, encourage your client to pay special attention to *set* and *setting*—set referring to one's mind*set* (open and accepting of emotions that may emerge) and setting referring to a quiet place free of distractions.

6. Review the "Hello Again" Letter

At the outset of the next session, inquire about the completion of the "hello again" letter assignment and ask the client to read it aloud to the extent they feel comfortable doing so. This serves the purpose of approaching difficult grief emotions and combatting potential avoidance. The "hello again" letter, which may be the first "correspondence" with the deceased loved one that a client has attempted since the death, will likely be highly evocative, particularly when themes of guilt, regret, or anger are included. Accordingly, while the client reads aloud, take note of any significant moments that may require greater attention.

You should allow for emotions and provide praise to the survivor for doing this difficult work. Following the client's reading of the assignment aloud in session, you will want to process the emotions of the activity—both the writing of the letter and the experience of reading it aloud. In addition, you will want to inquire about any insightful reactions from the assignment to explore the possibility of new ways of making sense of the death or the ongoing connection with the deceased.

7. Introduce and Assign the Response Letter

When the processing of the letter is complete, shift into describing the next assignment: the response letter. You should not introduce this when you provide the rationale for the "hello again" letter, as it may interfere with your client's approach and the details they provide in the initial letter. In the response letter, clients are instructed to respond to the letter they wrote from the perspective of the deceased loved one. Common prompts for this assignment are outlined in handout 7.3.

If the client struggles with completing the response letter for homework, create time in session for the client to complete the writing assignment.

> **Clinician Tip.** For relationships that were fraught with abuse or neglect, a response letter is typically not advised. In this scenario, the "hello again" letter should not be accompanied by a response from the perpetrator of the abuse or neglect and instead serve as a means for the survivor to have the "final word" in a way that repositions power dynamics in the survivor's favor.

8. Review the Response Letter

Just as you encourage your client to read the "hello again" letter out loud in session, encourage your client to read the response letter out loud as well, using the same rationale.

After your client reads the response letter, explore what it was like to write the letter and the experience of reading it out loud. You can also ask follow-up questions such as:

- *What did you learn about yourself through this activity?*

- *What did you learn about your relationship with your loved one?*

- *Any surprises in the response letter that came up?*

- *What do you make of how your loved one responded to your grief journey?*

Of note, for some clients the response letter can offer an opportunity to allow themselves to let go of challenging aspects of their grief, find meaning in the loss, or give permission to live a future life with hope.

> **Clinician Tip.** Readers familiar with process-experiential therapies may notice conceptual similarities between the "hello again" and response letter exercises to other experiential therapy techniques aimed at resolving emotional conflict, especially two-chair or empty-chair techniques. In these techniques, you guide your client through an imagined conversation with their loved one where they alternate speaking for themselves and their loved one, giving words to what they imagine their loved one might say. If you are knowledgeable and have adequate training in these kinds of techniques, you may find them helpful to use in session to augment letter writing exercises or, perhaps in some cases, use in lieu of these exercises.
>
> Be mindful, though, that many of the same clinical considerations regarding the use of the "hello again" and response letter exercises also apply to decisions regarding the use of other similar experiential exercises like chair work. Both exercises, and especially chair work, can be highly emotionally evocative and may bring out extremely painful emotions (Stiegler et al., 2018), so be sure your client has the ability to manage strong emotions using skills like those presented in module 4 before commencing with either activity.

9. Revising Connections

Revisit the idea that commemorative strategies can assist with reintegrating loved ones into clients' lives in ways that are not bound by the limits of a literal physical relationship. Often, clients struggle with developing this new relationship and remain connected through tangible past connections. Examples include keeping a loved one's bedroom and belongings exactly the same as when their loved one was living or visiting the gravesite every day. Clients will note feeling comforted by these types of connections, even though they may come at great personal expense. Validate the importance of feeling comforted by connections with their loved one and gently suggest finding ways of being connected with their loved one in their changed present lives. Remember: the rationale for revising bonds is to foster and maintain connection with the deceased in ways that are helpful to your client in their changed present lives while acknowledging and relinquishing aspects of the relationship that are unhelpful for clients and their loved ones.

Brainstorm ways your client can integrate their loved ones into daily-life rituals and during special occasions that honor them and maintain helpful aspects of the relationship but do not negatively impact their day-to-day lives. These can be activities, such as gardening their loved one's favorite flowers, journaling memories of their loved one, scrap booking photos, and so forth.

Revising connections can continue to build into meaningful behavioral activation (module 6). This exercise will need to entail survivor-specific, tangible ways of being connected with their loved one. It will help them to not only think of ways to connect with loved ones in present-day life but also consider ways to honor and feel connected with them during special days or holidays (see chapter 12 for more details). Of note, some clients may comment that there are positive symbols that remind them of their loved one or that they believe serve as a medium for connecting with their loved one. These could be in nature; for instance, butterflies, birds, or rainbows carry spiritual significance for many survivors depending on cultural and other factors and can serve as living reminders of a loved one's continuing presence. Support such comforting connections and present-focused observations through mindfulness (module 4).

10. Assign Activities for Revising Connections

Use handout 7.4 to list various ways your client can integrate a connection with their loved one in present-day life and assign several activities for them to engage in.

11. Continue Reviewing and Assigning New Activities

If a fifth session is needed to further review and brainstorm ways to integrate revising-bonds activities into your client's daily life, continue brainstorming activities with your client and discuss any barriers to engaging in connecting activities that may have emerged between sessions. This optional fifth session can also be useful if revising-bonds activities identified in the previous session were somewhat complex and need to be broken down into smaller actionable steps (for example, planting a memorial garden or starting a scrap book) as this allows follow-up discussion and reinforcement of those activities across multiple sessions. Continue to follow up and integrate activities across other modules and sessions as needed.

Cultural Considerations

The notion of revising the bond with the deceased loved one to maintain a connection and preserve the attachment functions afforded by that relationship is widely accepted across cultures. Indeed, cultural traditions from Mexico, Japan, and China, among others, embrace a nonstatic view of postdeath relationships with close attachment figures, such that there is an inherent fluid negotiation of the continuance of the bond between the deceased, the bereaved, and the broader community (Ahern, 1973). As such, survivors from these cultural backgrounds may be quite receptive to the idea of reconfiguring and maintaining a symbolic relationship, and you should lean heavily on their norms and practices to facilitate revising the bond.

Likewise, survivors who endorse the belief in an afterlife may more readily be able to revise the bond and envision a sustained connection despite the physical absence of the deceased (Root & Exline, 2014). Therefore, an assessment of your client's spiritual beliefs, or beliefs in life after death more specifically, is a crucial component to assessment and can help assess the possible function of revising and continuing bonds, including the selection of appropriate therapeutic activities (Benore & Park, 2004).

Conclusion

The desire to reconnect with a close loved one after their death is a nearly universal experience, and this is especially true when the death was sudden, unanticipated, and occurred under traumatic circumstances. Revising bonds entails a set of skills aimed at helping your client foster and maintain those connections in healthy ways through commemorative activities honoring the deceased and releasing unhelpful aspects of the relationship that may have created challenges for both survivors and their loved one in life. These activities can be quite emotionally evocative, however, and may be difficult for clients used to avoiding strong or painful emotions. In the next optional module—module 8—we will discuss techniques aimed at helping survivors regain control over situations and thoughts that evoke strong painful feelings, especially those related to the death event.

CHAPTER 11

Module 8: Therapeutic Exposure

Many survivors of traumatic loss suffer from elevated post-traumatic stress symptoms. They report significant intrusive thoughts and images of their loved one's death (whether they witnessed the death or imagined their loved one's death experience), the death notification, or the funeral and other memorial events. These intrusive thoughts and images may be accompanied by such intense pain and emotional distress that survivors make effortful attempts to avoid reminders of the death and loss of their loved one. Extreme avoidance of memories or things associated with the death may inhibit the integration or processing of the death event and, therefore, increase the likelihood that these reactions will become chronic. For many clients, fear and anxiety are core emotions that are maintained by the avoidance of internal stimuli (such as memories or thoughts of the death) and external stimuli (such as situations, places, and people associated with the death or the deceased).

During this component of treatment, clinicians assist clients in approaching internal and external reminders of the death that have been avoided and therefore limit the assimilation of the death event and engagement with restoration-oriented activities. Next, clinicians assist the client with an imaginal retelling of the death or related death events to elicit details of the event, as well as avoided thoughts, feelings, and reactions that were experienced by the client at the time. Through these therapeutic exposure exercises, clients learn (a) that certain stimuli are not necessarily dangerous, (b) that they can tolerate their emotional distress when confronted with reminders, and (c) that emotional distress can and will change over time. In addition, imaginal retelling assists with processing the reality of the death and helps survivors develop a tolerance to the distress associated with death-related thoughts and memories.

This module offers an approach-based process of managing distressing content related to post-traumatic stress symptoms and emotional avoidance around the death of a loved one. It is typically delivered across five to seven sessions and should be conducted concurrently until emotional distress and prevalence of intrusive reminders decrease, approach-based coping strategies increase, and mastery over managing trauma and grief cues develops.

Background and Related Literature

The role of avoidance in maintaining post-traumatic stress symptoms has been demonstrated across trauma-exposed populations (e.g., Cahill & Foa, 2007), including survivors of traumatic loss (e.g., Kaltman & Bonanno, 2003). Helping individuals approach avoided stimuli through exposure-based interventions may assist in decreasing not only fear and anxiety but also other emotions, such as guilt, sadness, and anger. PE is one such exposure-based, disorder-specific intervention developed from emotional processing theory (Foa & Kozak, 1986), which suggests that emotional, cognitive, and behavioral responses to traumatic events like the death of a loved one are organized into networks or fear structures in the mind. Over time, these fear structures can be activated by a wide range of people, places, situations, and memories that remind survivors of the death, all of which survivors may seek to avoid or escape because of the overwhelming emotions tied to the associated fear response. According to emotional processing theory, gradual exposure to these cues in a safe, supportive environment can create conditions where the meaning of these cues change to such a degree that the fear structure is no longer activated in the same way—a process called habituation.

PE has received considerable empirical support and is considered a frontline treatment for PTSD (see Powers et al., 2010). Exposure-based therapies, like PE, typically involve repeated contact with avoided memories, called imaginal exposure, and avoided people, places, and situations, called in vivo exposure. Exposure is considered therapeutically effective when the client experiences habituation of the stress response associated with environmental cues and memories following repeated presentation of these cues (for instance, looking at pictures of one's lost family member, talking to friends about the deceased, or resuming activities one used to do with the lost partner). In addition to emotional and physiological habituation, exposure techniques can provide a cognitive forum for integration of memories of the loved one that may allow for adaptive responses related to guilt, longing, and acceptance of loss (Foa & Rauch, 2004).

Both imaginal and in vivo exposures have been integrated into various treatment packages for PGD that have been shown to be effective in reducing PGD symptoms, as well as PTSD and depression symptoms in bereaved populations more broadly (e.g., Acierno et al., 2021; Boelen et al., 2007; Bryant et al., 2014). Of these various treatments, RR (Rynearson et al., 2015) was developed specifically for traumatic loss survivors and incorporates a variant of imaginal exposure in the form of a direct retelling of the imagined actions of a loved one's dying (Rynearson, 2001; Rynearson & Correa, 2008). Two open trials with traumatic loss survivors found RR was associated with reductions in PTSD, depression, and PGD symptoms (Rheingold et al., 2015; Saindon et al., 2014).

The current model was informed by emotional processing theory and existing literature on treatments for PTSD and PGD and adapts exposure-based techniques, including imaginal and in vivo exposure, for use with survivors. For readers interested in these stand-alone interventions and more specifics on implementation strategies, see Foa et al. (2007) for further details about PE and Rynearson (2001) for RR.

Presentation Appropriateness

This module is recommended for clients who lean excessively on avoidant coping strategies when confronted with death imagery, particularly those who report elevated PTSD symptoms. Clients with severe PGD symptoms who also actively avoid reminders of the permanence of the loss may also benefit from this module. Therapeutic exposures include approach-based strategies in the form of imaginal approach (death-imagery exposure and the retelling of the traumatic loss) and approach with action in vivo (real-life exposures).

Agenda for Sessions

This module is designed to be flexibly delivered in five to seven sessions. The number of sessions needed will likely depend on a number of factors, including the severity of the client's PTSD and avoidance symptoms, the range of avoided cues, and how quickly your client's distress decreases during exposure exercises. Clients who are primarily avoiding people, places, or activities that remind them of the death but who are not reporting recurring distress associated with death-related imagery, for example, may be able to complete this module in as few as five sessions focusing primarily on approach in action exposure activities. Contrary, clients reporting more severe PTSD symptoms, including avoidance of both memories and situational cues, will likely require the recommended seven sessions with follow-up across other sessions.

Module 8 first session:

1. Provide education on the role of avoidance.

2. Provide rationale for therapeutic exposure.

3. Provide rationale for approach with action.

4. Introduce SUDS (subjective units of distress scale).

5. Develop action hierarchy of avoided trauma and loss cues.

6. Assign approach with action.

Module 8 second session:

7. Review and practice approach with action if indicated.

8. Provide rationale for death-imagery approach.

9. Assign approach with action.

Module 8 third session:

10. Conduct death-imagery approach in session.

11. Conduct restorative processing of death imagery.

12. Assign approach with action.

13. Assign listening to imaginal recording.

Module 8 fourth and fifth sessions and additional sessions, as needed:

14. Conduct death-imagery approach with focus on hot spots.

15. Integrate restorative retelling components.

16. Assign approach with action and listening to imaginal recording.

Handouts

Handout 8.1: Education About Avoidance and Approaching Trauma and Loss Reminders

Handout 8.2: Hierarchy List of Trauma and Loss Reminders

Handout 8.3: Approach with Action Recording Form

Handout 8.4: Imaginal Recording Form

Module Components

1. Provide Education on the Role of Avoidance

Many clients heavily (or exclusively) use avoidant coping and have likely done so for quite some time. Clients may report that such strategies have been beneficial because it attenuates grief-related distress. However, it is critical to describe how this strategy, though possibly helpful in the short term, can be detrimental in the long term. For instance, consistently avoiding reminders of the death limits opportunities to habituate to grief-related distress and gather corrective emotional experiences (such as new knowledge about one's ability to tolerate distressing memories), as well as opportunities to consolidate or organize memories of the death in a manner that will foster acceptance and meaning making. In addition, from a pragmatic standpoint, an overreliance on avoidance strategies inherently constricts the client's (re)engagement with the world, which further hampers the adjustment to traumatic loss.

Below is a sample clinician-client dialogue related to the role of avoidance:

Clinician: You have told me that it's very difficult for you to go near Tonya's room.

Client: I just can't do it. It makes me so upset, so I've stopped going to that side of the apartment altogether... I sleep on the couch and basically have ever since I found her.

Clinician: Yeah, makes sense. Staying clear of Tonya's room has helped you to not think about her death and all the distressing emotions that come with those thoughts and memories. It's a pretty effective strategy to avoid the pain of her death. But what do you think will happen if you stick with that strategy over the long term?

Client: Hmm, I don't know. Since it's worked, I guess I haven't thought about that.

Clinician: I wonder if it actually has been working? Have you been feeling any less pain or is your trauma and grief still pretty intense?

Client: It's constant. It's always there.

Clinician: Yeah, so I'm wondering if avoiding the pain is actually working in the long run? We've also talked about how it's important for you to be able to move toward accepting the fact that Tonya died. How do you think this strategy fits with that goal?

Client: (after a long pause) I don't know if it does. I just shut it out, which is kind of the opposite.

Clinician: Right. I like the way you put that—avoiding her room, and that part of the home altogether, is sort of the opposite of acceptance. I wonder if that strategy of staying away comes with any other costs?

Client: Well, yeah, I guess it does. Since I only sleep on the couch, I have no privacy really and I'm constantly woken up by the kids and neighbors who are walking by our front door, so my sleep hasn't been great.

Clinician Tip. Alcohol and substance misuse are common avoidance strategies many survivors may have used at one point or another in their grief. Importantly, alcohol and substance misuse can increase the risk for a number of long-term health problems, contribute to the maintenance of bereavement-related mental health problems like PTSD, and interfere with the success of exposure exercises, if clients use substances as a way of tolerating exposures. If your client reports using alcohol or other substances to cope with trauma or grief-related cues, you should collaboratively assess whether they are able to reduce use on their own or consider whether a referral for more intensive substance use treatment is needed prior to moving forward with exposures.

2. Provide Rationale for Therapeutic Exposure

After providing education about the role of avoidance, you should describe how therapeutic exposure through approach aims to directly undermine avoidant coping and promote greater adjustment. Because this information is likely inconsistent with your client's previous efforts to cope, spend adequate time explaining this approach to increase motivation and adherence. Elements of motivational interviewing, such as assessing the balance between the benefits and drawbacks of avoidance and approach-based strategies in relation to goal attainment, may be especially useful for clients who experience greater reluctance to curb avoidance.

The clinician continues from explaining avoidance to the rationale for therapeutic exposure:

Clinician: Interesting. So, perhaps not only has avoiding Tonya's room made accepting her death challenging, but avoiding that area of the home has made life generally more difficult, like how it has negatively impacted your sleep. If avoidance comes with these costs, what then would a more effective strategy look like?

Client: I guess it may be better to stop avoiding...

Clinician: What would the advantage of that be? After all, you said how it helps you to avoid the emotional pain of the memory of her death and her absence now.

Client: Well, I suppose it's pretty hard to accept the fact that she died if I prevent myself from feeling the emotions that come with that horrific reality.

Clinician: I completely agree with that. Any other advantages to cutting down the avoidance?

Client: Well, like I said, my sleep has been horrible, so avoiding less might help me reclaim my home again. I mean, it's my home, and I want to be able to feel comfortable here again.

Clinician: Yes, and that's what I hope we can start to accomplish with these exercises to help you approach reminders of Tonya and your loss. It's almost like the painful memory of her death controls that space and so many other parts of your life. Together, if we can think of ways to approach her room and those memories on your terms, maybe we can start to take some control back. Maybe we can confront the pain on your terms, rather than it confronting you on its terms.

> **Clinician Tip.** Using terms other than "exposure" when presenting the rationale for these exercises may enhance client buy-in and engagement in exposure activities and help your client feel more empowered to engage in these activities. For example, you might refer to therapeutic exposure as the "practice of approach," which can include action-based approach (in vivo) or imaginal approach (Cox, 2024).

3. Provide Rationale for Approach with Action

Once you have described the rationale for therapeutic exposure as a remedy to the pitfalls of avoidance, you should explain how approach with action will be conducted in treatment. It is important to describe how approach blocks avoidance tendencies and provides corrective emotional experiences that disconfirm beliefs about the duration of the distress and the client's ability to effectively handle such distress. For instance, regardless of their valence, emotions do not last forever, and when clients consistently confront emotionally distressing situations, habituation occurs. Because exposure techniques reflect natural fear-modification processes, the use of examples from your client's life or the use of a metaphor (for example, fear of spiders or fear of heights) are often effective ways to improve understanding of the rationale for approach with action. Clinicians can use handout 8.1 to assist with explaining this rationale.

Below is a sample of how a clinician continues the conversation into the rationale for approach in action:

Clinician: So, rather than emotions dictating how you are in your own home, you want to be able to do what you want in your home again.

Client: Yeah, that sounds real nice...but that just doesn't seem possible.

Clinician: It seems like a big leap to just stop avoiding like that. (Clinician snaps fingers.) And you're right that it would be, but we can start small and take this one step at a time.

Module 8: Therapeutic Exposure

Client: I can try that, I guess.

Clinician: I wonder if there have been times in the past that you avoided something because it caused distress but at some point overcame it because it was important to you?

Client: I don't know if this fits, but my big brother loved those tall roller coasters growing up, but I was petrified of all of them, really. So I found myself waiting for him outside the exit each time. But I wanted to join him, and he knew how badly I wanted to ride with him, so for my eleventh birthday, he spent the whole day with me, riding the smaller kiddy-type coasters, and we went from one to the next until we got on the tallest one.

Clinician: And you were totally at ease the whole time?

Client: Not at all. (Client chuckles.) I remember being terrified—sweating, breathing heavy, all that. But during each of the taller rides, and especially after, I realized it wasn't as bad as I thought. And I guess that helped me go from one coaster to the next until we got to through the scariest one.

Clinician: That fits exactly with taking this one step at a time. That is a fantastic example! Let's follow your brother's lead in this situation. How does that sound to you?

4. Introduce SUDS (Subjective Units of Distress Scale)

Before clients engage in exposure activities, it is important to develop a method for assessing the degree of distress associated with different grief- and trauma-related cues to accurately assess whether specific exposure activities produced habituation. The Subjective Units of Distress Scale (SUDS) is a numerical scale for describing subjective levels of distress in a given situation. The scale typically ranges from 0 to 10 but can be expanded to a range of 0 to 100 to allow for greater variability in distress scores across approach activities.

You should guide clients through identifying approach targets (grief- or trauma-related cues and reminders) that represent a range of distress. Anchor points can be used to identify activities across the range of distress. For instance, 0, 25, 50, 75, and 100 are typical anchor points on a 100-point SUDS, with 0 representing a situation in which the client feels at complete ease (for example, taking a warm bath) while 100 represents a situation that causes or has caused the greatest degree of distress imaginable (for example, discovering the body of a deceased loved one). You could have a mix of trauma- and grief-related anchors with non-trauma- and non-grief-related anchors to help contextualize experiences into normal daily life.

133

5. Develop Action Hierarchy of Avoided Trauma and Loss Cues

When anchor points are established, collaborate to identify exposure targets that represent a range of SUDS scores and will promote adaptation to the loss and assist your client with achieving their therapy goals. Action targets are then placed in an action hierarchy in order, with activities and reminders associated with lower SUDS scores placed at the bottom, while more distressing items are placed at the top using handout 8.2. Situations can be related to avoidance about death or trauma reminders of how the loved one died, avoidance of reminders of the loss in general, and avoidance of (re)engagement in life activities. With your client, you should strive to identify ten to fifteen action targets that your client has been avoiding since the death, with the intention of moving up the hierarchy in a gradual fashion once habituation is achieved for each situation.

> **Clinician Tip.** If clients experience difficulty identifying ten to fifteen situations, provide recommendations or assign the identification of additional targets for homework in conjunction with the initial approach activities.

If the construction of the hierarchy is not completed in session, assign the review and completion of the hierarchy list for homework. Below is an example of such a hierarchy.

SUDS	Situation/Approach with Action
100	Talking about daughter's potential last moments.
100	Going into daughter's room.
95	Sleeping in own bed.
90	Walking by daughter's door.
90	Talking about good memories of daughter.
90	Looking at daughter's awards.
90	Completing headstone paperwork.
85	Talking and texting with parents of daughter's friends.
80	Baking apple pie (daughter's favorite).
75	Going to teen clothes section at department store.
75	Being around teens same age as daughter.
65	Saying the word *suicide* out loud.
50	Listening to gospel music (often listened together with daughter).
25	Looking at pictures of daughter.

> **Clinician Tip.** Many survivors report that going to the scene of their loved one's death helps them process the loss and maintain a sense of connection with their loved one (Kristensen et al., 2018). However, not all survivors wish to do so, nor is it always practical or safe for them to do so. In some cases, the death scene may be so far removed from where your client lives and works that it requires minimal, if any, effort to avoid the location and has minimal impact on their daily lives. Deciding whether visiting the death scene should be on your client's hierarchy should be a joint decision based on their goals, preferences, and ongoing impact of avoiding the location on their daily life and recovery.

6. Assign Approach with Action

You should emphasize to your client the importance of conducting approach activities outside of session each day. Completing approach activities, often with a great deal of repetition, will help promote habituation to trauma- and grief-related cues. For the first approach activity, assign activity that evokes moderate levels of distress (SUDS = 50/100). Instruct your client to remain in the situation for thirty to forty-five minutes if possible. Emphasize the importance of remaining in the situation until the SUDS score decreases by at least 50 percent. Additionally, ask your client to track their SUDS ratings before, their peak SUDS during, and their SUDS after each planned activity using handout 8.3.

7. Review and Practice Approach with Action

Review your client's homework and be sure to praise their efforts to practice these activities outside of session, whether they were initially successful in doing so or not. If your client is unable to complete actions, enlist the help of family members or friends, offer to accompany your client, or conduct approach activities during sessions, to the extent possible. For example, using the above hierarchy in session, you can ask your client to pull up gospel music on their phone to listen to with you during the session.

Of note, avoidance is powerfully self-reinforcing. Gently remind clients that the best way to get over avoidance is through approach. Validate the struggle and strong emotions they may feel when doing approach-related activities. Be sure to convey to your client that the more they continue approach, the easier it will get, and that emotions will come and will go, like ocean waves. This may take time and multiple attempts, so it is often helpful to remind your client that they can carry the trauma and grief with them toward the goal of living life.

8. Provide Rationale for Death-Imagery Approach

Death-imagery approach allows your client to experience the negative feelings, thoughts, and memories associated with the death in small doses in a safe, controlled environment. It can be helpful for clients who have recurrent distressing and intrusive thoughts, images, or nightmares about the death of their loved one, the notification of the death, or the funeral or other postdeath experiences that are intentionally and often effortfully avoided. Given the traumatic nature of the death, these memories may elicit fear and anxiety.

The goal is for clients to manage traumatic memories and associated effects without the need to avoid them. By doing so, clients develop a sense of mastery and control over death-related memories, which will pave the way for greater acceptance of the loss. The notion of intentionally "revisiting" the death through mental imagery may seem counterproductive for clients, so it is important to provide a rationale that includes the following concepts: a) *emotional processing* (retelling the death allows us to process and integrate the loss into our broader life story), b) *habituation* (we can remember trauma without such intense distress that we feel now), c) *repetition* (the memory does not result in loss of control, and that with continued approach, the memory becomes more tolerable), d) *differentiation* (we can learn that loss reminders are not truly dangerous and that remembering is not repeating), and e) *increased mastery* (we can gain mastery and confidence in managing intense distress associated with grief and trauma cues).

Below is a sample script of a clinician presenting a rationale for death-imagery:

Clinician: You've been doing such a nice job practicing action-based approach skills. I know it has been hard at times, but we're already seeing how some of the activities are getting easier based on your SUDS scores. Let's continue with approaching the trauma by talking through the story of how your daughter and granddaughter died. You've shared with me that you relive their experience in your head on a regular basis and even have nightmares, right?

Client: Yes. I just can't get their final moments out of my head.

Clinician: And what do you usually do when it pops in?

Client: I try to push it out. It just hurts so much.

Clinician: Yes. It's really painful. Has pushing it out of your mind been working over the long term? Has it gone away?

Client: Sometimes in the moment it works, but it keeps coming back.

Clinician: Right, this is another example of how avoidance in the short term may feel like it's working but long term may not be. The idea is that we approach these images by retelling the death, which will allow us to better make sense of it or to process it. When we push it away, it's not allowing us the ability to fully digest what happened.

(Pause.)

Client: Okay.

Clinician: Just like the action-based approach activities that we have been doing, retelling the death story will allow our body to habituate or get used to the story and memories so our emotions will not be as strong when these memories or images pop into our head. Of course, we can't prevent you from having these memories, and there may always be feelings of pain, anxiety, or grief associated with them when they come up. But by visiting and revisiting the death story together, these emotions will eventually not be as intense as they are now, and we don't have to feel so out of control when we think about your loved one.

    Often, when you think about your loved one, your mind will shift to how they died, as opposed to thinking about their life and positive memories. Processing the death in this way can free you of the constant return to the circumstances of their death. In addition, revisiting the death story allows our body to recognize the story of their death as a painful memory, but not one that has the power to keep overtaking us and the joyful memories of the time you had together.

    I recognize that this may be challenging, and I'm here to do it with you. By talking through the death story, you will gain confidence in yourself for doing such a hard thing. It's like someone who climbs a large mountain and makes it over the top. That way, when you think of your loved ones, you can connect with them rather than have your mind pull you to the way they died.

Provide an analogy to help relay the concepts of how approaching death-imagery may be useful. To use an analogy that a bereaved mother who lost her son in a motor vehicle crash gave us years ago when we were first developing this protocol: approach can almost be like learning to become a surgeon. You may pass out the first few times, but with practice, you can desensitize yourself and become a conduit for healing (Williams, Rheingold et al., 2018). Here are several examples of other analogies derived from exposure interventions that we have heard over the years in our own clinical training that may help explain the principles of this type of exposure:

Splinter Analogy

Clinician: Retelling the story of your loved one's death is like cleaning out an infected splinter. Imagine having a splinter in your finger that really hurts. You don't touch it because it hurts. Over time, your finger gets infected, and it's oozing and hurts more. You avoid touching it more, and in fact, you try to avoid doing anything that causes it to be touched. What do you need to do with the splinter to help reduce the pain and properly heal?

Client:　　　Pull it out.

Clinician:　　Right, for your finger to heal, you need to pull it out. And as you do, it may hurt even more as you may have to dig in there to really get it out. But once you do pull out the splinter, your finger will heal. Retelling the death of your loved one is kinda like digging in deep to remove an infected splinter. Right now, you're going through life trying not to touch the pain of your loss. But despite these efforts, it's always there, like the splinter. We will need dig into the death story and flush it out. Once we do, you may begin to heal. Now, unlike the splinter, you will always carry this loss, but perhaps we can clean out the wound to allow it to heal so the loss becomes less painful over time.

Shaken Soda Bottle Analogy

Clinician:　　Retelling the story of your loved one's death is like opening up a shaken soda bottle. Right now, when you feel overwhelmed with emotions, you put the cap back on that shaken bottle, perhaps for fear of what may come out or that it will keep flowing out forever. You may feel overwhelmed with emotions just like when opening a shaken bottle and all of the soda flows out. But what happens after some time of keeping the bottle open?

Client:　　　The soda stops coming out.

Clinician:　　Right, the soda doesn't keep flowing and flowing, it does eventually stop. The intense emotions of the death story are similar. Although it may seem scary to open the bottle of emotions and let all the messy emotions pour out, with time and keeping that cap open, the emotions will eventually slow down and stop fizzing so intensely.

Because approach-based activities are challenging, it is important to have clients explain in their own words the rationale for engaging in these activities.

Below is an example dialogue about the rationale of death-imagery approach:

Clinician:　　This can be tough work, and I want to make sure you understand why we're approaching this memory. Based on what we talked about today, what's your sense of why it may be important to talk about your loved one's dying story?

Client:　　　I guess so that over time, it becomes less and less painful to think about and talk about. So I don't have to avoid parts of my life, so that I can think about my loved one and have positive memories and not just think about the death. It sounds good, but I'm really not sure it will work for me.

Module 8: Therapeutic Exposure

Clinician: How come it may not work for you?

Client: I don't know. I just can't imagine ever feeling less pain about her death.

Clinician: So, it sounds like you understand how it could help but not sure if it will work for you.

Client: Yes.

Clinician: That makes sense. And to be honest, many survivors have the same doubts. I encourage us to lean in as we have done before in our work together, to approach those things we've been avoiding, and see what happens. As we've discovered together, avoidance isn't working, so let's approach your memory of this moment in your loved one's life so that you can think about your loved one and have positive memories and not just think about the death. Would you be willing to try?

Client: Okay. I don't think I will like it, but I will try.

> **Clinician Tip.** Some clinicians may be reluctant to recommend or use approach-based activities with their clients out of fear of harming or *retraumatizing* clients. However, prior work with traumatic loss survivors has shown they tend to view the conceptual process of therapeutic exposure favorably when conducted by a clinician who is sensitively attuned to their readiness to engage in this meaningful work (see Williams, Rheingold et al., 2018).

9. Assign Approach in Action

After reviewing your client's action activities from the previous week, reassign them. Continue tracking SUDS ratings during each planned activity using handout 8.3 and review during the next session.

10. Conduct Death-Imagery Approach in Session

Encourage your client to verbally tell the death story in session with as much detail as they would like. As you continue this imaginal approach, encourage your client to increase the details related to thoughts, emotions, and sensory experiences (such as heart racing, the temperature, and smells) they may have had during the death event.

Most often, death-imagery approach is conducted via verbal descriptions (sharing the story out loud). However, other approaches can be used, such as writing about the death, use of art to depict the death scene paired with verbal description of the art, or creating a *narrative book* where the client can create chapters about their loved one, starting with chapters on their life and then ones related to the death event.

Moreover, many survivors may choose to focus on the events of the dying in the story itself as the focus of the narrative, although the death notification (if the survivor was not present) and postdeath events, such as the funeral, can be important memories to detail, too, depending on what imagery causes the most distress for your client.

> **Clinician Tip.** Art or visual drawings of death-related imagery in lieu of verbal retellings may be useful for clients who are easily overwhelmed by the emotional intensity of verbal retellings. For some clients, visual drawings may offer a sense of safety and distance from the imagined events that help them gradually approach death imagery (Neimeyer & Rynearson, 2022).

If conducting imaginal approach via verbal retelling, make sure to record the audio of the retelling so that your client can listen to it at home between sessions for additional approach opportunities to the death story. In addition, to help gauge whether habituation to the death event is occurring, ask for and record your client's SUDS ratings every five minutes. It is often helpful to provide encouragement and limit interactions that interfere with the retelling to promote deeper engagement.

Conduct death-imagery approach for thirty to forty-five minutes and until SUDS scores either remain consistent or decrease. Do not stop if SUDS scores are increasing, as doing so may reinforce your client's tendency to avoid. Although there may not be a reduction these scores during the death-imagery approach, we would anticipate that, with repetition (including listening to the audio recording daily between sessions), we will see a reduction of SUDS ratings over time. Below are directions for procedures of the death-imagery approach:

Recall the memory with your eyes closed.

Imagine what you are seeing is happening now.

Engage in the feelings that the memory elicits.

If verbal, describe the scene in the present tense.

Recount as many details as you can.

Include your thoughts and feelings and any sensory perceptions.

Repeat the narrative as many times as possible in the allotted time.

Module 8: Therapeutic Exposure

Below is a sample script of beginning a death-imagery retelling:

Clinician: Okay, if you're willing, we're going to close our eyes so we're not distracted, and I would like you to imagine the day of your daughter's death is happening now. Go ahead and share the details of what you experience as if they are happening right now, with as many details as you are willing to share. Try to include the thoughts and feelings you were having that day, again, as if they were occurring right now. It may be helpful to provide details about what you sense, such as what you see, what you hear, taste, feel, or smell as well. I will be right here with you. If you get to the end, depending on time, I may ask you to start over again. I also will be asking your SUDS every so often. When I do, try to stay in the moment, just share your SUDS and keep going. What is your SUDS right now, 0–100?

Client: Like 100.

Clinician: Okay, remember I'm right here with you. We're getting that splinter out/ letting all the soda out. Let's close our eyes and begin.

TIPS FOR CONDUCTING DEATH-IMAGERY APPROACH

When guiding these exposures, ask open-ended questions to elicit aspects of the memory or to move the narrative along, such as *What are you thinking right now as you (example of a present-tense aspect of the memory)? How are you feeling in the moment as this is happening? What happens next?* Make clarifying and reflective statements to encourage details, such as *Tell me more about…*or *So the coroner asked you to sit down, then what happens next…* Provide supportive statements or briefly refer to the analogy you used when assessing SUDS if your client seems hesitant to move forward, such as *You're doing a great job sharing these details,* or *I am right here with you supporting you,* or *Keep approaching the memory, you've got this,* or *You're doing a great job keeping the soda cap off, let's keep going.*

Express empathy for your client's distress but keep comments to a minimum. If your client becomes very distressed or starts crying, periodically reassure them that they are safe. However, you should bear in mind that displays of strong emotions are normal and expected during death-imagery and actually indicate that your client is engaging fully with the memory. Make sure to have tissues and some water nearby.

11. Conduct Restorative Processing of Death Imagery

When your client completes the retelling of the death imagery, invite them to open their eyes. You should always begin by providing positive feedback and ask open-ended questions to elicit your client's thoughts and feelings about approaching the story such as, *What was that like for you?* Regardless of their response, normalize and help them to

141

understand their reactions associated with retelling the story, as well as during the death event and its aftermath. If your client reports that retelling the story was harder than they expected, validate and praise their effort, noting things like, *Even though that was harder than you thought it would be, you did such a good job sticking with it.* Comment on habituation you have (or have not) observed within or across sessions as you move forward in treatment. *Your SUDS remained high at 100 today. That is to be expected the first time doing this, and it shows that you weren't avoiding. I anticipate the more we do it, we will see it go down.* Or, *What do you make of the fact that last week your highest SUDS was 95 and this week it is 85?*

Ask questions about those aspects of the revisiting or your client's emotional responses that seem particularly surprising or meaningful. As therapy progresses, focus processing discussions on thoughts or beliefs that your client holds that may be contributing to their distress. It is important to lean on the principles outlined in module 2, such as Socratic dialogue and other related techniques of using open-ended questions.

12. Assign Approach with Action

Assign additional approach activities for homework and ask your client to track their SUDS ratings during each planned activity using handout 8.3 to review during the next session. Note that, by this point, you may start seeing signs of habituation to trauma and grief cues listed on the hierarchy, and you can begin assigning activities with slightly higher SUDS ratings on your client's hierarchy.

13. Assign Listening to Imaginal Recording

Encourage your client to listen to the recordings of their death-imagery story each day for homework to continue the process of habituation. Use handout 8.4 to track the activity and SUDS ratings. At the start of each session, review this recording form and problem-solve with your client if they were not able to listen to the recordings or experienced other challenges in completing the homework.

Common barriers to listening to these recordings include finding a private space or time to listen, which could be mitigated by planning ahead or scheduling when in the day to listen to the recording, as well as excessive avoidance, which can be addressed through explaining the rationale again or identifying a potential transition activity to engage in after listening (perhaps a behavioral activation task or rewarding activity). If clients continue to struggle with avoidance in listening to death-imagery recordings, validate the desire for avoidance while revisiting the long-term impact.

Clinician Tip. Timing and setting are important considerations for listening to the death-imagery recordings. Clients should be encouraged to find a private, quiet space where they will not be disrupted for the duration of the recording and will feel comfortable experi-

> encing emotions that come up during this homework. Related, clients should refrain from completing this homework before bedtime as the emotional valence and magnitude of the homework may negatively impact sleep.

14. Conduct Death-Imagery Approach with Focus on Hot Spots

After several iterations of the death-imagery retelling, identify parts of the narrative that seem to represent the worst or most distressing moments in the memory, which are referred to as *hot spots*. These spots may be when SUDS spike, when clients seem especially emotive, or parts that seem to be avoided. When a hot spot is identified, spend intentional time during the retelling solely focusing on the retelling or revisiting of these hot spots. During the imaginal approach, they may need to be repeated from start to finish multiple times to flush them out and promote habituation. Ask clients to slow down during hot spots and describe them in detail while continuing to gather SUDS ratings every five minutes. If there is more than one hot spot, start with one and work through it until SUDS ratings decrease to 30–40 and then move on to the next one.

15. Integrate Restorative Retelling Components

For some clients, assisting in the reframing of the dying narrative may be restorative in helping find meaning in the death experience or to reframe challenging thoughts or images they may be struggling with related to the death of their loved one. To assist with the process, you might ask your client to imagine themselves in the dying story even if they were not there during the dying. Ask them where they would want to be and what they would want to be doing. Encourage dialogue about this retelling of their role in their loved one's dying experience. You can also ask questions such as *If your loved one were here with us, how would they want you to remember them?* or *How would they help us get through this imagery?* This process of reflection may allow some clients the opportunity to challenge or process difficult thoughts.

16. Assign Approach with Action and Listening to Imaginal Recording

Continue assigning and reviewing action activities in additional sessions until your client habituates to activities that are listed as most distressing on the hierarchy. Also continue death-imagery exposures until SUDS ratings decrease to approximately 30–40. We would not anticipate ratings will ever decrease to 0, as there will always be some negative emotions tied to the death of a loved one. The goal is to decrease intense distress so that clients can revisit memories of the death without becoming consumed by anxiety and distress. This will allow for the ability of clients to recall their loved one without the interference of emotions related to the traumatic nature of the death once SUDS have substantially decreased from reviewing hot spots.

Working with Challenges in Therapeutic Exposure

A number of challenges in implementing therapeutic exposure may arise. As a result, it may be tempting to shy away from exposure activities or stop prematurely, but this may have a detrimental impact on your client's recovery. Below are several common challenges to consider when implementing therapeutic exposure and ways to address these challenges.

Clinician Avoidance. Therapeutic exposure can be challenging even for the seasoned clinician as it can be difficult for all to sit with the intense suffering of another human being. Our desire to reassure or decrease someone's distress or avoid direct discussion of trauma and loss events may interfere with client recovery. Reasons we avoid direct discussions of loss events with clients include the perceptions that as clinicians we are "causing" client discomfort. Recognize that while clients may display increases in distress during sessions of therapeutic exposure, allowing clients to engage in these activities allows them to engage with emotions that they already have and are experiencing. Through exposure and approach, we are merely encouraging direct contact with these emotions, so as to assist in processing and habituating to them.

Another reason clinicians may avoid engaging clients in exposure is our own discomfort in hearing the content and sitting with patient suffering. Practice similar coping skills we teach our clients, such as emotion regulation, managing reactions, challenging thoughts and beliefs about our clients' suffering, and mindfulness and acceptance.

Client Avoidance. Avoidance is a symptom of post-traumatic stress. Therefore, it is very common for clients to engage in avoidance during this module. In fact, it is to be expected. Ways to approach avoidance with clients include validating a client's distress and urges to avoid, reviewing the rationale for exposure and role of avoidance in the short and long term, remind clients that memories are not dangerous, and use analogies to support the rationale for exposure activities. You may also break down activities into smaller steps, when possible.

Underengagement. Some clients may not display or report significant distress when conducting imaginal approach. If they report post-traumatic symptoms but do not seem engaged in the approach exercises (for example, reporting low SUDS ratings or describing the narrative like a police report without much emotional descriptions), they may be emotionally avoiding the activity. This may be intentional or unintentional. Strategies to address underengagement include keeping eyes closed, telling the story in present tense, probing for detailed sensory information (but not so much that you are being too directive), revisiting the rationale, reminding that visualizing the memory is not the same as reencountering the trauma, exploring with the client what they fear might happen if they allow themselves to experience emotions, and noting that distress is not dangerous.

Overengagement. It is rarer, but some clients may overengage or display excessive emotional distress during the imaginal retelling. Displays of emotion and crying are typical emotional responses. However, overengagement may include dissociation, such as flashbacks during exposures or the client becomes unresponsive to clinician questions or directions, panic attacks, or crying hard for long periods of time. Remember that the goal of imaginal exposure is to help the client successfully recount some part of the memory while managing the distress for an optimal level of learning and habituation to occur.

If clients overengage in an exposure or have a history of dissociation, discuss ways to facilitate grounding and support prior to or after the exposure. Reiterate the rationale, if needed, with an emphasis on the aim of learning to discriminate the actual trauma from the memory of the trauma. Stress that memories are painful but not dangerous. Modify procedures to reduce emotional engagement in the memory, such as using past tense, keeping the eyes open, increasing the use of empathic statements, moving the memory forward to foster the realization that this moment ended by asking *and then what happened*, making it more conversational or letting them write the narrative, and integrating breathing or other grounding skills (such as holding a cold soda can or holding ice packs).

Culture Considerations

Several individual and cultural considerations need to be considered when delivering therapeutic exposure. Clinicians working with racially minoritized clients, for instance, should be mindful of the impact historical and current experiences of racial and ethnic discrimination may have on death-related imagery and narratives around traumatic loss. Obvious examples of ways discrimination can play into death imagery may be cases of race-based trauma, such as police-involved killings of Black Americans.

Experiences of racial, ethnic, or identity-based discrimination may factor into death imagery in other ways, though, including experiences before, during, or immediately after the death. For example, a Black client may have overheard a detective at the hospital following their loved one's death refer to their loved one using derogatory language. In such cases, you should take care not to minimize or discount the role of perceived racism in your client's experience and focus instead on how your client's racial identity may have affected how they felt in that moment (Williams et al., 2014).

Survivors from other marginalized communities, especially sexual and gender minority communities, may similarly face discrimination in ways that factor into death imagery and narratives around traumatic loss. Trans people in the US, for example, are at increased risk for suicide and homicide compared to the general population (James et al., 2016; Stotzer, 2009), and survivors, whether trans or cisgendered, may want to process ways that transphobic attitudes and violence factored into their loved one's death and how they process the dying story.

LGBTQIA2+ individuals may also face discrimination in ways that factor into death imagery and narratives, especially if a loved one's death within the community occurred as a result of a hate-based crime or anti-LGBTQIA2+ harassment that contributed to the death, as in cases of suicide. In some cases, partners in same-sex relationships may be excluded by the deceased's family, especially if the family was unsupportive of or unaware of the relationship, which can factor into intrusive death imagery and guilt.

When considering examples and analogies for exposure, it is important to consider cultural implications. For example, some clients may be more likely to engage if following a more medically integrated example as their belief system has less concerns related to medical care versus mental health care. Moreover, in some cultures, linear or timeline narratives are not as common, so it may be helpful to consider more thematic narratives with less emphasis on a timeline order.

For clients who have significant barriers outside of session, it may be important to assess, if homework is not complete, whether it was related to avoidance or logistical scheduling and time available outside of session. Increased problem solving may be necessary to mitigate these challenges. It also may be necessary to do more work in session (or have sessions more often) to ease with some of these challenges. It is also important in planning approach in action activities that you reassess not just safety but capacity for clients (such as transportation and doing activities during the day if nighttime isn't as safe in their neighborhood or community).

Conclusion

Therapeutic exposure is an effective way to help survivors feel more secure and in control when approaching previously avoided people, situations, and memories associated with their loved one's death. Exposures can be very challenging for survivors, though, and require considerable sensitivity and encouragement from empathically attuned clinicians.

To illustrate how this module and others we have presented in this manual can be integrated into a typical course of therapy for a survivor, we will present an example case study and offer suggestions for using the model in the next chapter.

CHAPTER 12

Putting It All Together

This chapter provides guidance for conducting a final session, as well as lessons learned and additional considerations that may arise as part of treatment for traumatic loss-related difficulties. We also provide a case example of how GRIEF Approach is applied with a client presenting with traumatic loss and varied symptoms to illustrate how you as a clinician can use this model in practice.

As we have noted throughout this manual, manifestations of grief, mental health symptoms, and cultural identities vary greatly among traumatic loss survivors. The following case example illustrates the ways in which GRIEF Approach can be utilized to address these complexities and achieve individualized, client-driven goals. In doing so, we return to the experiences of a traumatic loss survivor introduced in chapter 1: Donna.

Case Example: Donna (PTSD and PGD)

Donna is a sixty-four-year-old, Black, married woman who self-referred for mental health treatment approximately two years after her forty-two-year-old daughter was killed by a drunk driver. When Donna arrived at the clinic for her initial appointment, she was eager to begin treatment. She remarked to the clinician that she had "felt stuck and terrified for too long... I knew it was time for some professional help when my adult grandchildren said they were worried about me." During her initial visit, the clinician opened with an acknowledgment of the devastation her daughter's sudden death had caused and expressed curiosity about her, encouraging Donna to share what might be most important to know about her daughter, Denise.

Next, the clinician invited Donna to briefly describe the circumstances of her daughter's death and the challenges she had experienced since. Donna shared the story of the morning she learned her daughter had been killed by a drunk driver and the various ways she had been attempting to cope with being paralyzed by sadness, fear, anger at herself and the drunk driver, and a deep and desperate need to have Denise back. The clinician validated these experiences as being common given the circumstances of her daughter's death and inquired with Donna about following up on what she reported. Donna agreed.

The clinician conducted structured clinical interviews for PTSD, depression, and PGD. The result of these interviews indicated that Donna met criteria for co-occurring

PTSD and PGD. These findings were corroborated with her scores on the self-report instruments she had completed in the waiting room prior to the appointment.

At the end of the session, the clinician and Donna discussed her goals for treatment, which consisted of a desire to feel happy again from time to time, getting back to doing things she used to before Denise was killed (like attend weekly Bunco with former coworkers and drive at night or alone), and finding peace again, which she explained as feeling less bitter and angry toward the impaired driver and "not falling apart with that deep and desperate pain when I think of my baby."

Donna's treatment consisted of fourteen sessions and included the following modules:

- module 1: Psychoeducation About Grief, Types of Loss, and Traumatic Loss Reactions

- module 2: Identifying Emotions and Processing Thoughts

- module 3: Identifying and Building Strengths

- module 4: Managing Strong Emotions

- module 7: Revising Bonds

- module 8: Therapeutic Exposure

Session One

When Donna returned to the clinic, the clinician provided feedback on the previous assessment session, a review of Donna's goals for the treatment, and a description of GRIEF Approach. The clinician outlined Donna's symptoms and explained how they are common among survivors of traumatic loss and how they align with diagnoses of PTSD and PGD. Next, the clinician described GRIEF Approach and how treatment is tailored to her goals and symptoms.

The clinician and Donna then collaborated on the proposed sequencing of modules. Through this discussion, Donna agreed that while curbing trauma-related avoidance may be particularly useful, addressing her need to "make sense of how this happened and actually accept that it did" would be of greatest value and set the stage for exposure-based strategies. They agreed to complete the four core modules first, followed by modules focused on commemorating and revising bonds with Denise before moving to modules focused on traumatic-stress reactions.

Session Two

At the outset of the next session, the clinician inquired with Donna about questions that might have come up between sessions before introducing module 2. Although she didn't have any questions about the treatment or information that was shared during the first session, she was quickly able to describe the emotional ups and downs of her ongoing grief over Denise's death. Donna was then encouraged to identify and track the variety of emotions she experienced between sessions for homework using handouts 2.2 and 2.3.

Session Three

Donna and the clinician reviewed her completed homework. This suggested that she experienced distressing levels of guilt and fear throughout the week. The clinician introduced the cognitive behavioral triangle to help make sense of these emotional experiences and to introduce strategies to modulate affect. Through this discussion, Donna was able to identify those specific situations and thoughts from the past week associated with feelings of guilt and fear. The clinician introduced handout 2.4 and explained how practicing identifying emotions and the associated situations and thoughts is the foundation for beginning to modulate her emotional distress. The clinician fielded final questions and assigned handout 2.4 for homework throughout the week.

Session Four

The clinician began the session by leading a deep breathing exercise and briefly processing the experience before reviewing the assigned homework with the goal of introducing approach-focused coping strategies like those that would be covered in future sessions. Donna explained she had never "paid attention to my breathing like that" and found the experience to be helpful as she was "really not looking forward to the session" on this day. Next, the clinician and Donna reviewed her completed handout 2.4, and Donna noted how the most prominent emotion during the previous week was guilt as she grappled with the following thoughts: *I could have stopped this altogether, I should have told her to wait to leave until morning,* and *Because I didn't stop her, I'm responsible for her death.*

Referring to her homework, she was able to identify that these thoughts occur most often when her grandchildren mentioned how much they miss Denise. In addition, Donna was able to see how plans to commute on the interstate during the previous week provoked thoughts that elicited debilitating levels of fear and anxiety such as *I will be killed if I get into a car again.*

The clinician then led Donna through a discussion of helpful versus unhelpful thoughts and ways to develop or identify more helpful thoughts using handout 2.5, such as *I had no way of knowing my daughter would be killed, The man who decided to drive intoxicated is responsible for my daughter's death,* and *Although there is always a chance I may be in an accident, chances are very low, and I can do things to keep me more safe while driving.*

The session ended with another deep breathing exercise and a description of homework, which consisted of continued practice with handout 2.5 and daily deep breathing.

Session Five

To help Donna manage some of the intense emotions she described experiencing during the first few sessions of treatment, the clinician decided to next introduce module 4. The session began with a mindfulness exercise, which was briefly processed at its conclusion. Donna explained that while she was able to complete her homework from the previous week, she was not able to complete deep breathing at night because she was watching her grandchildren. The clinician and Donna worked together to establish she would carve out time each morning to complete deep breathing, which would also help set the stage for the day.

The clinician then introduced PMR and explained the theory and rationale behind the technique. Donna expressed how she felt less tense and how PMR could go hand in hand with her newly developed skill of identifying helpful thoughts to reduce the intensity and occurrence of anger directed at the drunk driver. Donna and the clinician worked together to decide that a combination of PMR practice in the afternoon with her daily morning deep breathing would be sufficient for homework given her new skills in identifying and reframing her thoughts.

Session Six

The clinician opened the session with a brief mindfulness exercise before inquiring about the homework. The clinician applauded Donna for sticking with the plan of practicing PMR and deep breathing each day. Next, the clinician introduced module 3 and the concept of resilience, as well as a discussion of ways in which Donna thinks others as well as herself have been resilient in the face of adversity and stress. In doing so, she illustrated how she would use prayer as a means of "remaining hopeful" during moments of great stress but that the practice had "fallen by the wayside" since her daughter's death. She also remarked how her newly developed relaxation and cognitive skills represent methods for coping that she feels confident in using. These strengths and strategies were noted on handout 3.2, and Donna was encouraged to continue with the deep breathing and PMR practice, as well as engaging in prayer each night before bed.

Session Seven

With the development and reinforcement of new coping skills and the clarification of prior skills and strengths, Donna was introduced to the concept of revising bonds and maintaining a connection with her daughter. She explained that this may be the most difficult part of treatment due to "fear of what it means to finally accept that she's gone forever." The clinician validated this fear and explained that the prior skills and strengths would make the process easier for her. The clinician then introduced handout 7.1 and assigned it for homework.

Session Eight

Donna returned the following week eager to share her completed handout with the clinician and remarked that although she experienced "huge waves" of grief this past week, she was able to utilize her newly developed skills to remain grounded and complete the activity. This brought about positive recollections and a sense of gratitude for "having her with me for as long as I did, but it was cut short... I wish I at least gave her a hug goodbye..." The clinician then introduced the "hello again" letter activity and assigned it for homework, explaining the importance of finding dedicated quiet time to feel the emotions that come up during the activity.

Session Nine

The session began with a brief mindfulness exercise before the clinician asked Donna to read the "hello again" letter aloud, which she did. The experience was processed before the clinician asked Donna to spend time in session constructing a response letter from Denise, using handout 7.3.

The process of writing the letter was discussed before the clinician asked Donna to read the response aloud. She expressed that taking Denise's perspective was "eye-opening," and helped her better understand that her role in life extends far beyond being Denise's mother. Even though she did not get a chance to say goodbye, she could engage in similar types of experiences to "like, literally say hello again" to feel more connected with Denise with the realization of how the relationship has dramatically changed.

The clinician then asked Donna what activities she could do during the following week that might help her "say hello" to Denise and feel connected with her. Donna mentioned that although she still spends time with friends, she no longer attends Bunco, which was a weekly activity she did with Denise, because the reality of not having Denise with her would be too painful. Encouraging the use of her coping skills, innate strengths, and benefits of experiencing a connection with Denise, the clinician suggested that Donna attend the upcoming weekly Bunco night with friends.

Session Ten

Donna arrived at the session with a palpable improvement in her mood. She stated that not only had she attended Bunco night, but she decided to accept an offer to attend the baby shower of Denise's best friend that weekend. The clinician inquired with Donna about the shift, since she had intentionally avoided Denise's friends because it made her death "that much more real when they were around." Donna mentioned that the anxiety she felt arriving to Bunco dissipated dramatically over the course of the night, and that she found herself enjoying without guilt, despite the absence of her daughter, which helped her attend the baby shower, producing a great sense of pride.

The clinician then asked Donna if she felt ready to begin addressing other things that she had been avoiding, largely due to traumatic-stress reactions. Donna quipped that they should "strike while the iron is hot" and before "my old habits come back." The clinician commended Donna for this perspective and provided a review of the role of avoidance and therapeutic exposure. Next, SUDS ratings were introduced, and Donna and the clinician constructed an approach in action hierarchy using handout 8.2. The clinician reviewed the principles of approach in action and habituation before they collaboratively decided on three items on the hierarchy to practice approaching over the next week (item SUDS range: 35–55) and record actions using handout 8.3.

Session Eleven

Handout 8.3 was reviewed, and Donna was applauded for completing the three action activities between session and adding additional activities. As the clinician and Donna reviewed the completed handout in session, Donna remarked that she was surprised at "how easy they got" over time. As such, it was mutually decided that Donna would complete items higher on the list for the next week, such as driving with a trusted friend at night on the street, driving alone on the street during the day, and driving with her friend on the interstate during the day. Donna was encouraged to continue recording her SUDS during these activities.

Session Twelve

Donna returned the following week with continued progress approaching trauma-related cues and expressed that she felt "oddly calm" during her final approach activity of the week, with her highest SUDS ratings being a 28 out of 100. Next, the clinician presented the rationale for death-imagery approach, particularly as a means to augment her work from the previous weeks.

Donna completed four death-imagery retellings centered on the death notification and reported SUDS ratings that ranged from 65 to 90. The clinician and Donna discussed these ratings, including points in which they were highest, which was when officers uttered the words "killed." The clinician noted how impressed she was at Donna's resilience and persistence in the face of distress, to which Donna remarked through tearful chuckles,

"Has been a theme of this whole thing, hasn't it?" Donna was instructed to review an audio recording of the death-imagery retelling made on her phone once each day and to continue approaching the final items on her action hierarchy while reporting SUDS ratings for both on the appropriate handouts.

Session Thirteen

After reviewing the final approach activities over the past week, the focus of the remainder of the session was on death-imagery centered around the identified hot spot of the death notification. Donna completed six iterations of imagery to the hot spot and mentioned during processing, to her surprise, that she "got kind of bored and a little frustrated actually that you had me do it so many times." The clinician validated this reaction and discussed the progress Donna had made so quickly with habituating to the images and memories of that moment. The session ended with instructions to continue listening to the recording each day, with a report of her SUDS ratings using handout 8.4.

Session Fourteen

During this session, the clinician reviewed Donna's SUDS ratings during her review of the recording during the previous week and was delighted to see that she completed the recording each day, with the highest SUDS rating being a 20. This was processed with Donna, who reported a great deal of self-efficacy and pride, and a review of Donna's goals for treatment.

Donna remarked that she was indeed now able to "feel peace" and to do so without guilt, that the guilt she had experienced in "failing to prevent" her daughter's death was nearly nonexistent, and that she had begun to drive on the interstate alone. However, she also mentioned that doing so at night was still "a bit difficult," producing SUDS ratings in the 35–40 range. The clinician applauded Donna for this progress and noted that a complete resolution of distress was unlikely, but that with continued practice, she was likely to experience more reductions.

Finally, the clinician reviewed Donna's self-report scores from the original assessment session and the scores she provided in the waiting room during what would be the final session of her treatment. When the clinician showed her a graph of her reduction of symptoms over time, she paused and then said through joyful tears, "I knew I was getting better, I could feel it and sense it, but seeing it like this is really eye-opening, like, wow. I know Denise would be so proud… Honestly, I'm really proud." The therapist expressed appreciation of Donna's consistency and dedication to her well-being and the treatment. She then reviewed skills and strategies that were learned over the course of treatment, as well as strategies that may be helpful during difficult moments in the future, such as the upcoming anniversary of Denise's death.

Considerations for Special Populations

As you begin treatment, you may find that there are several special considerations to keep in mind that affect the sequencing of modules, the amount of time spent on specific modules, and the content of different sessions. Here, we discuss some of these special considerations as they relate to special populations of traumatic loss survivors.

Multiple Traumatic Losses

Some clients may unfortunately be grieving the loss of multiple family members from one traumatic loss incident, such as a car crash or a homicide. This can be especially challenging as not only are they experiencing grief related to the multiple deaths, they also may have lost several important individuals in their social support network, which offers an additional layer to the complexity of the loss and their healing journey. Additional time may be needed with module 5 to be more creative and compassionately allow for more intentional expansion and revision of networks. In addition, module 2 may need extra time and attention. When there are multiple traumatic losses from a single incident some clients may have increased levels of survivor guilt, as they may indicate they "should have been there" with their family during their death. And finally, module 7 may need to be extended in length to allow clients to work through and process ways to be connected with each loved one that died and honor the relationship with individual loved ones.

Survivors Involved with the Justice System

If a loved one was killed, and there is an ongoing investigation or pending legal case against someone for their role in the death, your client may be involved in justice system proceedings. Court proceedings may span many years and could be a significant stressor and trauma cue for clients. As a clinician, learning more about the justice system and potential impact it could have on your client may be of value as you could assist them with preparation for difficult conversations with court personnel, sitting through court proceedings, creation of victim impact statements, and possible court testimony.

Most state, federal, or tribal prosecutor's offices have victim service professionals whose role is to help victims' families understand and navigate the justice system. They provide surviving family members with their victim rights, educate them about what to expect at court proceedings, attend court proceedings with family members, and can facilitate the development of a victim impact statement. Of note, the justice system is not always viewed as *just* or *fair* and can create a range of satisfaction or disappointment, especially for cold cases, cases that result in plea agreements, or for cases that do not get prosecuted. Even if a case reaches prosecution, the sentence may still result in ranges of satisfaction or disappointment, and this may be important to both prepare your client and to have time to process in session. Module 2 may assist in exploring such thoughts.

It may be helpful, with client permission, to contact your client's victim service professional to learn more about expectations of court proceedings and the requests of your client so you can best support them in navigating their emotional needs during such stressful experiences. Module 2 and module 4 could assist clients in proactively anticipating and planning for managing distress during such activities. You may also be able to include gradual approach exercises, such as visiting the courthouse prior to the beginning of a trial or other similar activities, into module 8.

Mass Violence Incidents

Some clients may have experienced the death of a loved one to mass violence incidents, which adds additional layers of complexity to death by homicide. Not only are clients grappling with the impact that their loved one has been killed, but they are also part of a collective trauma within a community affected by that mass violence incident. Collective traumas have challenges, including additional media coverage; deniers and conspiracy theorists; involvement of the city, county, state, or federal government officials; community commemoration or anniversary events; memorial planning; and interactions with other victims and survivors (which can be both helpful and unhelpful for survivors). Further, the dynamics of donation distribution may be a challenge for clients.

Sometimes, communities establish resiliency centers to support victims and survivors during recovery for several years after a mass violence incident. These centers may offer well-being and connection activities that could be of value to clients to support their grief journey. The National Mass Violence Center provides resources for victims, survivors, and family members through a virtual resource center available to anyone affected by mass violence at http://massviolence.help.

Other Considerations

Coping with Special Days, Holidays, and Anniversaries

There are a number of days or times of year that can be especially challenging for clients who have experienced traumatic loss. It is important during the assessment phase to note these special days. Instead of waiting for clients to bring up impending special days, proactively acknowledge upcoming days and create plans to manage reactions. Module 2 and module 4 can be used to recognize emotions and thoughts about special days and develop plans for managing emotions during such times.

In addition, strengthening social support during special days can assist clients with potential feelings of isolation and can be a focus of module 5. Module 7 can foster a sense of connection with loved ones to honor their memories and lives on special days. For instance, a client may choose to go shopping for shoes on the day of their mother's death to honor their mother who loved shoes. Creating space in activities or events to acknowledge loss and loved ones can also remove the potential elephant in the room on special occasions and allow a place for loved ones to be "present." For instance, at a wedding, taking pause during the rehearsal dinner to share a memory and light a candle may create space for connection.

Lessons Learned from Survivors

Over the course of the past two decades of clinical practice, we have heard suggestions from clients who have experienced traumatic loss and recognized their providers may have had good intentions but unfortunately and inadvertently made a misstep in their approach. First, do acknowledge the loss during the first session and use the name of the loved one as much as possible throughout sessions, so long as this is culturally appropriate and preferable to your client. Second, do allow time to talk about good memories. This is fostered in module 7; however, it can be integrated earlier in treatment.

Third, be careful in saying cliché supportive phrases to comfort. For example, statements such as *She is better off now* or *in a better place, God has a plan, At least she went quickly*, or *It could be worse*, may actually come across as invalidating of clients' emotions and experience. Instead, consider the use of silence. Fourth, be careful in using statements that attempt to offer empathy but often can be misinterpreted, such as, *I understand how you feel*.

And last, we are all human and, as providers, can have strong emotional reactions to the stories of our clients and the suffering they experience. While emotional reactions are normal and expected, it is important that we are intentional and thoughtful in the ways we show our emotions in therapeutic settings so as not to put responsibility on our clients to provide comfort. If emotions arise during a session, it is important to acknowledge and label that for the client and to explain the context. For example, *You might notice that I have tears in my eye. I want you to know that I am profoundly grateful that you trust me to hear your story and that my tears are reflective of that.* As providers, we do not want our clients to perceive that we cannot "handle" their stories and experiences. Tips for self-care in doing this work are discussed in more detail in the next chapter.

Wrapping Up Treatment and Looking Ahead

As noted in prior sessions, grief is a lifelong journey. It is not something that someone gets closure from or "gets over" but rather is a process that is a part of life. A final session could initially acknowledge this life journey with grief just as clients will have an ongoing life journey of love for their loved one.

Once you and your client have decided to end treatment, some clients may want to invite a supportive person, such as a family member or close friend, to this last session to share their accomplishments and skills learned in therapy, as well as to invite others into the conversation of visions for the future. This can serve as a nice transition from therapy to other supportive people in your client's life and to continue to model the value of healthy social connection and dialogue about their loved one and grief with others. Doing so is not required, but consider offering your client the opportunity to invite someone, if they wish.

During the final session, take some pause to review and list coping and resiliency strategies that were most helpful to your client. You could have your client write them out so they can reflect on them as needed. Discuss and write down anticipated future challenges, time periods, or situations where grief may be more difficult and what coping strategies they could use to assist in managing reactions going forward. This helps to acknowledge that intense emotions related to grief may increase in the future, potentially limiting future unhelpful beliefs such as *I am regressing* or *Here we go again*. It also allows for clients to anticipate future struggles, welcome them, and develop strategies to address them when they arise.

You can shift to a conversation about visions for the future or the next chapter in your client's life to allow them to reflect on their growth in therapy, their continued connection with their loved one, and giving life a more renewed sense of purpose and possible joy. You can foster this reflection by asking questions such as:

- *Have you done some things that you would have thought you could not do?*

- *Have you taken on any of the positive attributes of your loved one?*

- *You obviously no longer have the physical presence of your loved one. How do you now stay connected?*

- *If they were here now, what do you think they would say to you?*

Conclusion

In this chapter, we illustrated how to use this manual as a guide for implementing GRIEF Approach with traumatic loss survivors. We also discussed special considerations for treatment-based unique issues and circumstances associated with the loss, including being mindful of the emotional and personal impact that comes with the gift of healing. Being a clinician is a privilege, and to ensure that we give our best to the survivors that entrust us with their stories and experiences, we discuss strategies and recommendations for clinician self-care in the next chapter.

CHAPTER 13

Self-Care for Providers

Self-care is an incredibly important aspect of clinical practice; at the same time, it is often an aspect that is loosely defined and not always prioritized in the day-to-day. For some providers, the idea of self-care can feel frustrating and almost blaming (if you are burned-out or experience reactions to the work, then you are not doing enough). As a field, the approach to self-care has oscillated and, even more importantly, sometimes comes into direct contrast with the systemic structures in the mental health field (for instance, reimbursement and productivity models, scheduling structures, and organizational supports). While there are certainly challenges, it is essential that we understand the importance of self-care as it applies to our work, particularly when working with grieving and traumatized populations. After all, if we neglect our mental health and well-being, we are likely to be less effective clinicians for the survivors seeking our care.

If regular, effective, and realistic self-care is the destination, we should understand the journey. To start, let's consider some of the specific impacts for providers working with grief and trauma. Common concepts that may be familiar are *secondary traumatic stress* or *vicarious trauma*, *compassion fatigue*, and *burnout*.

Secondary Traumatic Stress and Vicarious Trauma

Secondary traumatic stress (STS) is typically described as the expected stress responses from either helping or wanting to help a person who has experienced a potentially traumatic event. Symptoms and responses of STS parallel PTSD symptoms, specifically intrusive imagery or thoughts, avoidance of associated cues, and arousal symptoms (Chrestman, 1999; Figley, 1999). Similarly, vicarious trauma is typically defined as the internal cognitive processes associated with the impact of helping professions, including the development of core beliefs associated with exposure to traumatic content (McCann & Pearlman, 1990).

Due to the nature of providing trauma and grief treatment interventions, STS and vicarious trauma may be experienced by providers (Baird & Kracen, 2006; Bride, 2007; Figley, 1999). More recently, empirical studies have investigated predictors, correlates, and strategies for mitigation of STS among helping professionals, demonstrating a shift in the field to both acknowledge and increase prevention efforts for the impact on providers (Arvay & Uhlemann, 1996; Brady et al., 1999; Bride, 2007; Baird & Kracen, 2006; Follette et al., 1994; Ghahramanlou & Brodbeck, 2000; Pearlman & Mac Ian, 1995; Schauben & Frazier, 1995). As the need for trained trauma and grief providers continues to grow, attention and prevention efforts related to the experience of STS are essential to reduce attrition of providers (Figley, 1999).

Compassion Fatigue

Compassion fatigue can be defined more actively as a reaction to the experience of STS where providers experience a reduction in their ability to provide empathy toward a client (Figley, 1995). If you have ever worked with a client where your ability to experience empathy and compassion toward them decreased (specifically tied to stress or the impact of your relationship with them), this is a potential sign of compassion fatigue. In practice, this might look like increased irritability toward a client, inability to hold space for client needs, promotion of our own needs before a client's needs, or indifference toward a client.

Burnout

While vicarious trauma and compassion fatigue tend to result more from helping people who have experienced potentially traumatic events, burnout refers to stress largely caused by the social environments in which people work. Common sources of burnout in the workplace include work overload, lack of control over different aspects of one's work, insufficient rewards for one's work, perceived unfairness in the workplace, a breakdown of community and lack of cohesion, and value conflicts (Maslach & Leiter, 1997).

These potential sources of burnout can emerge in many ways for clinicians working with traumatic loss survivors, especially those working in under-resourced community settings where heavy caseloads and lower than average wages are commonplace. You as a clinician might also experience sources of burnout when navigating interactions between professionals across different sectors serving your client. More than once, we have personally felt the lack of control that comes with trying to help under-resourced clients with unmet health-related social needs, only to be turned away or, worse yet, ignored by community-serving social services agencies. Signs of burnout include increased feelings of fatigue, pessimism about the future, cynicism, and irritability (Grosch & Olsen, 1995).

Ethical Considerations of Self-Care

In addition to the wellness of individual helping professions, there is an ethical tenet for us to consider when applying self-care practices. In most helping professions, our ethical mandates include the ideology of *do no harm*. When considering the impact of this work on providers, self-care is key, as both a prevention and intervention technique, in providing good, ethical clinical care to our clients. How we hear the stories our clients share and how we react to those stories has a direct impact on our work. Studies have shown that providers experiencing STS may exhibit impairment in clinical judgment and capacity to help clients seeking services, ultimately leading to poor outcomes (Bercier & Maynard, 2015; Bride, 2007; Figley, 1999; Rosenbloom et al., 1999). This is especially important to consider when working with survivors of traumatic loss.

Some of the death stories that are shared by clients can be emotionally difficult for clinicians to hear and process ourselves. We are human. We are compassionate and empathetic. We are helpers. However, the nature of horrific details of a death can be extraordinarily difficult to sit with even for the seasoned clinician. We, as clinicians, who are choosing to work with traumatic loss survivors, need to acknowledge the nature of this difficult work.

The implications of not acknowledging and preparing for our own empathetic distress could have a direct impact on the clients we serve. For example, over the years in the work we have done with homicide survivors, we have heard numerous times from clients that they had tried therapy before but stopped going because they made their therapist cry or felt like they were burdening their clinician with their suffering. To truly be present as helpers, we have to practice what we preach by paying attention to our emotions and distress to limit the potential negative impact on our clients. Doing so intentionally may also provide a much-needed model for clients who struggle with emotion identification and modulation.

Practical Strategies for Self-Care

As a provider specifically engaging in grief and trauma work, it is important for you to have tools and strategies at your disposal to engage in self-care. Below, we have highlighted areas for consideration and some example strategies for creating an effective, realistic self-care approach.

Self-Awareness

Acknowledgement and awareness of our internal thoughts, emotions, and processes is a skill that many providers demonstrate with clients; however, it is just as essential to practice this skill personally, especially when working with traumatic loss survivors. As helping professionals, we have developed a maladaptive lens to associate our needs as being unimportant or even selfish. We have to consider the importance of good clinical boundaries while holding space for ourselves to experience the normal responses to clinical work (Barnett et al., 2007; Sapienza & Bugental, 2000).

As providers, we should practice noticing and reflecting on our psychological and physiological needs as it relates to clinical work with survivors on a continuous basis to allow for us to monitor potential areas for intervention or support (Harrison & Westwood, 2009; Skovholt et al., 2001; Wityk, 2003). Awareness also involves being knowledgeable about the impact of the work, such as signs of emotional fatigue or ways to monitor our impairment (Smith & Moss, 2009; Wityk, 2003).

Utilizing mindfulness approaches as practitioners is associated with positive outcomes (Goodman & Schorling, 2012). Consider, in your own practice, finding ways to pay attention, on purpose, and without judgment, to be attuned to the emotional and physiological impact of the work. Some examples include:

- noticing body sensations and cues during moments of stress

- labeling sensations and cues

- reflecting on the thoughts and feelings you experience during sessions with a client

- asking reflective questions about underlying reasons for our thoughts and feelings in those moments

- journaling or creative writing (prompted or free form).

Engagement

While avoidance of stressful experiences is a common strategy, just like with avoidance of trauma- and grief-related cues and experiences, it does not work in the long term. Just as with our clients, as providers, it is beneficial for us to approach or engage when we might naturally avoid what is otherwise safe and likely beneficial. It is a common misconception that by avoiding the experience of negative emotions in a workplace or profession, we are able to sustain ourselves; it is actually quite the opposite. Providers who are willing to engage with negative or stressful experiences at work often experience greater job satisfaction, emotional intelligence, well-being, and sustainability over time (Colman et al., 2016; Donaldson-Feilder & Bond, 2004). Engagement is also connected to a sense of personal achievement or accomplishment and self-described clinical performance.

Strategies to increase engagement might include:

- setting an intention to be emotionally willing to engage in approaching negative or stressful experiences

- practicing real-time grounding or mindfulness techniques to allow your body to stay present-focused and engaged

- creating anticipatory excitement toward tasks instead of anticipatory anxiety or avoidance (*I get to* versus *I have to*)

Flexibility

Flexibility can be defined in a myriad of ways; however, as it applies to self-care, it is often referencing *cognitive flexibility,* or the ability of a provider to adapt one's thinking or mental processes to flexibly respond behaviorally in adaptive ways. As providers, we are often, and for good reason, expected to separate our emotional and cognitive experiences from those of our clients (Posluns & Gall, 2020). While this is still true, there are ways to better acknowledge these experiences and challenge our thinking while remaining true to the ethical responsibilities in a therapeutic relationship. Indeed, being mindful, that is, being aware and attuned to our internal and external experience in a nonjudgmental way, helps us be genuine and fully present with clients as they engage in difficult therapeutic work. Moreover, being mindful of our experiences can serve as a model to illustrate to clients how to accept and make room for difficult experiences. In fact, complete suppression of our emotional reactions has been linked to increases in anxiety and depression and higher reported levels of stress (Finlay-Jones et al., 2015; Moore et al., 2008).

An example of this practice is the strategy of cognitive reappraisal, a foundational tenet of the cognitive behavioral approach, which challenges us to attend to our emotions by challenging our thoughts and considering more helpful or accurate thoughts. Utilizing thought challenging is an adaptive technique that is associated with positive outcomes (Gross & John, 2003). Essentially, the way we think about our experiences can predict how we attune to information, what information we continue to think about (ruminations), and how we appraise that information (Yang et al., 2022). For example, a clinician working with a client who does not seem to be finding relief from their grief may say to themselves, *I cannot help her. Her grief is just too intense, and she will always struggle.* Taking pause to examine your thoughts and emotional reactions in the moment allows us to broaden our approach, consider alternative strategies, or even reframe the existing situation. In this example, a reframe may be, *Sitting alongside my client is providing hope. We can tolerate her intense grief together. Emotions are always changing. I can lean on my support just as she is leaning on me.*

Strategies to increase flexibility might include:

- reflective supervision

- thought challenging activities

- review of sessions and reflection of thoughts and feelings associated in the moment

- narrative work or journaling

- mindfulness exercises

Social Support

As with many facets of wellness, social support is integral to achieve a sense of connectedness and understanding. For providers, social support can occur across many domains, including colleagues, mentors, family, friends, and communities. Social connection across multiple domains creates a strong framework for providers to carry the weight of this work.

For helping professionals, support from colleagues can be crucial in creating spaces for wellness through a mechanism of shared understanding of the nature of the work and treatment, and it can help to protect providers from the impacts of trauma exposure. In some studies, peers at work were described as having a stronger role in providing support than personal connections due to that shared understanding of the nuances and complexities of the work environment (Caringi et al., 2017). Caringi and colleagues (2017) also noted that the informal nature of peer support is helpful due to the ability of providers to have quick, natural moments of support during the workday, which may align better with the realistic expectations in agencies and organizations. Support from friends and family may help us oscillate between work-related stress and life tasks in a fashion similar to the DPM. In this sense, their support may help us step away from the work and back into our lives, staying present with those who are important to us without being distracted by work-related stress.

While social support can be beneficial, it is important to note the limitations. For example, interactions perceived as unsupportive can have an opposite effect on a provider (Caringi et al., 2017). Additionally, social support can potentially lead to rumination when the emotional experience is magnified by a group dynamic, further exacerbating stress rather than resolving it (Harling et al., 2020). When considering peer support, it may be helpful to create a balanced approach to reduce the likelihood of rumination (for instance, time-limited interactions, establishing a goal for the discussion, and allowing for processing and then problem-solving).

Consider these strategies as you prioritize social connection into your workday:

- Identify supportive people across multiple domains (mentors, supervisors, peers, family, friends, community, faith practices) and tie specific support needs to those domains.

- Create space for natural connection at work (such as walks around the office, the breakroom, or lunch breaks).

- Establish social connection activities (such as group lunches, wellness activities, group texts, or team huddles).

- Engage in social activities with friends and family often to provide a break from clinical work.

Self-Compassion

The process of having compassion toward our clients is often easier than having compassion toward ourselves as providers. This is not a skill heavily practiced during our training and becomes increasingly more difficult to prioritize as we engage in clinical practice and meet the demands and expectations of our organizations. We are trained to prioritize our empathy and compassion in a unidirectional way to support the needs of our clients without any expectation of reciprocation (Skovholt et al., 2001). While clinical boundaries require a separation of our needs from our clients, it does not preclude us from engaging in compassion and empathy toward ourselves in appropriate settings and with supports. In fact, providers who engage in self-compassion and acceptance of their roles and capabilities to sit with their experiences are better able to recognize both their professional restrictions, as well as areas for growth (Patsiopoulos & Buchanan, 2011).

Professionally, we may be hesitant to engage in self-compassion due to our perceived need to appear professionally competent, particularly to supervisors and mentors (de Figueiredo et al., 2014). Self-compassion, as a practice, does not mean that we cannot learn, grow, and hold ourselves accountable to expectations for good clinical care; however, it does suggest that when we approach our work, outcomes, and struggles with a compassionate and empathetic stance rather than a judgmental and critical one, this can mitigate the impact of stressful environments and experiences.

Strategies to engage in self-compassion might include:

- creating self-compassion statements

- mindfulness practice

- perspective taking activities, where providers observe their thoughts, feelings, and emotions through the lens of a friend or loved one

Harmonious Balance

Work-life balance is an idea that has become more widely adopted in the workplace, with an intentional emphasis on employee wellness and organizational culture. The foundational idea behind a balance or harmony of work versus personal aims is to allow for a "recovery phase" for providers. Studies have shown that providers who create a sense of balance between work and life domains experience increased resilience (Skovholt & Trotter-Mathison, 2010).

As providers, there seems to be a sweet spot for balancing work and personal life in a way that is conducive to our needs and allows us to have a manageable level of perceived stress. Perception is key here; for example, studies have shown that when professionals perceive the expectations at work to be disproportionate, they are more likely to experience stress and burnout. However, when professionals perceive their jobs as reasonably challenging, they report a sense of independence and satisfaction (MacKinnon & Murray, 2018).

It is important to note that what is considered a healthy work-life balance and perception of stress levels will vary widely from person to person. One potential mitigating factor that should be considered, in combination with task and expectations, is the personal meaning a person attributes to those tasks or expectations. In fact, it may be less about the specific expectations but rather how a person views them that should weigh more heavily.

Strategies for finding your harmony or balance at work:

- Identify your tasks and goals and create realistic timelines to accomplish this.

- Create space in your day to incorporate self-care practices (such as mindfulness, breathing, and relaxation) across the day instead of at the end of the day.

- Create moments of meaning in your day (for example, write down meaningful moments or share meaningful experiences with colleagues).

- Practice flexibility within your organizational structure—can you work with your organization to have flexible hours, hybrid schedules, and room for recovery in your day?

- Find a way to create space when coming and going from work that brings meaning or even joy (such as music, a scenic drive, or speaking to someone you love on the phone).

Consultation and Supervision

Consultation and supervision can help to provide both support and problem solving to address challenges in our field. For helping professionals, it is common to have clinical supervision or mentorship that can be utilized for process-oriented discussions. This is also a great place for discussion around the risk factors for STS, compassion fatigue, and vicarious trauma when working with traumatic loss survivors (Merriman, 2015). The structure of consultation and supervision can vary across organizations; however, it is important to consider that both acknowledgment and strategies to address these stressors for professions should be a part of an organizational culture, particularly in agencies where trauma and grief work is being done (Sutton et al., 2022).

Consider strategies for consultation and supervision:

- Balance case supervision with process-oriented supervision.

- Discuss the impact of trauma on you as a provider and solicit feedback on strategies for managing distress.

- Explore emotions and thoughts surrounding exposure to trauma and grief content with your supervisor.

- Engage in thought-challenging activities together.

Conclusion

In this chapter, we discussed the impact of working with traumatic loss survivors on clinicians and suggested domains and skills that might be employed to bolster resiliency and create meaning in the work. Sustaining ourselves in this profession is not only personally important, but also essential in providing adequate care for survivors.

Many interventions and models of self-care exist for helping professionals. As a provider, it can be overwhelming to identify a starting place or to sift through a myriad of models and recommendations. For providers working specifically with trauma-exposed clients, Miller and Sprang's components for enhancing clinician engagement and reducing trauma model (CE-CERT; 2017) may serve as a foundational model to address the impact of this work. In this model, based on decades of research and provider experiences, Miller and Sprang (2017) identify five skill domains essential to providers: 1) experiential engagement, 2) reducing rumination, 3) conscious narration, 4) reducing emotional labor, and 5) parasympathetic recovery. This constellation of strategies helps to orient providers to maintain *conscious oversight* through their work and employ strategies in real time throughout their day to address the impact of working with trauma.

Moreover, personal engagement in these strategies conveys our conviction of their effectiveness and reflects the process of approaching difficult experiences. This is underscored as a general principle throughout this manual and hopefully enables us to continue the important work of supporting survivors as long as we have the privilege to continue doing so.

References

Acierno, R. (2015). *BATE-G manual*. Medical University of South Carolina.

Acierno, R., Kauffman, B., Muzzy, W., Tejada, M. H., & Lejuez, C. (2021). Behavioral activation and therapeutic exposure vs. cognitive therapy for grief among combat veterans: A randomized clinical trial of bereavement interventions. *The American Journal of Hospice & Palliative Care, 38*(12), 1470–1478. http://doi.org/10.1177/1049909121989021

Acierno, R., Rheingold, A., Amstadter, A., Kurent, J., Amella, E., Resnick, H., Muzzy, W., & Lejuez, C. (2012). Behavioral activation and therapeutic exposure for bereavement in older adults. *The American Journal of Hospice & Palliative Care, 29*(1), 13–25. http://doi.org/10.1177/1049909111411471

Ahern, E. M. (1973). *The cult of the dead in a Chinese village*. Stanford University Press.

American Psychiatric Association. (2022). *Diagnostic and statistical manual of mental disorders* (5th ed., text rev.). http://doi.org/10.1176/appi.books.9780890425787

Arvay, M. J., & Uhlemann, M. R. (1996). Counsellor stress in the field of trauma: A preliminary study. *Canadian Journal of Counselling, 30*(3), 193–210.

Baddeley, J. L., Williams, J. L., Rynearson, T., Correa, F., Saindon, C., & Rheingold, A. A. (2015). Death thoughts and images in treatment-seekers after violent loss. *Death Studies, 39*(2), 84–91. http://doi.org/10.1080/07481187.2014.893274

Baird, K., & Kracen, A. C. (2006). Vicarious traumatization and secondary traumatic stress: A research synthesis. *Counselling Psychology Quarterly, 19*(2), 181–188. http://doi.org/10.1080/09515070600811899

Baker, A. W., Keshaviah, A., Horenstein, A., Goetter, E. M., Mauro, C., Reynolds, C. F. III, Zisook, S., Shear, M. K., & Simon, N. M. (2016). The role of avoidance in complicated grief: A detailed examination of the Grief-Related Avoidance Questionnaire (GRAQ) in a large sample of individuals with complicated grief. *Journal of Loss and Trauma, 21*(6), 533–547. http://doi.org/10.1080/15325024.2016.1157412

Banks, K., Newman, E., & Saleem, J. (2015). An overview of the research on mindfulness-based interventions for treating symptoms of posttraumatic stress disorder: A systematic review. *Journal of Clinical Psychology, 71*(10), 935–963. http://doi.org/10.1002/jclp.22200

Barnett, J. E., Baker, E. K., Elman, N. S., & Schoener, G. R. (2007). In pursuit of wellness: The self-care imperative. *Professional Psychology: Research and Practice, 38*(6), 603–612. http://doi.org/10.1037/0735-7028.38.6.603

Beck, A. T. (1970). Cognitive therapy: Nature and relation to behavior therapy. *Behavior Therapy, 1*(2), 184–200. http://doi.org/10.1016/S0005-7894(70)80030-2

Beck, A. T., Rush A. J., Shaw B. F., Emery, G., DeRubeis, R. J., & Hollon, S. D. (2024). *Cognitive therapy of depression* (2nd ed.). Guilford Press.

Beck, J.S. (2020). *Cognitive behavior therapy: Basics and beyond* (3rd ed.). Guilford Press.

Benore, E. R., & Park, C. L. (2004). Death-specific religious beliefs and bereavement: Belief in an afterlife and continued attachment. *International Journal for the Psychology of Religion, 14*(1), 1–22. http://doi.org/10.1207/s15327582ijpr1401_1

Bercier, M. L., & Maynard, B. R. (2015). Interventions for secondary traumatic stress with mental health workers: A systematic review. *Research on Social Work Practice, 25*(1), 81–89. http://doi.org/10.1177/1049731513517142

Berking, M., Wupperman, P., Reichardt, A., Pejic, T., Dippel, A., & Znoj, H. (2008). Emotion-regulation skills as a treatment target in psychotherapy. *Behaviour Research and Therapy, 46*(11), 1230–1237. http://doi.org/10.1016/j.brat.2008.08.005

Berkowitz, S., Bryant, R., Brymer, M., Hamblen, J., Jacobs, A., Layne, C., Macy, R., Osofsky, H., Pynoos, R., Ruzek, J., Steinberg, A., Vernberg, E., & Watson, P. (2010). *Skills for psychological recovery: Field operations guide.* National Center for PTSD and National Child Traumatic Stress Network. http://www.nctsn.org and http://www.ptsd.va.gov

Blevins, C. A., Weathers, F. W., Davis, M. T., Witte, T. K., & Domino, J. L. (2015). The Posttraumatic Stress Disorder Checklist for DSM-5 (PCL-5): Development and initial psychometric evaluation. *Journal of Traumatic Stress, 28*(6), 489–498. http://doi.org/10.1002/jts.22059

Boelen, P. A., de Keijser, J., & Smid, G. (2015). Cognitive-behavioral variables mediate the impact of violent loss on post-loss psychopathology. *Psychological Trauma: Theory, Research, Practice and Policy, 7*(4), 382–390. http://doi.org/10.1037/tra0000018

Boelen, P. A., de Keijser, J., van den Hout, M. A., & van den Bout, J. (2007). Treatment of complicated grief: A comparison between cognitive-behavioral therapy and supportive counseling. *Journal of Consulting and Clinical Psychology, 75*(2), 277–284. http://doi.org/10.1037/0022-006X.75.2.277

Boelen, P. A., & Lenferink, L. I. (2020). Symptoms of prolonged grief, posttraumatic stress, and depression in recently bereaved people: Symptom profiles, predictive value, and cognitive behavioural correlates. *Social Psychiatry and Psychiatric Epidemiology, 55*(6), 765–777. http://doi .org/10.1007/s00127-019-01776-w

Boelen, P. A., & Lensvelt-Mulders, G. J. L. M. (2005). Psychometric properties of the Grief Cognitions Questionnaire (GCQ). *Journal of Psychopathology and Behavioral Assessment, 27*(4), 291–303. http:// doi.org/10.1007/s10862-005-2409-5

Boelen, P. A., Olff, M., & Smid, G. E. (2019). Traumatic loss: Mental health consequences and implications for treatment and prevention. *European Journal of Psychotraumatology, 10*(1), 1591331 . http://doi.org/10.1080/20008198.2019.1591331

Boelen, P. A., Reijntjes, A., J Djelantik, A. A. A. M., & Smid, G. E. (2016). Prolonged grief and depression after unnatural loss: Latent class analyses and cognitive correlates. *Psychiatry Research, 240,* 358–363. http://doi.org/10.1016/j.psychres.2016.04.012

Boelen, P. A., van den Hout, M. A., & van den Bout, J. (2006). A cognitive-behavioral conceptualization of complicated grief. *Clinical Psychology: Science and Practice, 13*(2), 109–128. http://doi.org/10 .1111/j.1468-2850.2006.00013.x

Bonanno, G. A. (2005). Resilience in the face of potential trauma. *Current Directions in Psychological Science, 14*(3), 135–138. http://doi.org/10.1111/j.0963-7214.2005.00347.x

Bonanno, G. A., & Kaltman, S. (2001). The varieties of grief experience. *Clinical Psychology Review, 21*(5), 705–734. http://doi.org/10.1016/s0272-7358(00)00062-3

Bordere, T., Rheingold, A. A., & Williams, J. (2021). Grief following homicide. In H. L. Servaty-Seib & H. S. Chapple (Eds.). *Handbook of thanatology* (3rd ed., pp. 388–416). Association for Death Education and Counseling.

Bottomley, J. S., Feigelman, W. T., & Rheingold, A. A. (2022). Exploring the mental health correlates of overdose loss. *Stress and Health: Journal of the International Society for the Investigation of Stress, 38*(2), 350–363. http://doi.org/10.1002/smi.3092

Bottomley, J. S., Smigelsky, M. A., Campbell, K. W., Neimeyer, R. A., & Rheingold, A. A. (2024). Bereavement-related needs and their relation to mental health symptoms among adults bereaved by suicide and fatal overdose. *Journal of Loss and Trauma,* 1–22. http://doi.org/10.1080/15325024 .2024.2357776

Bowlby, J. (1980). *Attachment and loss. Vol. 3: Loss, sadness and depression.* Basic Books.

Boyd, J. E., Lanius, R. A., & McKinnon, M. C. (2018). Mindfulness-based treatments for posttraumatic stress disorder: A review of the treatment literature and neurobiological evidence. *Journal of Psychiatry & Neuroscience: JPN, 43*(1), 7–25. http://doi.org/10.1503/jpn.170021

Brady, J. L., Guy, J. D., Poelstra, P. L., & Brokaw, B. F. (1999). Vicarious traumatization, spirituality, and the treatment of sexual abuse survivors: A national survey of women psychotherapists. *Professional Psychology: Research and Practice, 30*(4), 386–393. http://doi.org/10.1037/0735-7028.30.4.386

Brancu, M., Mann-Wrobel, M., Beckham, J. C., Wagner, H. R., Elliott, A., Robbins, A. T., Wong, M., Berchuck, A. E., & Runnals, J. J. (2016). Subthreshold posttraumatic stress disorder: A meta-analytic

References

review of DSM–IV prevalence and a proposed DSM–5 approach to measurement. *Psychological Trauma: Theory, Research, Practice and Policy, 8*(2), 222–232. http://doi.org/10.1037/tra0000078

Bretherton, I. (1992). The origins of attachment theory: John Bowlby and Mary Ainsworth. *Developmental Psychology, 28*(5), 759–775. http://doi.org/10.1037/0012-1649.28.5.759

Bride, B. E. (2007). Prevalence of secondary traumatic stress among social workers. *Social Work, 52*(1), 63–70. http://doi.org/10.1093/sw/52.1.63

Bryant, R. A., Galatzer-Levy, I., & Hadzi-Pavlovic, D. (2023). The heterogeneity of posttraumatic stress disorder in DSM-5. *JAMA Psychiatry, 80*(2), 189–191. http://doi.org/10.1001/jamapsychiatry.2022.4092

Bryant, R. A., Kenny, L., Joscelyne, A., Rawson, N., Maccallum, F., Cahill, C., Hopwood, S., Aderka, I., & Nickerson, A. (2014). Treating prolonged grief disorder: A randomized clinical trial. *JAMA Psychiatry, 71*(12), 1332–1339. http://doi.org/10.1001/jamapsychiatry.2014.1600

Burke, L. A., & Neimeyer, R. A. (2014). Complicated spiritual grief I: Relation to complicated grief symptomatology following violent death bereavement. *Death Studies, 38*(4), 259–267. http://doi.org/10.1080/07481187.2013.829372

Burke, L. A., Neimeyer, R. A., & McDevitt-Murphy, M. E. (2010). African American homicide bereavement: Aspects of social support that predict complicated grief, PTSD, and depression. *OMEGA - Journal of Death and Dying, 61*(1), 1–24. http://doi.org/10.2190/OM.61.1.a

Cacciatore, J., Thieleman, K., Fretts, R., & Jackson, L. B. (2021). What is good grief support? Exploring the actors and actions in social support after traumatic grief. *PloS One, 16*(5), e0252324. http://doi.org/10.1371/journal.pone.0252324

Cahill, S. P., & Foa, E. B. (2007). Psychological theories of PTSD. In M. J. Friedman, T. M. Keane & P. A. Resick (Eds.), *Handbook of PTSD: Science and practice* (pp. 55–77). Guilford Press.

Caringi, J. C., Hardiman, E. R., Weldon, P., Fletcher, S., Devlin, M., & Stanick, C. (2017). Secondary traumatic stress and licensed clinical social workers. *Traumatology, 23*(2), 186–195. http://doi.org/10.1037/trm0000061

Carlson, C. R., & Hoyle, R. H. (1993). Efficacy of abbreviated progressive muscle relaxation training: A quantitative review of behavioral medicine research. *Journal of Consulting and Clinical Psychology, 61*(6), 1059–1067. http://doi.org/10.1037//0022-006x.61.6.1059

Centers for Disease Control and Prevention. (2023a). *Injuries and violence are leading causes of death.* http://www.cdc.gov/injury/wisqars/animated-leading-causes.html

Centers for Disease Control and Prevention. (2023b). *WISQARS fatal and nonfatal injury reports.* http://wisqars.cdc.gov/reports/

Centers for Medicare and Medicaid Services. (2023). *A guide to using the Accountable Health Communities Health-Related Social Needs Screening Tool: Promising practices and key insights.* http://www.cms.gov/priorities/innovation/media/document/ahcm-screeningtool-companion

Cerel, J., Brown, M. M., Maple, M., Singleton, M., van de Venne, J., Moore, M., & Flaherty, C. (2019). How many people are exposed to suicide? Not six. *Suicide and Life-Threatening Behavior, 49*(2), 529–534. http://doi.org/10.1111/sltb.12450

Chandla, S. S., Sood, S., Dogra, R., Das, S., Shukla, S. K., & Gupta, S. (2013). Effect of short-term practice of pranayamic breathing exercises on cognition, anxiety, general well being and heart rate variability. *Journal of the Indian Medical Association, 111*(10), 662–665.

Chen, Y.-F., Huang, X.-Y., Chien, C.-H., & Cheng, J.-F. (2017). The effectiveness of diaphragmatic breathing relaxation training for reducing anxiety. *Perspectives in Psychiatric Care, 53*(4), 329–336. http://doi.org/10.1111/ppc.12184

Cherpitel, C. J., Ye, Y., & Kerr, W. C. (2021). Shifting patterns of disparities in unintentional injury mortality rates in the United States, 1999–2016. *Pan American Journal of Public Health, 45*, e36. http://doi.org/10.26633/RPSP.2021.36

Chorpita, B. F., Daleiden, E. L., & Weisz, J. R. (2005). Modularity in the design and application of therapeutic interventions. *Applied and Preventive Psychology, 11*(3), 141–156. http://doi.org/10.1016/j.appsy.2005.05.002

Chrestman, K. R. (1999). Secondary exposure to trauma and self-reported distress among therapists. In B. H. Stamm (Ed.), *Secondary traumatic stress: Self-care issues for clinicians, researchers, and educators* (2nd ed., pp. 29–36). Sidran Press.

Ciharova, M., Furukawa, T. A., Efthimiou, O., Karyotaki, E., Miguel, C., Noma, H., Cipriani, A., Riper H., & Cuijpers, P. (2021). Cognitive restructuring, behavioral activation and cognitive-behavioral therapy in the treatment of adult depression: A network meta-analysis. *Journal of Consulting and Clinical Psychology, 89*(6), 563–574. http://doi.org/10.1037/ccp0000654

Cohen, S. (2004). Social relationships and health. *American Psychologist, 59*(8), 676–684. http://doi.org/10.1037/0003-066X.59.8.676

Cohen, S., & Wills, T. A. (1985). Stress, social support, and the buffering hypothesis. *Psychological Bulletin, 98*(2), 310–357. http://doi.org/10.1037/0033-2909.98.2.310

Colman, I., Kingsbury, M., Garad, Y., Zeng, Y., Naicker, K., Patten, S., Jones, P. B., Wild, T. C., & Thompson, A. H. (2016). Consistency in adult reporting of adverse childhood experiences. *Psychological Medicine, 46*(3), 543–549. http://doi.org/10.1017/S0033291715002032

Conrad, A., & Roth, W. T. (2007). Muscle relaxation therapy for anxiety disorders: It works but how? *Journal of Anxiety Disorders, 21*(3), 243–264. http://doi.org/10.1016/j.janxdis.2006.08.001

Cox, K. S. (2024). Repackaging exposure therapy as the practice of approach: A new idea for an old problem. *The Behavior Therapist, 47*(7), 341–348.

Cribb, G., Moulds, M. L., & Carter, S. (2006). Rumination and experiential avoidance in depression. *Behaviour Change, 23*(3), 165–176. http://doi.org/10.1375/bech.23.3.165

de Figueiredo, S., Yetwin, A., Sherer, S., Radzik, M., & Iverson, E. (2014). A cross-disciplinary comparison of perceptions of compassion fatigue and satisfaction among service providers of highly traumatized children and adolescents. *Traumatology, 20*(4), 286–295. http://doi.org/10.1037/h0099833

DiGiuseppe, R., & Tafrate, R. C. (2003). Anger treatment for adults: A meta-analytic review. *Clinical Psychology: Science and Practice, 10*(1), 70–84. http://doi.org/10.1093/clipsy.10.1.70

Djelantik, A. A. A. M. J., Robinaugh, D. J., & Boelen, P. A. (2022). The course of symptoms in the first 27 months following bereavement: A latent trajectory analysis of prolonged grief, posttraumatic stress, and depression. *Psychiatry Research, 311*, 114472. http://doi.org/10.1016/j.psychres.2022.114472

Djelantik, A. A. A. M. J., Smid, G. E., Kleber, R. J., & Boelen, P. A. (2017). Symptoms of prolonged grief, post-traumatic stress, and depression after loss in a Dutch community sample: A latent class analysis. *Psychiatry Research, 247*, 276–281. http://doi.org/10.1016/j.psychres.2016.11.023

Djelantik, A. A. A. M. J., Smid, G. E., Mroz, A., Kleber, R. J., & Boelen, P. A. (2020). The prevalence of prolonged grief disorder in bereaved individuals following unnatural losses: Systematic review and meta regression analysis. *Journal of Affective Disorders, 265*, 146–156. http://doi.org/10.1016/j.jad.2020.01.034

Donaldson-Feilder, E. J., & Bond, F. W. (2004). The relative importance of psychological acceptance and emotional intelligence to workplace well-being. *British Journal of Guidance & Counselling, 32*(2), 187–203. http://doi.org/10.1080/08069880410001692210

Donker, T., Griffiths, K. M., Cuijpers, P., & Christensen, H. (2009). Psychoeducation for depression, anxiety and psychological distress: A meta-analysis. *BMC Medicine, 7*, 79. http://doi.org/10.1186/1741-7015-7-79

Eisma, M. C., Stelzer, E.M., Lenferink, L. I. M., Knowles, L. M., Gastmeier, S. K., Angelopoulou, M., Doering, B. K., & O'Connor, M.F. (2020). *Yearning in Situations of Loss Scale--Short Form (YSL-SF)* [Database record]. APA PsycTests.

Eisma, M. C., & Stroebe, M. S. (2021). Emotion regulatory strategies in complicated grief: A systematic review. *Behavior Therapy, 52*(1), 234–249. http://doi.org/10.1016/j.beth.2020.04.004

Eisma, M. C., Stroebe, M. S., Schut, H. A. W., Stroebe, W., Boelen, P. A., & van den Bout, J. (2013). Avoidance processes mediate the relationship between rumination and symptoms of complicated grief and depression following loss. *Journal of Abnormal Psychology, 122*(4), 961–970. http://doi.org/10.1037/a0034051

Ekers, D., Webster, L., Van Straten, A., Cuijpers, P., Richards, D., & Gilbody, S. (2014). Behavioural activation for depression; An update of meta-analysis of effectiveness and sub group analysis. *PloS One, 9*(6), e100100. http://doi.org/10.1371/journal.pone.0100100

Ennis, N., Bottomley, J., Sawyer, J., Moreland, A. D., & Rheingold, A. A. (2023). Measuring grief in the context of traumatic loss: A systematic review of assessment instruments. *Trauma, Violence, & Abuse, 24*(4), 2346–2362. http://doi.org/10.1177/15248380221093694

References

Feeney, B. C., & Collins, N. L. (2015). A new look at social support: A theoretical perspective on thriving through relationships. *Personality and Social Psychology Review, 19*(2), 113–147. http://doi.org/10.1177/1088868314544222

Ferguson, A., Dinh-Williams, L.-A., & Segal, Z. (2021). Mindfulness-based cognitive therapy. In A. Wenzel (Ed.), *Handbook of cognitive behavioral therapy: Overview and approaches* (pp. 595–615). American Psychological Association.

Field, J. (2006). Lifelong learning and the new educational order. *British Journal of Educational Technology, 37*(6), 973–990. http://doi.org/10.1111/j.1467-8535.2006.00660_18.x

Figley, C. R. (1995). Compassion fatigue: Toward a new understanding of the costs of caring. In B. H. Stamm (Ed.), *Secondary traumatic stress: Self-care issues for clinicians, researchers, and educators* (pp. 3–28). Sidran Press.

Figley, C. R. (1999). Police compassion fatigue (PCF): Theory, research, assessment, treatment, and prevention. In J. M. Violanti & D. Paton (Eds.), *Police trauma: Psychological aftermath of civilian combat* (pp. 37–53). Charles C Thomas Publisher, Ltd.

Fincham, G.W., Strauss, C., Montero-Marin, J., & Cavanagh, K. (2023). Effect of breathwork on stress and mental health: A meta-analysis of randomised-controlled trials. *Scientific Reports, 13*(1), 432. http://doi.org/10.1038/s41598-022-27247-y

Finlay-Jones, A. L., Rees, C. S., & Kane, R. T. (2015). Self-compassion, emotion regulation and stress among Australian psychologists: Testing an emotion regulation model of self-compassion using structural equation modeling. *PloS One, 10*(7), e0133481. http://doi.org/10.1371/journal.pone.0133481

First, M. B., Williams, J. B. W., Karg, R. S., & Spitzer, R. L. (2016). *Structured Clinical Interview for DSM-5 Disorders—Clinician Version (SCID-5-CV).* American Psychiatric Association Publishing.

Foa, E. B., Hembree, E, & Rothbaum, B. (2007). *Prolonged exposure therapy for PTSD: Emotional processing of traumatic experiences, therapist guide.* Oxford Academic. http://doi.org/10.1093/med:psych/9780195308501.001.0001

Foa, E. B., & Kozak, M. J. (1986). Emotional processing of fear: Exposure to corrective information. *Psychological Bulletin, 99*(1), 20–35.

Foa, E. B., & Rauch, S. A. (2004). Cognitive changes during prolonged exposure versus prolonged exposure plus cognitive restructuring in female assault survivors with posttraumatic stress disorder. *Journal of Consulting and Clinical Psychology, 72*(5), 879–884. http://doi.org/10.1037/0022-006X.72.5.879

Follette, V. M., Polusny, M. M., & Milbeck, K. (1994). Mental health and law enforcement professionals: Trauma history, psychological symptoms, and impact of providing services to child sexual abuse survivors. *Professional Psychology: Research and Practice, 25*(3), 275–282. http://doi.org/10.1037/0735-7028.25.3.275

Freud, S. (1917). Mourning and melancholia. In J. Strachey (Ed.), *The standard edition of the complete psychological works of Sigmund Freud, volume XIV* (pp. 243–58). Hogarth Press.

Galatzer-Levy, I.R., & Bonanno, G.A. (2012). Beyond normality in the study of bereavement: Heterogeneity in depression outcomes following loss in older adults. *Social Science and Medicine, 74*(12), 1987–1994. http://doi.org/10.1016/j.socscimed.2012.02.022

Gamino, L. A., Mowll, J., & Hogan, N. S. (2021). Grief following sudden nonvolitional deaths. In H. L. Servaty-Seib & H. S. Chapple (Eds.), *Handbook of thanatology* (3rd ed., pp. 336–361). Association for Death Education and Counseling.

Gariépy, G., Honkaniemi, H., & Quesnel-Vallée, A. (2016). Social support and protection from depression: Systematic review of current findings in Western countries. *The British Journal of Psychiatry, 209*(4), 284–293. http://doi.org/10.1192/bjp.bp.115.169094

Ghahramanlou, M., & Brodbeck, C. (2000). Predictors of secondary trauma in sexual assault trauma counselors. *International Journal of Emergency Mental Health, 2*(4), 229–240.

Glad, K. A., Stensland, S., Czajkowski, N. O., Boelen, P. A., & Dyb, G. (2022). The longitudinal association between symptoms of posttraumatic stress and complicated grief: A random intercepts cross-lag analysis. *Psychological Trauma: Theory, Research, Practice, and Policy, 14*(3), 386–392. http://doi.org/10.1037/tra0001087

Gobaud, A. N., Mehranbod, C. A., Dong, B., Dodington, J., & Morrison, C. N. (2022). Absolute versus relative socioeconomic disadvantage and homicide: A spatial ecological case-control study of US zip codes. *Injury Epidemiology, 9*(1), 7. http://doi.org/10.1186/s40621-022-00371-z

Goodman, M. J., & Schorling, J. B. (2012). A mindfulness course decreases burnout and improves well-being among healthcare providers. *The International Journal of Psychiatry in Medicine, 43*(2), 119–128. http://doi.org/10.2190/PM.43.2.b

Gould, M., Greenberg, N., & Hetherton, J. (2007). Stigma and the military: Evaluation of a PTSD psychoeducational program. *Journal of Traumatic Stress, 20*(4), 505–515. http://doi.org/10.1002/jts.20233

Goyal, M., Singh, S., Sibinga, E. M. S., Gould, N. F., Rowland-Seymour, A., Sharma, R., Berger, Z., Sleicher, D., Maron, D. D., Shihab, H. M., Ranashinghe, P. D., Linn, S., Saha, S., Bass, E. B., & Haythornthwaite, J. A. (2014). Meditation programs for psychological stress and well-being: A systematic review and meta-analysis. *JAMA Internal Medicine, 174*(3), 357–368. http://doi.org/10.1001/jamainternmed.2013.13018

Graham, J. R., Sorenson, S., & Hayes-Skelton, S. A. (2013). Enhancing the cultural sensitivity of cognitive behavioral interventions for anxiety in diverse populations. *The Behavior Therapist, 36*(5), 101–108.

Grosch, W. N., & Olsen, D. C. (1995). Prevention: Avoiding burnout. In M. B. Sussman (Ed.), *A perilous calling: The hazards of psychotherapy practice* (pp. 275–287). John Wiley & Sons.

Gross, J. J., & John, O. P. (2003). Individual differences in two emotion regulation processes: implications for affect, relationships, and well-being. *Journal of Personality and Social Psychology, 85*(2), 348-362. http://doi.org/10.1037/0022-3514.85.2.348

Gutner, C. A., Galovski, T., Bovin, M. J., & Schnurr, P. P. (2016). Emergence of transdiagnostic treatments for PTSD and posttraumatic distress. *Current Psychiatry Reports, 18*(10), 95. http://doi.org/10.1007/s11920-016-0734-x

Gutner, C. A., & Presseau, C. (2019). Dealing with complexity and comorbidity: Opportunity for transdiagnostic treatment for PTSD. *Current Treatment Options in Psychiatry, 6*(2), 119–131. http://doi.org/10.1007/s40501-019-00170-2

Hardt, M. M., Jobe-Shields, L., & Williams, J. L. (2020). Complications in bereavement following motor vehicle crash fatalities in a sample of young adults. *Traumatology, 26*, 388–395. http://doi.org/10.1037/trm0000271

Harling, G., Kobayashi, L. C., Farrell, M. T., Wagner, R. G., Tollman, S., & Berkman, L. (2020). Social contact, social support, and cognitive health in a population-based study of middle-aged and older men and women in rural South Africa. *Social Science & Medicine, 260*, 113167. http://doi.org/10.1016/j.socscimed.2020.113167

Harlow, H. F., & Zimmermann, R. R. (1959). Affectional responses in the infant monkey; Orphaned baby monkeys develop a strong and persistent attachment to inanimate surrogate mothers. *Science, 130*, 421–432. http://doi.org/10.1126/science.130.3373.421

Harris, D. L., & Bordere, T.C. (Eds.). (2016). *Handbook of social justice in loss and grief: Exploring diversity, equity, and inclusion* (1st ed.). Routledge.

Harris, R. (2021). *When life hits hard: How to transcend grief, crisis, and loss with acceptance and commitment therapy.* New Harbinger Publications.

Harrison, R. L., & Westwood, M. J. (2009). Preventing vicarious traumatization of mental health therapists: Identifying protective practices. *Psychotherapy: Theory, Research, Practice, Training, 46*(2), 203–219. http://doi.org/10.1037/a0016081

Harrop, E., Medeiros Mirra, R., Goss, S., Longo, M., Byrne, A., Farnell, D. J. J., Seddon, K., Penny, A., Machin, L., Sivel, S., & Selman, L. E. (2023). Prolonged grief during and beyond the pandemic: Factors associated with levels of grief in a four time-point longitudinal survey of people bereaved in the first year of the COVID-19 pandemic. *Frontiers in Public Health, 11*, 1215881. http://doi.org/10.3389/fpubh.2023.1215881

Hayes, S. C., Bond, F. W., Barnes-Holmes, D., & Austin, J. (Eds.). (2006). *Acceptance and mindfulness at work: Applying acceptance and commitment therapy and relational frame theory to organizational behavior management.* Routledge.

Hayes, S. C., Strosahl, K. D., & Wilson, K. G. (2011). *Acceptance and commitment therapy: The process and practice of mindful change*. Guilford Press.

Hayes, S.C, Strosahl, K.D., & Wilson, K.G. (2012). *Acceptance and commitment therapy: The process and practice of mindful change* (2nd ed.). Guilford Press.

Hayes, S. C., Wilson, K. G., Gifford, E. V., Follette, V. M., & Strosahl, K. (1996). Experiential avoidance and behavioral disorders: A functional dimensional approach to diagnosis and treatment. *Journal of Consulting and Clinical Psychology, 64*(6), 1152–1168. http://doi.org/10.1037//0022-006x.64.6.1152

Hays, P. A. (2008). *Addressing cultural complexities in practice: Assessment, diagnosis, and therapy* (2nd ed.). American Psychological Association. http://doi.org/10.1037/11650-000

Heeke, C., Stammel, N., Heinrich, M., & Knaevelsrud, C. (2017). Conflict-related trauma and bereavement: Exploring differential symptom profiles of prolonged grief and posttraumatic stress disorder. *BMC Psychiatry, 17*(1), 118. http://doi.org/10.1186/s12888-017-1286-2

Hobfoll, S. E., Freedy, J., Lane, C., & Geller, P. (1990). Conservation of social resources: Social support resource theory. *Journal of Social and Personal Relationships, 7*(4), 465–478. http://doi.org/10.1177/0265407590074004

Hofmann, S. G., Asnaani, A., Vonk, I. J. J., Sawyer, A. T., & Fang, A. (2012). The efficacy of cognitive behavioral therapy: A review of meta-analyses. *Cognitive Therapy and Research, 36*(5), 427–440. http://doi.org/10.1007/s10608-012-9476-1

Holland, J. M., Klingspon, K. L., Lichtenthal, W. G., & Neimeyer, R. A. (2020). The Unfinished Business in Bereavement Scale (UBBS): Development and psychometric evaluation. *Death Studies, 44*(2), 65–77. http://doi.org/10.1080/07481187.2018.1521101

Holland, J. M., & Neimeyer, R. A. (2011). Separation and traumatic distress in prolonged grief: The role of cause of death and relationship to the deceased. *Journal of Psychopathology and Behavioral Assessment, 33*(2), 254–263. http://doi.org/10.1007/s10862-010-9214-5

Holland, J. M., Plant, C. P., Klingspon, K. L., & Neimeyer, R. A. (2020). Bereavement-related regrets and unfinished business with the deceased. *Death Studies, 44*(1), 42–47. http://doi.org/10.1080/07481187.2018.1521106

House, J. S. (1983). *Work stress and social support*. Addison-Wesley.

House, J. S., Umberson, D., & Landis, K. R. (1988). Structures and processes of social support. *Annual Review of Sociology, 14*, 293–318. http://doi.org/10.1146/annurev.so.14.080188.001453

Iacoviello, B. M., & Charney, D. S. (2014). Psychosocial facets of resilience: implications for preventing posttrauma psychopathology, treating trauma survivors, and enhancing community resilience. *European Journal of Psychotraumatology, 5*, 23970. http://doi.org/10.3402/ejpt.v5.23970

James, S. E., Herman, J. L., Rankin, S., Keisling, M., Mottet, L., & Anafi, M. (2016). *The report of the 2015 U.S. transgender survey*. National Center for Transgender Equality. http://ustranssurvey.org/download-reports/

Jordan, J. R., & McGann, V. (2017). Clinical work with suicide loss survivors: Implications of the U.S. postvention guidelines. *Death Studies, 41*(10), 659–672. http://doi.org/10.1080/07481187.2017.1335553

Kabat-Zinn, J. (1994). *Wherever you go, there you are: Mindfulness meditation in everyday life*. Hyperion.

Kabat-Zinn, J. (2003). Mindfulness-based stress reduction (MBSR). *Constructivism in the Human Sciences, 8*(2), 73–107.

Kabat-Zinn, J. (2005). *Wherever you go, there you are: Mindfulness meditation in everyday life* (10th edition). Hachette.

Kabat-Zinn, J. (2012). *Mindfulness for beginners: Reclaiming the present moment—and your life*. Sounds True.

Kaltman, S., & Bonanno, G. A. (2003). Trauma and bereavement: Examining the impact of sudden and violent deaths. *Journal of Anxiety Disorders, 17*(2), 131–147. http://doi.org/10.1016/s0887-6185(02)00184-6

Kaplow, J. B., Gipson, P. Y., Horwitz, A. G., Burch, B. N., & King, C. A. (2014). Emotional suppression mediates the relation between adverse life events and adolescent suicide: implications for prevention. *Prevention Science, 15*(2), 177–185. http://doi.org/10.1007/s11121-013-0367-9

Kaplow, J. B., Layne, C. M., Pynoos, R. S., Cohen, J. A., & Lieberman, A. (2012). DSM-V diagnostic criteria for bereavement-related disorders in children and adolescents: Developmental considerations. *Psychiatry, 75*(3), 243–266. http://doi.org/10.1521/psyc.2012.75.3.243

Kaplow, J. B., Layne, C. M., Saltzman, W. R., Cozza, S. J., & Pynoos, R. S. (2013). Using multidimensional grief theory to explore effects of deployment, reintegration, and death on military youth and families. *Clinical Child and Family Psychology Review, 16*(3), 322–340. http://doi.org/10.1007/s10567-013-0143-1

Karb R. A., Subramanian, S. V., & Fleegler, E. W. (2016) County poverty concentration and disparities in unintentional injury deaths: A fourteen-year analysis of 1.6 million U.S. fatalities. *PLoS One, 11*(5), e0153516. http://doi.org/10.1371/journal.pone.015351

Keng, S. L., Smoski, M. J., & Robins, C. J. (2011). Effects of mindfulness on psychological health: A review of empirical studies. *Clinical Psychology Review, 31*(6), 1041–1056. http://doi.org/10.1016/j.cpr.2011.04.006

Kessler, R. C., Aguilar-Gaxiola, S., Alonso, J., Benjet, C., Bromet, E. J., Cardoso, G., Degenhardt, L., de Girolamo, G., Dinolova, R. V., Ferry, F., Florescu, S., Gureje, O., Haro, J. M., Huang, Y., Karam, E. G., Kawakami, N., Lee, S., Lepine, J.-P., Levinson, D., … Koenen, K. C. (2017). Trauma and PTSD in the WHO World Mental Health Surveys. *European Journal of Psychotraumatology, 8*(sup5), 1353383. http://doi.org/10.1080/20008198.2017.1353383

Keyes, K. M., McLaughlin, K. A., Demmer, R. T., Cerdá, M., Koenen, K. C., Uddin, M., & Galea, S. (2013). Potentially traumatic events and the risk of six physical health conditions in a population-based sample. *Depression and Anxiety, 30*(5), 451–460. http://doi.org/10.1002/da.22090

Keyes, K. M., Pratt, C., Galea, S., McLaughlin, K. A., Koenen, K. C., & Shear, M. K. (2014). The burden of loss: Unexpected death of a loved one and psychiatric disorders across the life course in a national study. *American Journal of Psychiatry, 171*(8), 864–871. http://doi.org/10.1176/appi.ajp.2014.13081132

Kilpatrick, D. G., Resnick, H. S., Milanak, M. E., Miller, M. W., Keyes, K. M., & Friedman, M. J. (2013). National estimates of exposure to traumatic events and PTSD prevalence using DSM-IV and DSM-5 criteria. *Journal of Traumatic Stress, 26*(5), 537–547. http://doi.org/10.1002/jts.21848

Kristensen, P., Dyregrov, A., Weisæth, L., Straume, M., Dyregrov, K., Heir, T., & Bugge, R. G. (2018). Optimizing visits to the site of death for bereaved families after disasters and terrorist events. *Disaster Medicine and Public Health Preparedness, 12*(4), 523–527.

Kroenke, K., Spitzer, R. L., & Williams, J. B. (2001). The PHQ-9: Validity of a brief depression severity measure. *Journal of General Internal Medicine, 16*(9), 606-613. http://doi.org/10.1017/dmp.2017.94

Kübler-Ross, E. (1969). *On death and dying: What the dying have to teach doctors, nurses, clergy and their own families.* Macmillan.

Kumar, S. M. (2005). *Grieving mindfully: A compassionate and spiritual guide to coping with loss.* New Harbinger Publications.

Lang, A. J., Strauss, J. L., Bomyea, J., Bormann, J. E., Hickman, S. D., Good, R. C., & Essex, M. (2012). The theoretical and empirical basis for meditation as an intervention for PTSD. *Behavior Modification, 36*(6), 759–786. http://doi.org/10.1177/0145445512441200

Layne, C. M., Kaplow, J. B., Oosterhoff, B., Hill, R., & Pynoos, R. S. (2017). The interplay between posttraumatic stress and grief reactions in traumatically bereaved adolescents: When trauma, bereavement, and adolescence converge. *Adolescent Psychiatry, 7*(4), 266–285. http://doi.org/10.2174/2210676608666180306162544

LeJeune, J. (2012). *Leaves on a stream* [Audio]. Portland Psychotherapy Clinic. http://www.portlandpsychotherapyclinic.com/counseling/mindfulness_and_acceptance_exercises

Lejuez, C. W., Hopko, D. R., Acierno, R., Daughters, S. B., & Pagoto, S. L. (2011). Ten year revision of the brief behavioral activation treatment for depression: Revised treatment manual. *Behavior Modification, 35*(2), 111–161. http://doi.org/10.1177/0145445510390929

Lenferink, L. I. M., Eisma, M. C., Buiter, M. Y., de Keijser, J., & Boelen, P. A. (2023). Online cognitive behavioral therapy for prolonged grief after traumatic loss: A randomized waitlist-controlled trial. *Cognitive Behaviour Therapy, 52*(5), 508–522. http://doi.org/10.1080/16506073.2023.2225744

References

Lewinsohn, P. M., Sullivan, J. M., & Grosscup, S. J. (1980). Changing reinforcing events: An approach to the treatment of depression. *Psychotherapy: Theory, Research & Practice, 17*(3), 322–334. http://doi.org/10.1037/h0085929

Linehan, M. M. (2015). *DBT skills training manual* (2nd ed.). Guilford Press.

Lord, J., Hook, M., Alkhateeb, S., & English, S. J. (2008). *Spiritually sensitive caregiving: A multi-faith handbook*. Compassion Books.

Maciejewski, P. K., Zhang, B., Block, S. D., & Prigerson, H. G. (2007). An empirical examination of the stage theory of grief. *JAMA, 297*(7), 716–723. http://doi.org/10.1001/jama.297.7.716

MacKinnon, M., & Murray, S. (2018). Reframing physician burnout as an organizational problem: A novel pragmatic approach to physician burnout. *Academic Psychiatry, 42*(1), 123–128. http://doi.org/10.1007/s40596-017-0689-1

Mancini, A. D., Prati, G., & Black, S. (2011). Self-worth mediates the effects of violent loss on PTSD symptoms. *Journal of Traumatic Stress, 24*(1), 116–120. http://doi.org/10.1002/jts.20597

Masferrer, L., Garre-Olmo, J., & Caparrós, B. (2017). Is complicated grief a risk factor for substance use? A comparison of substance-users and normative grievers. *Addiction Research & Theory, 25*(5), 361–367.

Maslach, C., & Leiter, M. P. (1997). *The truth about burnout: How organizations cause personal stress and what to do about it*. Jossey-Bass.

Mason, T. M., Tofthagen, C. S., & Buck, H. G. (2020). Complicated grief: Risk factors, protective factors, and interventions. *Journal of Social Work in End-of-Life & Palliative Care, 16*(2), 151–174. http://doi.org/10.1080/15524256.2020.1745726

McCann, I. L., & Pearlman, L. A. (1990). Vicarious traumatization: A framework for understanding the psychological effects of working with victims. *Journal of Traumatic Stress, 3*(1), 131–149. http://doi.org/10.1007/BF00975140

McDevitt-Murphy, M. E., Neimeyer, R. A., Burke, L. A., Williams, J. L., & Lawson, K. (2012). The toll of traumatic loss in African Americans bereaved by homicide. *Psychological Trauma: Theory, Research, Practice, and Policy, 4*(3), 303–311. http://doi.org/10.1037/a0024911

McGann, V. L., Sands, D. C., & Gutin, N. (2021). Grief following suicide. In H. L. Servaty-Seib & H. S. Chapple (Eds.), *Handbook of thanatology* (3rd ed., pp. 362–387). Association for Death Education and Counseling.

Merriman, J. (2015). Enhancing counselor supervision through compassion fatigue education. *Journal of Counseling & Development, 93*(3), 370–378. http://doi.org/10.1002/jcad.12035

Miller, B., & Sprang, G. (2017). A components-based practice and supervision model for reducing compassion fatigue by affecting clinician experience. *Traumatology, 23*(2), 153–164. http://doi.org/10.1037/trm0000058

Monk, T. H., Houck, P. R., & Shear, M. K. (2006). The daily life of complicated grief patients--what gets missed, what gets added? *Death Studies, 30*(1), 77–85. http://doi.org/10.1080/07481180500348860

Moore, S. A., Zoellner, L. A., & Mollenholt, N. (2008). Are expressive suppression and cognitive reappraisal associated with stress-related symptoms?. *Behaviour Research and Therapy, 46*(9), 993–1000. http://doi.org/10.1016/j.brat.2008.05.001

Naht Hahn, T. (1996). *The miracle of mindfulness: An introduction to the practice of meditation*. Beacon Press.

Naht Hahn, T. (2010). *You are here: Discovering the magic of the present moment*. Shambhala.

Neimeyer, R. A. (2012). The life imprint. In R. A. Neimeyer (Ed.), *Techniques of grief therapy* (pp. 274–276). Routledge.

Neimeyer, R. A. (2019). Meaning reconstruction in bereavement: Development of a research program. *Death Studies, 43*(2), 79–91. http://doi.org/10.1080/07481187.2018.1456620

Neimeyer, R. A. (2023). Grief therapy as a quest for meaning. In E. M. Steffen, E. Milman, & R. A. Neimeyer (Eds.), *Handbook of grief therapies* (pp. 53–68). Sage.

Neimeyer, R. A., Baldwin, S. A., & Gillies, J. (2006). Continuing bonds and reconstructing meaning: Mitigating complications in bereavement. *Death Studies, 30*(8), 715–738. http://doi.org/10.1080/07481180600848322

Neimeyer, R. A., & Rynearson, E. (T.) (2022). From retelling to reintegration: Narrative fixation and the reconstruction of meaning. In L. A. Burke & E. K. Rynearson (Eds.), *The restorative nature of ongoing connections with the deceased: Exploring presence within absence* (pp. 95–110). Routledge.

O'Connor, M., Piet, J., & Hougaard, E. (2014). The effects of mindfulness-based cognitive therapy on depressive symptoms in elderly bereaved people with loss-related distress: A controlled pilot study. *Mindfulness, 5*(4), 400–409. http://doi.org/10.1007/s12671-013-0194-x

O'Connor, M.-F., & Sussman, T. J. (2014). Developing the yearning in situations of loss scale: Convergent and discriminant validity for bereavement, romantic breakup, and homesickness. *Death Studies, 38*(7), 450–458. http://doi.org/10.1080/07481187.2013.782928

Orcutt, H. K., Reffi, A. N., & Ellis, R. A. (2020). Experiential avoidance and PTSD. In M. T. Tull & N. A. Kimbrel (Eds.), *Emotion in posttraumatic stress disorder: Etiology, assessment, neurobiology, and treatment* (pp. 409–436). Elsevier Academic Press. http://doi.org/10.1016/B978-0-12-816022-0.00014-4

Papa, A., Rummel, C., Garrison-Diehn, C., & Sewell, M. T. (2013). Behavioral activation for pathological grief. *Death Studies, 37*(10), 913–936. http://doi.org/10.1080/07481187.2012.692459

Papa, A., Sewell, M. T., Garrison-Diehn, C., & Rummel, C. (2013). A randomized open trial assessing the feasibility of behavioral activation for pathological grief responding. *Behavior Therapy, 44*(4), 639–650. http://doi.org/10.1016/j.beth.2013.04.009

Parkes, C. M. (2009) *Love and loss: The roots of grief and its complications.* Routledge.

Patsiopoulos, A. T., & Buchanan, M. J. (2011). The practice of self-compassion in counseling: A narrative inquiry. *Professional Psychology: Research and Practice, 42*(4), 301–307. http://doi.org/10.1037/a0024482

Pearlman, L. A., & Mac Ian, P. S. (1995). Vicarious traumatization: An empirical study of the effects of trauma work on trauma therapists. *Professional Psychology: Research and Practice, 26*(6), 558–565. http://doi.org/10.1037/0735-7028.26.6.558

Pompoli, A., Furukawa, T. A., Efthimiou, O., Imai, H., Tajika, A., & Salanti, G. (2018). Dismantling cognitive-behaviour therapy for panic disorder: A systematic review and component network meta-analysis. *Psychological Medicine, 48*(12), 1945–1953. http://doi.org/10.1017/S0033291717003919

Posluns, K., & Gall, T. L. (2020). Dear mental health practitioners, take care of yourselves: A literature review on self-care. *International Journal for the Advancement of Counselling, 42*(1), 1–20. http://doi.org/10.1007/s10447-019-09382-w

Powers, M. B., Halpern, J. M., Ferenschak, M. P., Gillihan, S. J., & Foa, E. B. (2010). A meta-analytic review of prolonged exposure for posttraumatic stress disorder. *Clinical Psychology Review, 30*(6), 635–641. http://doi.org/10.1016/j.cpr.2010.04.007

Price, M., Lancaster, C. L., Gros, D. F., Legrand, A. C., van Stolk-Cooke, K., & Acierno, R. (2018). An examination of social support and PTSD treatment response during prolonged exposure. *Psychiatry, 81*(3), 258–270. http://doi.org/10.1080/00332747.2017.1402569

Prigerson, H. G., Boelen, P. A., Xu, J., Smith, K. V., & Maciejewski, P. K. (2021). Validation of the new DSM-5-TR criteria for prolonged grief disorder and the PG-13-Revised (PG-13-R) scale. *World Psychiatry, 20*(1), 96–106. http://doi.org/10.1002/wps.20823

Redmond, L.M. (1989). *Surviving: When someone you love was murdered: A professional guide to group grief therapy or families and friends of murder victims.* Psychological Consultations and Educational Services.

Resick, P. A., Galovski, T. E., Uhlmansiek, M. O., Scher, C. D., Clum, G. A., & Young-Xu, Y. (2008). A randomized clinical trial to dismantle components of cognitive processing therapy for posttraumatic stress disorder in female victims of interpersonal violence. *Journal of Consulting and Clinical Psychology, 76*(2), 243–258. http://doi.org/10.1037/0022-006X.76.2.243

Resick, P. A., Monson, C. M., & Chard, K. M. (2017). *Cognitive processing therapy for PTSD: A comprehensive manual.* Guilford Press.

Rheingold, A. A., Baddeley, J. L., Williams, J. L., Brown, C., Wallace, M. M., Correa, F., & Rynearson, E. K. (2015). Restorative retelling for violent death: An investigation of treatment effectiveness, influencing factors, and durability. *Journal of Loss and Trauma, 20*(6), 541–555. http://doi.org/10.1080/15325024.2014.957602

References

Rheingold, A. A., & Williams, J. L. (2015). Survivors of homicide: Mental health outcomes, social support, and service use among a community-based sample. *Violence and Victims*, 30(5), 870–883. http://doi.org/10.1891/0886-6708.VV-D-14-00026

Rheingold, A. A., & Williams, J. L. (2018). Module-based comprehensive approach for addressing heterogeneous mental health sequelae of violent loss survivors. *Death Studies*, 42(3), 164–171. http://doi.org/10.1080/07481187.2017.1370798

Rheingold, A. A., Williams, J. L., & Bottomley, J. S. (2024). Prevalence and co-occurrence of psychiatric conditions among bereaved adults. *JAMA Network Open*, 7(6), e2415325. http://doi.org/10.1001/jamanetworkopen.2024.15325

Roberts, B. K., Nofi, C. P., Cornell, E., Kapoor, S., Harrison, L., & Sathya, C. (2023). Trends and disparities in firearm deaths among children. *Pediatrics*, 152(3), e2023061296. http://doi.org/10.1542/peds.2023-061296

Root, B. L., & Exline, J. J. (2014). The role of continuing bonds in coping with grief: Overview and future directions. *Death Studies*, 38(1), 1–8. http://doi.org/10.1080/07481187.2012.712608

Rosenbloom, D. J., Pratt, A. C., & Pearlman, L. A. (1999). Helpers' responses to trauma work: Understanding and intervening in an organization. In B. H. Stamm (Ed.), *Secondary traumatic stress: Self-care issues for clinicians, researchers, and educators* (2nd ed., pp. 65–79). Sidran Press.

Rosner, R., Pfoh, G., & Kotoučová, M. (2011). Treatment of complicated grief. *European Journal of Psychotraumatology*, 2(1), 7995. http://doi.org/10.3402/ejpt.v2i0.7995

Rynearson, E. K. (2001). *Retelling violent death*. Routledge.

Rynearson, E. K. (2012). The narrative dynamics of grief after homicide. *OMEGA - Journal of Death and Dying*, 65(3), 239–249. http://doi.org/10.2190/OM.65.3.f

Rynearson, E. K., & Correa, F. (2008). *Accommodation to violent dying: A guide to restorative retelling and support*. Violent Death Bereavement Society. http://www.ojp.gov/ncjrs/virtual-library/abstracts/accommodation-violent-dying-guide-restorative-retelling-and-support

Rynearson, E. K., Correa, F., Favell, J., Saindon, C., & Prigerson, H. (2006). Restorative retelling after violent dying. In E. K. Rynearson (Ed.), *Violent death: Resilience and intervention beyond crisis* (pp. 195–216). Routledge. http://doi.org/10.4324/9780203961469-13

Rynearson, E. K., Correa, F., & Takacs, L. (2015). *Accommodation to violent dying: A guide to restorative retelling and support* (4th rev.). Virginia Mason Medical Center.

Saindon, C., Rheingold, A. A., Baddeley, J., Wallace, M. M., Brown, C., & Rynearson, E. K. (2014). Restorative retelling for violent loss: An open clinical trial. *Death Studies*, 38(4), 251–258. http://doi.org/10.1080/07481187.2013.783654

Saltzman, W., Layne, C. M., Pynoos, R., Olafson, E., Kaplow, J., & Boat, B. (2017). *Trauma and grief component therapy for adolescents: A modular approach to treating traumatized and bereaved youth*. Cambridge University Press.

Sapienza, B. G., & Bugental, J. F. T. (2000). Keeping our instruments finely tuned: An existential–humanistic perspective. *Professional Psychology: Research and Practice*, 31(4), 458–460. http://doi.org/10.1037/0735-7028.31.4.458

Schauben, L. J., & Frazier, P. A. (1995). Vicarious trauma: The effects on female counselors of working with sexual violence survivors. *Psychology of Women Quarterly*, 19(1), 49–64. http://doi.org/10.1111/j.1471-6402.1995.tb00278.x

Shear, M. K., Frank, E., Houck, P. R., & Reynolds, C. F. (2005). Treatment of complicated grief: A randomized controlled trial. *JAMA*, 293(21), 2601–2608. http://doi.org/10.1001/jama.293.21.2601

Shear, M. K., Jackson, C. T., Essock, S. M., Donahue, S. A., & Felton, C. J. (2006). Screening for complicated grief among Project Liberty service recipients 18 months after September 11, 2001. *Psychiatric Services*, 57(9), 1291–1297. http://doi.org/10.1176/ps.2006.57.9.1291

Shear, M. K., & Mulhare, E. (2008). Complicated grief. *Psychiatric Annals*, 38(10), 662–670. http://doi.org/10.3928/00485713-20081001-10

Simon, N. M., Hoeppner, S. S., Lubin, R. E., Robinaugh, D. J., Malgaroli, M., Norman, S. B., Acierno, R., Goetter, E. M., Hellberg, S. N., Charney, M. E., Bui, E., Baker, A. W., Smith, E., Kim, H. M., & Rauch, S. A. M. (2020). Understanding the impact of complicated grief on combat related posttraumatic stress disorder, guilt, suicide, and functional impairment in a clinical trial of post-9/11 service members and veterans. *Depression and Anxiety, 37*(1), 63–72. http://doi.org/10.1002/da.22911

Skovholt, T. M., Grier, T. L., & Hanson, M. R. (2001). Career counseling for longevity: Self-care and burnout prevention strategies for counselor resilience. *Journal of Career Development, 27*(3), 167–176. http://doi.org/10.1177/08948453010270030

Skovholt, T. M., & Trotter-Mathison, M. (2010). *The resilient practitioner: Burnout prevention and self-care strategies for counselors, therapists, teachers, and health professionals* (2nd ed.). Routledge. http://doi.org/10.4324/9780203893326

Smid, G. E., Groen, S., de la Rie, S. M., Kooper, S., & Boelen, P. A. (2018). Toward cultural assessment of grief and grief-related psychopathology. *Psychiatric Services, 69*(10), 1050–1052. http://doi.org/10.1176/appi.ps.201700422

Smith, A. J., Abeyta, A. A., Hughes, M., & Jones, R. T. (2015). Persistent grief in the aftermath of mass violence: The predictive roles of posttraumatic stress symptoms, self-efficacy, and disrupted worldview. *Psychological Trauma: Theory, Research, Practice, and Policy, 7*(2), 179–186. http://doi.org/10.1037/tra0000002

Smith, P. L., & Moss, S. B. (2009). Psychologist impairment: What is it, how can it be prevented, and what can be done to address it? *Clinical Psychology: Science and Practice, 16*(1), 1–15. http://doi.org/10.1111/j.1468-2850.2009.01137.x

Sobczak, L. R., & West, L. M. (2013). Clinical considerations in using mindfulness- and acceptance-based approaches with diverse populations: Addressing challenges in service delivery in diverse community settings. *Cognitive and Behavioral Practice, 20*(1), 13–22. http://doi.org/10.1016/j.cbpra.2011.08.005

Soydas, S., Smid, G. E., Goodfellow, B., Wilson, R., & Boelen, P. A. (2019). Prevalence and predictors of psychiatric disorders in a large help-seeking sample of homicidally bereaved persons. *European Journal of Psychotraumatology, 10*(sup1), 11–12. http://doi.org/10.1080/20008198.2019.1613834

Stein, A. T., Carl, E., Cuijpers, P., Karyotaki, E., & Smits, J. A. J. (2021). Looking beyond depression: A meta-analysis of the effect of behavioral activation on depression, anxiety, and activation. *Psychological Medicine, 51*(9), 1491–1504. http://doi.org/10.1017/S0033291720000239

Stewart, A. E. (1999). Complicated bereavement and posttraumatic stress disorder following fatal car crashes: Recommendations for death notification practice. *Death Studies, 23*(4), 289–321. http://doi.org/10.1080/074811899200984

Stiegler, J. R., Binder, P.-E., Hjeltnes, A., Stige, S. H., & Schanche, E. (2018). 'It's heavy, intense, horrendous and nice': Clients' experiences in two-chair dialogues. *Person-Centered & Experiential Psychotherapies, 17*(2), 139–159. http://doi.org/10.1080/14779757.2018.1472138

Stotzer, R. L. (2009). Violence against transgender people: A review of United States data. *Aggression and Violent Behavior, 14*(3), 170–179. http://doi.org/10.1016/j.avb.2009.01.006

Stroebe, M., & Schut, H. (1999). The dual process model of coping with bereavement: Rationale and description. *Death Studies, 23*(3), 197–224. http://doi.org/10.1080/074811899201046

Stroebe, M., Schut, H., & Boerner, K. (2017). Cautioning health-care professionals: Bereaved persons are misguided through the stages of grief. *OMEGA - Journal of Death and Dying, 74*(4), 455–473. http://doi.org/10.1177/0030222817691870

Sun, J., Kang, J., Wang, P., & Zeng, H. (2013). Self-relaxation training can improve sleep quality and cognitive functions in the older: A one-year randomised controlled trial. *Journal of Clinical Nursing, 22*(9–10), 1270–1280. http://doi.org/10.1111/jocn.12096

Sutton, L., Rowe, S., Hammerton, G., & Billings, J. (2022). The contribution of organisational factors to vicarious trauma in mental health professionals: A systematic review and narrative synthesis. *European Journal of Psychotraumatology, 13*(1), 2022278. http://doi.org/10.1080/20008198.2021.2022278

Tal, I., Mauro, C., Reynolds, C. F., 3rd, Shear, M. K., Simon, N., Lebowitz, B., Skritskaya, N., Wang, Y., Qiu, X., Iglewicz, A., Glorioso, D., Avanzino, J., Wetherell, J. L., Karp, J. F., Robinaugh, D., & Zisook, S. (2017). Complicated grief after suicide bereavement and other causes of death. *Death Studies, 41*(5), 267–275. http://doi.org/10.1080/07481187.2016.1265028

Tarrier, N., & Humphreys, A.-L. (2004). PTSD and the social support of the interpersonal environment: The development of social cognitive behavior therapy. In S. Taylor (Ed.), *Advances in the treatment of posttraumatic stress disorder: Cognitive-behavioral perspectives* (pp. 113–127). Springer.

Taylor, D. J., & Pruiksma, K. E. (2014). Cognitive and behavioural therapy for insomnia (CBT-I) in psychiatric populations: A systematic review. *International Review of Psychiatry, 26*(2), 205–213. http://doi.org/10.3109/09540261.2014.902808

Thrasher, S., Power, M., Morant, N., Marks, I., & Dalgleish, T. (2010). Social support moderates outcome in a randomized controlled trial of exposure therapy and (or) cognitive restructuring for chronic posttraumatic stress disorder. *The Canadian Journal of Psychiatry, 55*(3), 187–190. http://doi.org/10.1177/070674371005500311

Titlestad, K. B., Kristensen, P., O'Connor, M., Hystad, S., & Dyregrov, K. (2022). Paths to positive growth in parents bereaved by drug-related death: A mixed-method study. *Frontiers in Psychology, 13*, 982667. http://doi.org/10.3389/fpsyg.2022.982667

Toussaint, L., Nguyen, Q. A., Roettger, C., Dixon, K., Offenbächer, M., Kohls, N., Hirsh, J., & Sirois, F. (2021). Effectiveness of progressive muscle relaxation, deep breathing, and guided imagery in promoting psychological and physiological states of relaxation. *Evidence-based Complementary and Alternative Medicine, 2021*, 5924040. http://doi.org/10.1155/2021/5924040

Tracy, E. M., & Whittaker, J. K. (1990). The social network map: Assessing social support in clinical practice. *Families in Society, 71*(8), 461-470. http://doi.org/10.1177/104438949007100802

Turner, R. J., & Brown, R. L. (2010). Social support and mental health. In T. L. Scheid & T. N. Brown (Eds.), *A handbook for the study of mental health: Social contexts, theories, and systems* (pp. 200–212). Cambridge University Press.

Tursi, M. F. de S., Baes, C. von W., Camacho, F. R. de B., Tofoli, S. M. de C., & Juruena, M. F. (2013). Effectiveness of psychoeducation for depression: A systematic review. *The Australian and New Zealand Journal of Psychiatry, 47*(11), 1019–1031. http://doi.org/10.1177/0004867413491154

Tyler, J. M., Darrow, N. E. T., Outlaw, A. B., & Guffin, J. P. (2023). Lived experiences of utilizing cultural resiliency to navigate traumatic loss. *Journal of Counseling & Development, 101*(2), 180–192. http://doi.org/10.1002/jcad.12462

van Denderen, M., de Keijser, J., Huisman, M., & Boelen, P. A. (2016). Prevalence and correlates of self-rated posttraumatic stress disorder and complicated grief in a community-based sample of homicidally bereaved individuals. *Journal of Interpersonal Violence, 31*(2), 207–227. http://doi.org/10.1177/0886260514555368

Varela, R. E., & Hensley-Maloney, L. (2009). The influence of culture on anxiety in Latino youth: A review. *Clinical Child and Family Psychology Review, 12*(3), 217–233. http://doi.org/10.1007/s10567-009-0044-5

Vergara-Lopez, C., & Roberts, J. E. (2015). An application of behavioral activation therapy for major depressive disorder in the context of complicated grief, low social-economic status, and ethnic minority status. *Clinical Case Studies, 14*(4), 247–261. http://doi.org/10.1177/1534650115593847

Walsh, J. (2010). *Psychoeducation in mental health*. Oxford University Press.

Wang, Y., Chung, M. C., Wang, N., Yu, X., & Kenardy, J. (2021). Social support and posttraumatic stress disorder: A meta-analysis of longitudinal studies. *Clinical Psychology Review, 85*, 101998. http://doi.org/10.1016/j.cpr.2021.101998

Waters, E., Bond, C. & Eriksson, L. (2017). Examining the accuracy of print media representations of homicide in Australia. *Current Issues in Criminal Justice, 29*(2), 137–153. http://doi.org/10.1080/10345329.2017.12036092

Waters, E., & Cummings, E. M. (2000). A secure base from which to explore close relationships. *Child Development, 71*(1), 164–172. http://doi.org/10.1111/1467-8624.00130

Weathers, F. W., Bovin, M. J., Lee, D. J., Sloan, D. M., Schnurr, P. P., Kaloupek, D. G., Keane, T. M., & Marx, B. P. (2018). The Clinician-Administered PTSD Scale for DSM–5 (CAPS-5): Development and initial psychometric evaluation in military veterans. *Psychological Assessment, 30*(3), 383–395. http://doi.org/10.1037/pas0000486

Wen, F. H., Prigerson, H. G., Chou, W.-C., Huang, C.-C., Hu, T.-H., Chiang, M. C., Chuang, L.-P., & Tang, S. T. (2023). Comorbid prolonged grief, PTSD, and depression trajectories for bereaved family surrogates. *JAMA Network Open, 6*(11), e2342675. http://doi.org/10.1001/jamanetworkopen.2023.42675

White, M. (1988). *Saying hullo again: The incorporation of the lost relationship in the resolution of grief.* Dulwich Centre Publications.

Whitworth J. D. (2016). The role of psychoeducation in trauma recovery: Recommendations for content and delivery. *Journal of Evidence-Informed Social Work, 13*(5), 442–451. http://doi.org/10.1080/23761407.2016.1166852

Wilkins, N. J., Zhang, X., Mack, K. A., Clapperton, A. J., Macpherson, A., Sleet, D., Kresnow-Sedacca, M.-J., Ballesteros, M. F., Newton, D., Murdoch, J., Mackay, J. M., Berecki-Gisolf, J., Marr, A., Armstead, T., & McClure, R. (2019). Societal determinants of violent death: The extent to which social, economic, and structural characteristics explain differences in violence across Australia, Canada, and the United States. *SSM - Population Health, 8,* 100431. http://doi.org/10.1016/j.ssmph.2019.100431

Williams, J. L., Eddinger, J. R., Rynearson, E. K., & Rheingold, A. A. (2018). Prevalence and correlates of suicidal ideation in a treatment-seeking sample of violent loss survivors. *Crisis, 39*(5), 377385. http://doi.org/10.1027/0227-5910/a000520

Williams, J. L., Hardt, M. M., Henschel, A. V., Jamison, J. R., Brymer, M. J., & Rheingold, A. A. (2024). An open trial of skills for psychological recovery for sudden loss survivors. *Cognitive and Behavioral Practice, 31*(1), 58–71. http://doi.org/10.1016/j.cbpra.2022.06.003

Williams, J. L., Hardt, M. M., Milman, E., Rheingold, A. A., & Rynearson, E. K. (2022). Development and psychometric validation of the Dying Imagery Scale-Revised. *Death Studies, 46*(5), 1243–1252. http://doi.org/10.1080/07481187.2020.1812135

Williams, J. L., & Rheingold, A. A. (2020). Novel application of skills for psychological recovery as an early intervention for violent loss: Rationale and case examples. *OMEGA - Journal of Death and Dying, 81*(2), 179–196. http://doi.org/10.1177/0030222818766138

Williams, J .L., Rheingold, A. A., McNallan, L. J., & Knowlton, A. W. (2018). Survivors' perspectives on a modular approach to traumatic grief treatment. *Death Studies, 42*(3), 155–163. http://doi.org/10.1080/07481187.2017.1370796

Williams, M. T., Malcoun, E., Sawyer, B. A., Davis, D. M., Nouri, L. B., & Bruce, S. L. (2014). Cultural adaptations of prolonged exposure therapy for treatment and prevention of posttraumatic stress disorder in African Americans. *Behavioral Sciences, 4*(2), 102–124. http://doi.org/10.3390/bs4020102

Wityk, T. L. (2003). Burnout and the ethics of self-care for therapists. *Alberta Counsellor, 28*(1), 4-11.

World Health Organization. (2024). *Injuries and violence* [Fact sheet]. http://www.who.int/news-room/fact-sheets/detail/injuries-and-violence

Yang, X., Xu, Y., Tan, R., & Zhou, X. (2022). Event centrality and post-traumatic stress symptoms among college students during the COVID-19 pandemic: The roles of attention to negative information, catastrophizing, and rumination. *European Journal of Psychotraumatology, 13*(1), 2078563. http://doi.org/10.1080/20008198.2022.2078563

Young, L. J & Xiang, H. (2022). US racial and sex-based disparities in firearm-related death trends from 1981–2020. *PLoS One, 17*(12), e0278304. http://doi.org/10.1371/journal.pone.0278304

Zalta, A. K., Tirone, V., Orlowska, D., Blais, R. K., Lofgreen, A., Klassen, B., Held, P., Stevens, N. R., Adkins, E., & Dent, A. L. (2021). Examining moderators of the relationship between social support and self-reported PTSD symptoms: A meta-analysis. *Psychological Bulletin, 147*(1), 33–54. http://doi.org/10.1037/bul0000316

Zhu, H., Xie, S., Liu, X., Yang, X., & Zhou, J. (2022). Influencing factors of burnout and its dimensions among mental health workers during the COVID-19 pandemic. *Nursing Open, 9*(4), 2013–2023. http://doi.org/10.1002/nop2.1211

Zisook, S., & Shear, K. (2009). Grief and bereavement: What psychiatrists need to know. *World Psychiatry, 8*(2), 67–74. http://doi.org/10.1002/j.2051-5545.2009.tb00217.x

Zuckoff, A., Shear, K., Frank, E., Daley, D. C., Seligman, K., & Silowash, R. (2006). Treating complicated grief and substance use disorders: A pilot study. *Journal of Substance Abuse Treatment, 30*(3), 205–211. http://doi.org/10.1016/j.jsat.2005.12.001

Index

A

acceptance, 17; commemorative-imagery strategies, 119; death-imagery approach, 136; education on role of avoidance, 129; exposure techniques, 127, 129, 136, 144; introducing concept of, 90–91; Kübler-Ross's stages of grief, 10; loss from unintentional injuries, 38–39; problematic relationships, 120; self-care for providers, 164; support networks, 96; timing of treatment, 24. See also module 4

acceptance and commitment therapy (ACT), 79, 90

Accountable Health Communities Health-Related Social Needs Screen Tool (AHC HRSN), 35

activity-tracking worksheets, 105, 107–110; assigning, 107, 109; reassigning, 110; reviewing, 108, 110; values-based activities, 109

ADDRESSING model, 27–28

afterlife, belief in, 8, 125

AHC HRSN (Accountable Health Communities Health-Related Social Needs Screen Tool), 35

American Foundation for Suicide Prevention (AFSP), 99

anger, 42, 44–45; acceptance of, 90; case example, 147, 150; "hello again" letters, 122; Kübler-Ross's stages of grief, 10; primary versus secondary emotions, 58–59; relaxation strategies, 79, 81; traumatic loss from intentional injuries, 37; traumatic loss from unintentional injuries, 38; unanswered questions surrounding loss, 27

anniversaries, coping with, 153, 155

appraisal support, 98–99, 101

approach concept and activities, 16; case example, 152–153; exposure techniques, 133–135, 137, 139, 142

Ask Suicide-Screening Questions (ASQ) Toolkit, 30

assertiveness skills, 101

attachment bonds, revision of, 113–125; to-be-maintained or relinquished aspects of relationships, 119–120; commemorative-imagery strategies, 117–119; felt security, 113; "hello again" letters, 120–122; human hardwiring for, 113; impact of deceased's life, 114; messages of moving on or letting go, 114;

problematic relationships, 114, 119–120, 122; rationale for revising, 116; response letters, 122–123

avoidance (avoidant coping), 129–131; acceptance, 90–91; action hierarchy of avoided trauma and loss cues, 134; approach concept, 16, 31; approach-based coping versus, 16–17; case example, 148, 152; client avoidance, 144; clinician avoidance, 144; cognitive behavioral triangle, 63; cultural considerations, 91–92; dual process model of bereavement, 6; early interventions, 32; emotion management, 78–79; grief-related, 13; "hello again" letters, 122; loss-oriented coping, 7; multidimensional grief theory, 9; post-traumatic stress, 10, 28; prolonged grief, 13; psychoeducation, 40–41, 45–49, 51; resiliency strategies, 75–76; safety concerns versus, 111; secondary emotions, 59; self-care for providers, 161. See also Therapeutic Exposure

B

bargaining, 10

behavioral activation. See Meaningful Behavioral Activation

bodily sensations (physical symptoms) of grief, 40, 43

Brief Grief Questionnaire (BGQ), 30

Building Healthy Support Networks (module 5), 94–112; communication challenges, 101; content and selection parameters, 23; cultural considerations, 102; education about kinds of social support, 98; exploring supportive relationships, 98–100; handouts, 96; multiple traumatic losses, 154; overview, 94–95; presentation appropriateness, 95; rationale for, 96–97; session agenda, 95; social support engagement plans, 100–101; social support mapping, 98–100; special days, holidays, and anniversaries, 155; summary of, 21

burnout, 159, 165

C

CAPS-5 (Clinician-Administered PTSD Scale for DSM-5) assessment, 29

Caringi, J. C., 163

chair work, 123

Charney, D. S., 71

circumstance-related distress, 8

cliché supportive phrases, 156
client avoidance, 144
clinical supervision, 165–166
Clinician-Administered PTSD Scale for DSM-5 (CAPS-5) assessment, 29
clinicians: clinician avoidance, 144; defined, 2; self-care, 158–166; treatment-planning flowchart for, 36
cognitive behavioral triangle, 62–64, 149
cognitive flexibility, 71, 162
cognitive processing therapy (CPT), 18
cognitive reappraisal, 162
cognitive symptoms of grief, 43
commemorative-imagery strategies, 115, 117–120; introducing, 117–119; reviewing, 119; revisiting, 123–124
communication, challenges to, 101
compassion fatigue, 159, 165
complicated spiritual grief, 77
conscious oversight, 166
consultation strategies, 165–166
CPT (cognitive processing therapy), 18
Cultural Bereavement Interview, 28
cultural considerations: behavioral activation, 111; emotion identification and thought processing, 69–70; emotion management, 91–92; psychoeducation, 52–53; revising bonds, 125; strengths identification and building, 77; support networks, 102; therapeutic exposure, 145–146

D

DBT (dialectical behavior therapy), 79
death-imagery approach, 135–144; case example, 152–153; conducting in session, 139–141; cultural considerations, 145–146; focusing on hot spots, 143; listening to imaginal recording, 142–143; rationale for, 135–139; restorative processing and retelling, 141–143; shaken soda bottle analogy, 138; splinter analogy, 137–138; tips for conducting, 141
deep breathing exercises, 79, 81–85, 149–150
denial, 10, 45–46
depression: behavioral activation, 104; co-occurrence with PTSD and PGD, 14–15; exposure techniques, 127; Kübler-Ross's stages of grief, 10; major, 22–23, 29, 31–32, 36, 103–104; mindfulness, 79; overview, 11–12; pretreatment assessment of, 29–30; social support and, 95; timing of treatment, 33; treatment rationale, 17–18
dialectical behavior therapy (DBT), 79
differentiation, 136
discrimination: death-imagery approach, 145–146; emotion identification and thought processing,

70; emotion management, 91. See also cultural considerations
DIS-R (Dying Imagery Scale-Revised), 34
distressing thoughts and emotions, 17. See also Identifying Emotions and Processing Thoughts; Managing Strong Emotions
doggie paddle metaphor, 86
dual process model of bereavement (DPM), 6–7, 9, 45
Dying Imagery Scale-Revised (DIS-R), 34

E

emotion identification. See Identifying Emotions and Processing Thoughts
emotion regulation. See Managing Strong Emotions
emotional processing, 18, 127, 136
emotional support, 94, 98–99, 101
empty-chair techniques, 123
engagement: behavioral activation, 106–107; exposure techniques, 144–145; self-care for providers, 161; social support engagement plans, 100–102
Ennis, N., 30
existential/identity-related distress, 8–9
exposure techniques. See Therapeutic Exposure

F

felt security, 113
flexibility: cognitive, 71, 162; self-care for providers, 162, 165
Freud, Sigmund, 113
fun, functional, and fulfilling activities, 107–101

G

GCQ (Grief Cognitions Questionnaire), 35
GRAQ (Grief-Related Avoidance Questionnaire), 35
GRIEF (Grief Recovery with Individualized Evidence-Based Formulation) Approach, 19; case example, 146–153; finishing treatment and looking ahead, 156–157; lessons learned from survivors, 156; modules and sessions, 20–23; overview, 16–17; rationale, 17–19; timing for, 24–25; treatment development, 19–20. See also *names of specific modules*
Grief Cognitions Questionnaire (GCQ), 35
grief cues, 60
grief reminders, 60
grief symptoms, 32–33, 43
Grief-Related Avoidance Questionnaire (GRAQ), 35
guilt: case example, 149, 152–154; depression and, 12; emotion identification and thought processing, 58–61, 65, 67; exposure techniques, 127; revising bonds, 120–121; traumatic loss from intentional injuries, 37, 44;

Index

traumatic loss from unintentional injuries, 38, 44

H

habituation, 127, 132–136, 140, 142–143, 145, 152

handouts: Activities Calendar, 105, 109; Activity Schedule, 105–106; Additional Assessment Questions for Clinicians, 27; Approach with Action Recording Form, 129, 135, 139, 142, 152; Cognitive Behavioral Triangle and Thought Identification, 56, 66, 149; Deep Breathing Recording Form, 81, 83; downloading, 17; Dual Process Model of Grief, 42, 45; Education About Avoidance and Approaching Trauma and Loss Reminders, 129, 132; Emotion Education, 56, 59; Emotion Identification, 56, 60, 149; "Hello Again" Letter Activity, 116, 120; Hierarchy List of Trauma and Loss Reminders, 129, 134, 152; Imaginal Recording Form, 129, 142, 153; Instructions for Deep Breathing, 81, 83; Instructions for Mindfulness, 81, 89; Instructions for Progressive Muscle Relaxation, 81, 84; Life Imprint Activity, 116, 119, 151; List of Commonly Noted Strengths and Coping Strategies, 72, 74; Mindfulness Recording Form, 81, 89, 91; Mood and Thought Tracking with Helpful Thought Identification, 56, 69, 149–150; Mood Log, 56, 61, 149; My Strengths, 72, 74, 150; Overview of GRIEF Approach, 42, 50; Progressive Muscle Relaxation Recording Form, 81, 84; Response Letter Activity, 116, 122, 151; Revising Connections, 116, 124; Social Support Engagement Plan, 96, 100; Social Support Map, 96, 98; Summary of Depression Symptoms, 42, 48; Summary of Post-Traumatic Stress Symptoms, 42, 48; Summary of Prolonged Grief Symptoms, 42, 48; Types of Behavioral Activities, 105–106; Types of Social Support, 96, 98; Valued Activities, 105, 109; What Makes Traumatic Loss Different? 42–43

harmonious balance (work-life balance), 164–165

healthy support networks. See Building Healthy Support Networks

"hello again" letters, 120–122; case example, 151; introducing and assigning, 120–121; response letters, 122–123; reviewing, 122; set and setting, 121

helpful thoughts, 53; case example, 149–150; education about, 66–67; examples of, 67–68; identifying, 68–69; mood and thought tracking and, 69. See also Identifying Emotions and Processing Thoughts

holidays, coping with, 124, 155

homicide: firearm incidents, 3, 5; PTSD among survivors, 8; social justice, 8; special populations, 154–155; specific reactions associated with, 44, 52; traumatic loss from, 37

hot spots, in death-imagery approach, 143–144, 153

I

Iacoviello, B. M., 71

Identifying and Building Strengths (module 3), 71–77; assessing strengths, 73–74; assigning resilience strategies, 74–77; case example, 150; content and selection parameters, 22; cultural considerations, 77; overview, 71–72; past coping strategies, 74; presentation appropriateness, 72; problem solving barriers to, 76; session agendas, 72; summary of, 21

Identifying Emotions and Processing Thoughts (module 2), 54–70; case example, 149–150; cognitive behavioral triangle, 62–64; content and selection parameters, 22; cultural considerations, 69–70; educating clients about grief emotions, 57–61; handouts, 56; helpful thoughts, 66–69; justice system involvement, 154–155; mood tracking, 61–62, 66; multiple traumatic losses, 154; overview, 54–55; presentation appropriateness, 55; rationale for, 57; reframing and helpful responses, 68; session agendas, 55–56; special days, holidays, and anniversaries, 155; summary of, 21; thought tracking, 66; unhelpful thoughts, 65–66

imaginal exposure and approaches: death-imagery approach, 135–144; "hello again" letters, 120–123; imaginal recordings, 142–143; restorative processing and retelling, 141–143. See also Therapeutic Exposure

increased mastery concept, 136

informational support, 98

instrumental support, 94, 98–99, 101

intentional injuries, 2–3, 5–6, 8, 37–38

isolation, 94–96, 106, 155. See also Building Healthy Support Networks

J

Jacobson, Edmund, 79

justice system involvement, 44–45, 154–155

K

Kabat-Zinn, Jon, 85

Kübler-Ross, Elisabeth, 10

L

Leaves on a Stream guided meditation, 89–91

Lejuez, C. W., 108

life-imprint activities, 119

loneliness, 11, 13, 60, 95–96, 101

183

Lord, Janice, 70
loss-oriented coping, 6–7, 9

M

major depressive disorder (MDD): behavioral activation, 103–104; module content and, 22–23; symptoms of, 29; treatment planning, 31–32, 36. See also depression
maladaptive cognitions, 54
Managing Strong Emotions (module 4), 78–93; acceptance, 90–91; case example, 150; clinician scripts, 81; content and selection parameters, 23; cultural considerations, 91–92; deep breathing exercises, 82–83; handouts, 81; justice system involvement, 155; mindfulness, 85–91; overview, 78–79; presentation appropriateness, 79; problem solving barriers to, 84–85; progressive muscle relaxation, 83–84; relaxation strategies, 81–85; session agendas, 80; special days, holidays, and anniversaries, 155; summary of, 21
mass violence incidents, 154–155
MBCT (mindfulness-based cognitive therapy), 79
MBSR (mindfulness-based stress reduction), 79
MDD. See depression; major depressive disorder
meaning and purpose, 17; harmonious balance, 165; meaning reconstruction model of bereavement, 7–8; timing of treatment, 24. See also Meaningful Behavioral Activation
meaning reconstruction model of bereavement, 7–8
Meaningful Behavioral Activation (module 6), 103–112; activity-tracking, 107–108, 110–111; content and selection parameters, 23; cultural considerations, 111; education about activities, 106; fun, functional, and fulfilling activities, 107–101; goal of, 107; handouts, 105; overview, 103–104; personal values across life domains, 108–110; presentation appropriateness, 104; problem-solving barriers to, 108, 110; rationale for, 105–107; session agenda, 104–105; summary of, 21; values-consistent activities, 109–111
mental health complications of traumatic loss, 10–15; co-occurrence of mental health problems, 14–15; depression, 11–12; post-traumatic stress, 10–11; prolonged grief, 12–13
Miller, B., 166
mindful breathing, 87–89, 91
mindfulness, 39, 78–79, 85–91; acceptance, 90–91; books on, 93; case example, 150–151; components of, 86; cultural considerations, 91–92; in daily living, 88–89; education about, 85–86, 88–89; guided meditation, 89–90; mobile apps, 93; online resources, 93; practicing, 86–90; self-care for providers, 144,

161–162, 164–165. See also Managing Strong Emotions
mindfulness-based cognitive therapy (MBCT), 79
mindfulness-based stress reduction (MBSR), 79
module 1. See Psychoeducation About Grief, Types of Loss, and Traumatic Loss Reactions
module 2. See Identifying Emotions and Processing Thoughts
module 3. See Identifying and Building Strengths
module 4. See Managing Strong Emotions
module 5. See Building Healthy Support Networks
module 6. See Meaningful Behavioral Activation
module 7. See Revising Bonds
module 8. See Therapeutic Exposure
mood tracking, 61–62, 66, 107
motivational interviewing, 31, 131
multidimensional grief theory, 8–9
multiple traumatic losses, 154

N

narrative books, 140
narrative model of traumatic dying, 7–8
National Center for PTSD, 33
National Child Traumatic Stress Network, 33
National Institute of Mental Health, 30
National Mass Violence Center, 155
natural loss, traumatic loss versus, 44
Neimeyer, R. A., 7

O

open-ended questions: death-imagery approach, 141–142; pretreatment assessment, 27; values-consistent activities, 109
overdose-related deaths, 2–3, 11, 48; revising bonds, 120; specific reactions associated with, 38, 43–44; support networks, 96
overengagement, 145

P

Parents of Murdered Children (POMC), 99
Patient Health Questionnaire-9 (PHQ-9), 29–30
PCL-5 (PTSD Checklist for DSM-5) assessment, 29
PE (prolonged exposure), 18, 127–128
personal values. See Meaningful Behavioral Activation; values
PG-13-R (Prolonged Grief Disorder 13-Item-Revised), 30
PGD. See prolonged grief and prolonged grief disorder
PHQ-9 (Patient Health Questionnaire-9), 29–30
physical symptoms (bodily sensations) of grief, 40, 43
PMR (progressive muscle relaxation), 79, 81, 83–85, 150
POMC (Parents of Murdered Children), 99

post-traumatic stress and post-traumatic stress disorder (PTSD), 10–15; behavioral activation and, 104; case example, 146–153; cognitive behavioral therapies, 55; co-occurrence with depression and PGD, 14–15; exposure techniques, 127–128; GRIEF Approach, 17–23; mindfulness, 79; module content and, 22–23; psychoeducation, 41; secondary traumatic stress and, 159; support networks, 95; symptoms of, 28–29; treatment planning, 31–33, 36

pretreatment assessment, 26–31; ADDRESSING model, 27–28; case example, 146–147; Cultural Bereavement Interview, 28; depression symptoms, 29–30; overview, 26; post-traumatic stress symptoms, 28–29; prolonged grief symptoms, 30; reviewing results of, 46; using open-ended questions, 27

primary emotions, 58–59

problem-solving machine metaphor, 87

process-experiential therapies, 123

progressive muscle relaxation (PMR), 79, 81, 83–85, 150

prolonged exposure (PE), 18, 127–128

prolonged grief and prolonged grief disorder (PGD), 12–15; behavioral activation, 104; case example, 146–153; co-occurrence with PTSD and depression, 14–15; exposure techniques, 127–128; GRIEF Approach, 17–20; module content and, 22–23; psychoeducation, 41; revising bonds, 114–115; support networks, 95; symptoms of, 30; treatment planning, 31–33, 36

Prolonged Grief Disorder 13-Item-Revised (PG-13-R), 30

Psychoeducation About Grief, Types of Loss, and Traumatic Loss Reactions (module 1): case example, 148; clarifying treatment goals, 49–50; content and selection parameters, 22; cultural considerations, 52–53; describing treatment approach, 50–51; discussing symptoms, 46–48; handouts, 42; overview, 40–41; presentation appropriateness, 41; providing overview of grief and impact of traumatic loss, 42–46; reviewing handouts, 48–49; reviewing pretreatment assessments, 46; secondary stressors, 51; session agenda, 41–42; summary of, 21

psychological adaptation, 6–10, 17

PTSD. See post-traumatic stress and post-traumatic stress disorder

PTSD Checklist for DSM-5 (PCL-5) assessment, 29

R

reenactment imagery, 8

relaxation strategies, 78–89; deep breathing exercises, 79, 81–85, 149–150; education about, 81–82; mindful breathing, 87–89, 91; problem solving barriers to, 84–85; progressive muscle relaxation, 79, 81, 83–85, 150. See also Managing Strong Emotions

repetition concept, 136

resiliency strategies: assessing strengths, 73–74; assigning for practice, 74–77; case example, 150, 152; cultural considerations, 77; educating clients about, 73; education about, 73; overview, 71–72; problem solving barriers to, 74–77; psychosocial factors that promote resilience, 71; reviewing use of, 76. See also Identifying and Building Strengths

response letters, 122–123, 151

restoration-oriented coping, 6–7, 9

restorative retelling (RR), 19, 141–143

Retelling Violent Death (Rynearson), 19

Revising Bonds (module 7), 113–125; case example, 150–151; commemorative-imagery strategies, 117–119; content and selection parameters, 23; cultural considerations, 125; good memories, 156; handouts, 116; "hello again" letters, 120–122; multiple traumatic losses, 154; overview, 113–114; presentation appropriateness, 115; rationale for, 116; response letters, 122–123; reviewing and assigning new activities, 124; revising connections, 123–124; session agenda, 115–116; special days, holidays, and anniversaries, 155–156; summary of, 21; to-be-maintained or relinquished aspects of relationships, 119–120

RR (restorative retelling), 19, 141–143

rumination, 6, 78, 89, 162–163

Rynearson, E., 7–8, 19

S

Schut, H., 6

SCID-5 (Structured Clinical Interview for DSM-5) interview, 29

secondary emotions, 58–61

secondary stressors, 6, 52

secondary traumatic stress (STS), 158–160, 165

self-awareness, 160–161

self-care for providers, 158–166; burnout, 159; cognitive flexibility, 162; compassion fatigue, 159; consultation and supervision, 165–166; emotional reactions to client stories, 156, 160; engagement, 161; ethical considerations, 159–160; flexibility, 162; harmonious balance, 164–165; secondary traumatic stress, 158–160; self-awareness, 160–161; self-compassion, 164; social support, 163; vicarious trauma, 158–159

self-compassion, 78–79, 164

self-efficacy, 17, 60, 71, 75, 81, 111, 153
separation distress, 9, 18, 115
shaken soda bottle analogy, 138
Skills for Psychological Recovery (SPR), 25, 33, 95
social justice conceptualizations of loss, 9
social support: anticipated barriers to, 100–101; availability of, 99; benefits of perceived, 94–95; clinicians, 163; community resources, 99; defined, 94; direction of, 99; education about kinds of, 98; engagement plans, 100–101; identifying, 98; mapping, 98–100; rationale for building healthy networks, 96–97; self-care for providers, 163; strength of, 99
special days, coping with, 124, 155
special populations, 154–155
spiritual reactions to grief, 43
Spiritually Sensitive Caregiving (Lord), 70
splinter analogy, 137–138
SPR (Skills for Psychological Recovery), 25, 33, 95
Sprang, G., 166
stage-based model of grief, 9–10
strengths-based approach. See Identifying and Building Strengths
Stroebe, M., 6
Structured Clinical Interview for DSM-5 (SCID-5) interview, 29
STS (secondary traumatic stress), 158–160, 165
Subjective Units of Distress Scale (SUDS): action hierarchy, 134; approach activities, 135; case example, 152–153; death-imagery approach, 140–144; defined, 133
suicide, 2–3, 5–6, 120; cultural considerations, 146; "hello again" letters, 120–121; posttraumatic stress, 11; prolonged grief, 12; revising bonds, 120–121; risk screening, 30; specific reactions associated with, 43–44; traumatic loss, 37. See also intentional injuries
survivors, defined, 2
survivor/survival guilt, 65, 67, 154

T

Therapeutic Exposure (module 8), 126–146; action hierarchy of avoided trauma and loss cues, 134; approach activities, 135, 139; avoidance, 129–131; case example, 152–153; challenges in, 144–145; client avoidance, 144; clinician avoidance, 144; content and selection parameters, 23; cultural considerations, 145–146; death-imagery approach, 135–144; handouts, 129; justice system involvement, 155; overengagement, 144–145; overview, 126–128; presentation appropriateness, 128; rationale for, 131–133; session agendas, 128–129; Subjective Units of Distress Scale, 133; summary of, 21; underengagement, 144–145
thought challenging, 162
thought processing. See Identifying Emotions and Processing Thoughts
thought tracking, 66, 69
trauma cues, 60, 83, 154
trauma reminders, 60, 134
traumatic loss: contemporary theories of psychological adaptation to, 6–10; health disparities in, 4–6; from intentional injuries, 37–38; mental health complications of, 10–15; natural loss versus, 44; prevalence of, 3–4; racial disparities, 5; socioeconomic status and, 6; from unintentional injuries, 38–39. See also Psychoeducation About Grief, Types of Loss, and Traumatic Loss Reactions
treatment planning, 31–39; challenges to, 32–34; flowchart, 36; overview, 31–32; supplemental modules and symptom measures, 34–35; for traumatic loss from intentional injuries, 37–38; for traumatic loss from unintentional injuries, 38–39
tug-of-war metaphor, 90
two-chair technique, 123

U

underengagement, 144–145
unhelpful thoughts, 54–55, 59, 61, 83; case example, 149; education about, 65; examples of, 67–68; helpful responses, 68; identifying, 66, 69
unintentional injuries, 2–6, 38–39
untrained puppy metaphor, 87

V

validation, 17, 22, 24; case example, 147, 151, 153; of clients with marginalized identities, 53; of emotions, 91–92, 135, 144; revisiting bonds, 116, 124; of thoughts, 67
values: assigning values-based activities, 109; cultural considerations, 111; discussing across life domains, 108–110; identifying values-based activities, 109. See also Meaningful Behavioral Activation
vicarious trauma, 158–159, 165

W

withdrawal, 16–17, 31, 106
work-life balance (harmonious balance), 164–165
World Health Organization (WHO), 3

Y

Yearning in Situations of Loss Scale (YSL)-Bereaved version, 35

Alyssa A. Rheingold, PhD, is a licensed clinical psychologist, professor, and associate director of the National Crime Victims Research and Treatment Center at the Medical University of South Carolina. She is director of the Response, Recovery & Resilience division of the National Mass Violence Center providing support to communities impacted by mass violence. Rheingold has been working in the traumatic loss field for over two decades, and has numerous federally funded service and research grants supporting her work. She has published over one hundred peer-reviewed articles and book chapters in the areas of trauma, interpersonal violence, traumatic grief, death by homicide, and anxiety.

Joah L. Williams, PhD, is a licensed clinical psychologist, and associate professor in the department of psychology at The University of Memphis in Memphis, TN. He has published more than fifty peer-reviewed articles and book chapters related to the assessment, prevention, and treatment of trauma-related mental health problems; and received the Robert Magwood Jr., Outstanding Service to Crime Victims Award in 2015 in recognition of his work with victims of violence. He is also actively involved in clinical training, and regularly conducts trainings and workshops on clinical interventions for victims of violence and traumatic loss survivors.

Megan M. Wallace, LISW-CP, is a licensed independent social worker for the state of South Carolina. She is clinical assistant professor and director of clinical operations for the National Crime Victims Research and Treatment Center within the department of psychiatry and behavioral sciences at the Medical University of South Carolina, and associate director for the Community Outreach Program-Esperanza. Wallace is trained in evidence-based treatment of trauma-related mental health issues, specifically focusing on child abuse and loss by homicide. She has expertise in traumatic loss, evidence-based trauma treatment approaches, telehealth service delivery, and community- and school-based mental health approaches.

Jamison S. Bottomley, PhD, is a licensed clinical psychologist, and research assistant professor at the National Crime Victims Research and Treatment Center within the department of psychiatry and behavioral sciences at the Medical University of South Carolina. His research expertise includes the study of traumatic loss with an emphasis on bereavement following suicide and fatal opioid-related overdose. His program of research has been generously supported by the American Foundation for Suicide Prevention (AFSP) and the National Institute on Minority Health and Health Disparities (NIMHD).

Foreword writer **Robert A. Neimeyer, PhD**, is professor emeritus in the department of psychology at the University of Memphis. He maintains an active consulting practice, and directs the Portland Institute for Loss and Transition, which provides global online training in grief therapy.

TherapyAssist

BY NEW HARBINGER

Improve Client Treatment Outcomes with Resources by the Greatest Minds in Psychology and Research

A Better Way to Assign and Deliver Homework

Designed by clinicians for clinicians. TherapyAssist is a groundbreaking platform, empowering clinicians to easily find, assign, and deliver the best evidence-based client resources for between-session and in-session use, track their completion, and improve therapeutic outcomes.

- ✓ More than 2,500 Resources
- ✓ Secure Homework Tracking
- ✓ Interactive Client Portal
- ✓ Curated Protocols
- ✓ Custom Workbooks
- ✓ Downloadables/Printables
- ✓ HIPPA-Compliant
- ✓ Unlimited Clients

"I am beyond thrilled with TherapyAssist! It is by far the best online resource for therapist/client interactions! The protocols for OCD and panic are of the highest quality in particular!"

—Trisha A. Blecich, LPC, LMHC, CMHC

Start your free trial today!
therapyassist.com

MORE BOOKS from NEW HARBINGER PUBLICATIONS

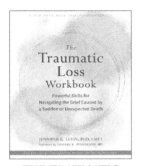

THE TRAUMATIC LOSS WORKBOOK

Powerful Skills for Navigating the Grief Caused by a Sudden or Unexpected Death

978-1648484926 / US $25.95

INTEGRATING MINDFULNESS INTO PSYCHOTHERAPY FOR TRAUMA

A Clinician's Guide to Using Mindfulness Processes to Facilitate Healing and Reduce Suffering

978-1648484650 / US $64.45

CONTEXT PRESS
An Imprint of New Harbinger Publications

TRAUMA-FOCUSED ACT

A Practitioner's Guide to Working with Mind, Body, and Emotion Using Acceptance and Commitment Therapy

978-1684038213 / US $64.95

CONTEXT PRESS
An Imprint of New Harbinger Publications

THE SUICIDAL THOUGHTS WORKBOOK

CBT Skills to Reduce Emotional Pain, Increase Hope, and Prevent Suicide

978-1684037025 / US $21.95

THE POLYVAGAL THEORY WORKBOOK FOR TRAUMA

Body-Based Activities to Regulate, Rebalance, and Rewire Your Nervous System Without Reliving the Trauma

978-1648484162 / US $25.95

THE EMDR WORKBOOK FOR TRAUMA AND PTSD

Skills to Manage Triggers, Move Beyond Traumatic Memories, and Take Back Your Life

978-1684039586 / US $24.95

newharbingerpublications
1-800-748-6273 / newharbinger.com

(VISA, MC, AMEX / prices subject to change without notice)

Follow Us

QUICK TIPS for THERAPISTS

Written by leading clinicians, Quick Tips for Therapists are free e-mails, sent twice a month, to help enhance your client sessions.

Visit **newharbinger.com/quicktips** to sign up today!

Did you know there are **free tools** you can download for this book?

Free tools are things like **worksheets**, **guided meditation exercises**, and **more** that will help you get the most out of your book.

You can download free tools for this book— whether you bought or borrowed it, in any format, from any source—from the New Harbinger website. All you need is a NewHarbinger.com account. Just use the URL provided in this book to view the free tools that are available for it. Then, click on the "download" button for the free tool you want, and follow the prompts that appear to log in to your NewHarbinger.com account and download the material.

You can also save the free tools for this book to your **Free Tools Library** so you can access them again anytime, just by logging in to your account! Just look for this button on the book's free tools page.

+ Save this to my free tools library

If you need help accessing or downloading free tools, visit **newharbinger.com/faq** or contact us at **customerservice@newharbinger.com.**